teach yourself...

Excel 5.0

John Weingarten

MIS:
PRESS

A Subsidiary of
Henry Holt and Co., Inc.

D1293877

First Edition—1994

ISBN 1-55828-332-3

Printed in the United States of America.

10 9 8 7 6 5 4 3

MIS:Press books are available at special discounts for bulk purchases for sales promotions, premiums, fund-raising, or educational use. Special editions or book excerpts can also be created to specification.

For details contact: Special Sales Director
                          MIS:Press
                          a subsidiary of Henry Holt and Company, Inc.
                          115 West 18th Street
                          New York, New York 10011

Publisher, *Steve Berkowitz*
Development Editor, *Judy Brief*
Production Editor, *Patricia Wallenburg*
Associate Production Editor, *Kevin Latham*
Copy Editor, *Janey Brand*
Technical Editor, *John Wiemann*

ACKNOWLEDGEMENTS

This book was a team effort and I want to thank everyone who helped make it possible. If I've left anyone out of the following list, please know that you are appreciated.

Matt Wagner, of Waterside Productions, is more than just a great agent. I can't thank him enough for his encouragement and guidance.

Ron Varela, who spent countless hours pouring over the manuscript to make sure I didn't say anything too stupid, helped with many suggestions and endless encouragement. He's a great guy and I'm honored that he is my friend.

Judy Brief, of MIS Press, shepherded this project from beginning to end. Her wonderful sense of humor made working with her a joy. Her hard work and genuine concern for the quality of the product have been inspiring.

Patty Wallenburg, of MIS Press, applied great skill and dedication to make this a great looking book. She even handled last minute changes with amazing grace and humor.

John Wiemann helped to ensure the technical accuracy of this book. His help and suggestions were greatly appreciated.

Steve Berkowitz, of MIS Press, had the immense wisdom and good taste to have me write this book. But seriously, as the publisher, he provided the leadership necessary to ensure that this book is consistent with all the other top-notch MIS books.

Finally, my wife Pam, and children, Sarah and Joshua, provided love and encouragement. For their support and patience, they deserve the most thanks of all.

Table of Contents

v

CHAPTER 1

EXCEL: THE BIG PICTURE (A LITTLE PERSPECTIVE) 1

CHAPTER 2

GETTING STARTED—EXCEL AND WINDOWS BASICS 7

CHAPTER 3

CREATING A WORKSHEET 43

CHAPTER 4

MODIFYING A WORKSHEET 67

CHAPTER 8

CHAPTER 9

CHAPTER 10

Introduction

This book is for people who want to learn the essentials of Excel 5.0 quickly. You do not find detailed discussions of arcane and seldom-used features here. What you find are step-by-step procedures for putting Excel to work for you.

The examples in the book are based on real world situations and should provide you with enough practical insight to tailor the procedures to your own requirements. Tasks and concepts are presented in a logical order, progressing from simple navigation and data entry to more complex tasks, such as charting, database manipulation, and linking multiple worksheets. Don't be intimidated if some of these terms seem foreign to you. They are all clearly defined and explained in the appropriate part of the book.

I hope you find the writing style clear, concise and friendly, with even a bit of humor thrown in. You should not have to be bored to tears to learn the basics of Excel. It should be fun!

WHO SHOULD READ THIS BOOK

No previous knowledge of spreadsheets or computers is required. If you have never even seen a spreadsheet before, you will easily be able to follow the procedures. You will be amazed at how quickly you will become comfortable working with Excel.

If you have worked with a previous version of Excel, or another spreadsheet program without mastering the ins and outs, this book helps you learn version 5.0 while providing a refresher on general spreadsheet basics.

THE HIGHLIGHTS OF VERSION 5.0

This version of Excel offers many powerful new features, as well as refinements to make working with the program easier and more intuitive. The following are some of more interesting new features that are covered in this book.

Improved Help Facilities

The help Excel provides is more extensive and helpful than in previous versions. Help has even acquired some intelligence. With the new TipWizard feature, Excel can tell you a better way to do what you just did.

More and Better Wizards

Excel 4.0 introduced Wizards for stepping you through the completion of several tasks. Version 5.0 enhances the Wizards' capabilities and now includes Wizards for applying functions, applying formats to charts and creating PivotTables.

In-Cell Editing

Editing the contents of a cell has become easier now that you can edit in the cell itself, instead of having to use the formula bar.

Enhanced List Management

Working with lists and databases is easier now that you can work in an automatically created form dialog box. The form dialog box even lets you find, edit, and delete records in the database. The new AutoFilter feature makes it a snap to display just the records you want.

PivotTables

The new PivotTable feature, with its own Wizard for creating them, replaces the Crosstab feature in Excel 4.0. PivotTables make analyzing and summarizing list data easier than ever.

CONVENTIONS USED IN THIS BOOK

Keyboard combinations are separated by commas and/or plus signs (+). A combination separated by commas means press and release the first key and then press and release the second key. A combination separated by a plus sign means, press and hold down the first key, then press the second key, and then release both keys. For example, if you are instructed to press **Ctrl+X**, press and hold down the **Ctrl** key and then, while still pressing the Ctrl key, tap the **X** key. **Ctrl+X, Y** means press and hold the **Ctrl** key while pressing the **X** key, then release them and then tap the **Y** key.

The first time an important term is used in the book, it appears in italics. The term is defined and explained in the chapter and in the glossary at the end of the book.

A FINAL THOUGHT

If you take the time to work through all the chapters in this book, you are rewarded with a new skill that allows you to perform many of your business and personal tasks in much less time than you currently spend. You have more time for the things you really enjoy. And don't let this book be the last of your Excel explorations. Excel is a rich program with vast capabilities. You have plenty to explore when you finish. Enjoy the journey.

John Weingarten
Spokane, Washington

Chapter 1

Excel: The Big Picture (A Little Perspective)

* SPREADSHEETS: HOW THE COMPUTER REVOLUTION STARTED
* WHAT SPREADSHEETS ARE (AND AREN'T) GOOD FOR
* WHAT SETS EXCEL APART FROM THE COMPETITION
* GRAPHING AND DATA MANAGEMENT
* WHAT YOU SEE IS WHAT YOU GET

SPREADSHEETS: HOW THE COMPUTER REVOLUTION STARTED

The spreadsheet is a formidable computer tool that lets you record the past, analyze the present, and predict the future. Spreadsheets allow for easy preparation of accounting records and financial statements, as well as budgets and forecasts.

Because of their ability to use mathematical formulas and functions to calculate results when numbers are changed, spreadsheets are marvelous facilities for playing *what if.* In a business, you might want to know the answer to, "What if our supplies costs increase by ten percent next year?", or "What if we increased our selling price by three percent?".

Before the development of the first spreadsheet program about 15 years ago, few people thought of computers as *personal.* Large corporations used huge mainframe computers, often costing millions of dollars, for very specific accounting applications such as accounts receivable and inventory control. The only contact most corporate workers had with these computers was by way of printed reports or, perhaps, entering data through terminals.

When the first spreadsheet program, *Visicalc,* appeared on the scene shortly after the introduction of the first Apple personal computers, small and medium-sized businesses quickly realized that they now had the ability to have greater control over their business. They could do budgeting and forecasting on their own desktop computers.

Computers and software have come a long way since those early Visicalc days. Other categories of software, such as word processing, database, and desktop publishing programs now share spots on the software best seller lists along with spreadsheets. But spreadsheets remain one of the primary reasons for the tremendous proliferation of personal computers.

WHAT SPREADSHEETS ARE (AND AREN'T) GOOD FOR

Almost any task that requires numeric calculations is a good candidate for spreadsheet consideration. Budgeting and forecasting are the tasks that come to mind first when thinking about what spreadsheets are good for, but virtually anything requiring the storage and manipulation of data can be done with a spreadsheet. This doesn't mean that a spreadsheet is the *best* tool for any of these tasks.

It has become increasingly difficult in recent years to choose the most appropriate software category for a particular task. Many word processing programs offer spreadsheet-like features, and database programs include the ability to work with data in rows and columns, which makes them look like spreadsheets.

If the work you need to perform is heavily text-oriented, where reporting on certain aspects of the document's contents isn't required, a word processing program is likely your best bet.

A database program would make more sense if:

1. You need to share your information with many other people but don't want two people updating the same data at the same time.

2. You want to be able to restrict the types of data being entered, as in an inventory control system.

    As we explore Excel, you'll see that you can accomplish most word processing and database tasks with this powerful spreadsheet program, but the fact that you *can* do it doesn't mean you *should* do it.

WHAT SETS EXCEL APART FROM THE COMPETITION

Excel 5 includes virtually every feature and refinement you could imagine a spreadsheet containing. You'll find a wide variety of powerful functions for almost any type of business, with financial or scientific calculation. Charting and database facilities, as well as proofing tools such as spell checking and spreadsheet analysis, round out Excel's impressive capabilities.

However, none of these features truly sets Excel apart from the competition. There are several other products that include practically the same feature set. So what does set Excel apart? Ease of use and integration.

Excel 5 introduces a number of features that make the program easier to use, and to troubleshoot when you run into problems. These ease-of-use features—such as Tip Wizards, tabbed dialog boxes, tool tips, and tracing—are covered in detail later in the book.

For those seeking ease of use, there is the ability to switch easily to other types of computers without having to spend a great deal of time learning a new program. Excel is practically identical on both IBM compatible computers and

Macintosh computers. If your business uses both types of machines, you'll be able to use Excel on either without giving a thought to which machine you're using.

Excel works smoothly with other Windows applications, especially other Microsoft applications. Microsoft, the company that makes Excel, has gone to great lengths to make Excel work like its other Windows programs. An example of this is the similarity of menu structure between Excel and Microsoft's word processing program called Word. Excel is one of the first applications to support the new standard for sharing data with other Windows programs, OLE 2.0. OLE is discussed later.

CHARTING AND DATA MANAGEMENT

When you think of spreadsheets, you generally think of the rows and columns of text and numbers that create a worksheet document. Back in the early days of spreadsheet programs that was the only capability they had.

Most modern spreadsheet programs include at least basic facilities for turning numbers into charts and graphs and for performing database functions and manipulation. Many programs include charting and database facilities that rival the most powerful stand-alone programs in these categories.

No spreadsheet program has gone further in these areas than Excel 5. Excel's competitors cannot create a wider variety of charts and graphs or customize them in such seemingly endless ways. The data management capabilities (including easy creation of lists and almost automatic sorting) let you do more with your normal worksheet data, and may prove powerful enough to save you the dollar and time investment of a stand-alone database program.

WHAT YOU SEE IS WHAT YOU GET

Thanks to advances in both computer hardware and software, it's now much easier to create great-looking documents than it once was. In the old days, if you wanted to print your documents with special fonts, characters, and graphic embellishments, you had to enter arcane printer codes into the spreadsheet program. As if that wasn't bad enough, you often didn't see the results of these codes until you actually printed your document. The result was a sense of *flying blind*, requiring repeated experimentation, as well as wasted time and paper, until you attained the desired results.

With the introduction of computers that displayed reasonably accurate representations of what would be on the printed page, you no longer had to guess at what would come out of your printer. It was right there in front of you on your screen.

The acronym WYSIWYG (What You See Is What You Get) has become as meaningless as the ubiquitous *user friendly.* Many programs claiming to be WYSIWYG don't provide a very accurate view of the printed output. In this area, as in many others, Excel has raised the standard by providing a greater measure of accuracy and detail than was available before.

A FINAL THOUGHT

This chapter set the stage for a better understanding of Excel's place in the computing world. While you can certainly use Excel productively without this information, this background should help shed some light on the big picture.

Chapter 2

Getting Started—Excel and Windows Basics

WHAT WINDOWS CAN DO FOR YOU

As mentioned in the previous chapter, Windows lets you accurately see what your printed documents look like before you print them. But, what the heck is Windows?

Glad you asked. Windows is a software program in your computer that creates an environment that is friendly, intuitive, and graphical. Windows is called a *GUI* (pronounced "gooey"), *Graphic User Interface*. Friendly and intuitive means you can choose commands from menus and dialog boxes by simply pointing and clicking with a *mouse*, without typing anything on the keyboard.

Windows also displays everything on your screen as a graphic image and can use visual images and cues to lead you through the use of the application you're working with.

Finally, Windows makes your computing life easier by providing a consistent *user interface*. The user interface is just a fancy term for the way you and your computer interact. Without Windows, you normally communicate with the computer by typing commands on the keyboard. Aside from making it easier to enter commands, the user interface makes it easier to learn new programs.

Most Windows programs adhere, more or less, to the same structure of menus and other tools for communicating with Windows. Once you learn how to use one Windows program, you've already gone a long way toward learning the next program. For example, the procedures for opening, closing, and saving documents are virtually identical from one Windows program to another.

Windows can increase your productivity by allowing you to run more than one program at a time and share information among them. This may seem trivial, but imagine you are working in your word processing program on a report that requires a portion of a worksheet from Excel. The ability to move between the two programs without having to exit one before starting the other saves time and effort.

N O T E   If you're used to the old-style user interface, it may feel as if Windows is getting in your way and slowing you down. Let me assure you that, as you become familiar with the myriad shortcuts available to you, you'll be flying through Windows commands as quickly as you used to enter them without Windows.

The next few sections provide a brief tutorial for using Windows. I know you want to dive right in and start using Excel, but please work through the tutorial if you're not familiar with Windows basics. You'll find that learning Excel and other Windows programs is much easier if you have a good understanding of the Windows environment. Keep in mind that the following sections just scratch the surface of what Windows has to offer. If you want to learn more of the ins and outs of Windows, take a look at *Teach Yourself...Windows 3.1* from MIS:Press, or use the Windows tutorial that is included with Windows.

STARTING WINDOWS

Many computers are set up to start Windows automatically. If this is the case with your system, you may skip this section. On second thought, at some point you could find yourself dumped out of Windows and needing a way to get back in, so follow along.

If your computer doesn't automatically start Windows, you probably see a DOS prompt on your screen that looks something like this:

```
C:\>
```

To start Windows from the DOS prompt, type **WIN** and press the **Enter** key.

The Windows Program Manager appears on your screen as displayed in Figure 2.1.

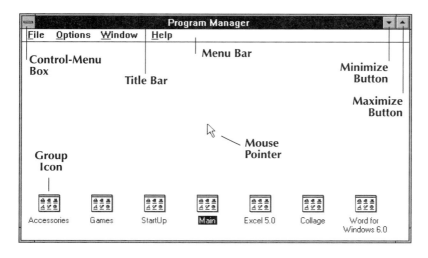

Figure 2.1 *The Program Manager screen.*

Windows is highly customizable, so your opening Windows screen may look different than what you see in Figure 2.1. As you learn to work in the Windows environment, you'll discover ways to tailor Windows to suit your needs. For now, don't worry if your screen bears little resemblance to the example.

FINDING YOUR WAY IN THE WINDOWS ENVIRONMENT

Normally, when you first start Windows, you are in the Program Manager. Think of the Program Manager as the control center or cockpit from where you begin most of your Windows operations, launch applications, and perform procedures for customizing and optimizing the system for your needs.

The large rectangle in Figure 2.1 is the Program Manager's *application window*. There are two basic types of windows that can be displayed: application and document windows. You can easily identify an application window because it has its own menu bar.

Telling Windows What to Do

You communicate with Windows using either the keyboard, the mouse, or both. In this book, the mouse method is emphasized, but that doesn't mean it is always the most efficient way to carry out an operation. Where there is a keyboard method that is clearly a shortcut, I'll point it out. However, most people who are new to Windows find the mouse action more intuitive and easier to remember.

The mouse pointer on the screen moves as you move the mouse on the surface of your desk. In addition to moving the mouse to reposition the pointer, there are several basic mouse operations you need to master:

✳ **Dragging** Moving the mouse while holding down the left mouse button.

✳ **Clicking** Pressing and releasing the left mouse button.

✳ **Right-clicking** Pressing and releasing the right mouse button.

✳ **Double-clicking** Clicking the left mouse button twice in rapid succession.

As the mouse is moved over various portions of the screen, its shape changes to indicate the sort of action that can be performed. As the pointer is positioned over the border on the side of a window, it changes to a double-headed arrow. That indicates that you can change the height or width of the window by dragging the mouse in one of the directions the arrow is pointing. Placing the pointer over one of the corners of a window transforms it into a diagonal double-headed arrow, indicating that you can change both the height and width at the same time.

Resizing a Window

Let's try changing the size of the Program Manager window.

1. Position the mouse pointer over the right border of the window as displayed in Figure 2.2.

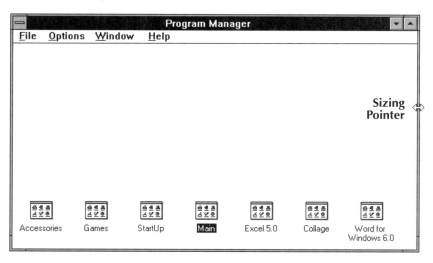

Figure 2.2   *The mouse pointer as a double-headed sizing arrow.*

N O T E   If the Program Manager window occupies your entire screen and you have no borders, it is probably maximized. Click on the double arrow in the upper-right corner of the window or double-click on the title bar to restore it to a size you can work with.

2. Drag the mouse to the left as shown in Figure 2.3.

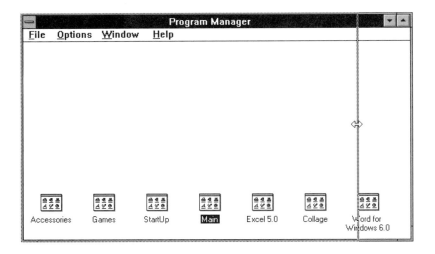

Figure 2.3   *The outline of the new right border's position.*

3.   Release the mouse button to complete the resizing process.

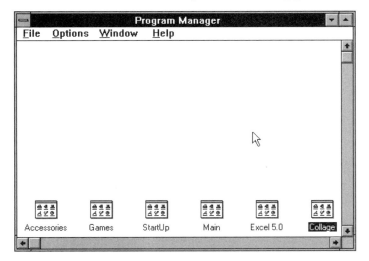

Figure 2.4   *The resized Program Manager window.*

Because the window is no longer large enough to display all the *group icons* in their current positions, Windows adds *scroll bars* to allow navigation to portions of the window that aren't currently visible.

Depending on its size, your Program Manager window may have already had scroll bars, or you may need to reduce it further to make the scroll bars appear. If you don't have scroll bars, follow the steps above to reduce the window's size until you do have scroll bars.

Using Scroll Bars

Changing the view of the window's contents so you can see a portion of the window that isn't currently visible is easily accomplished by clicking on the scroll bar buttons, the scroll bar itself, or dragging the scroll box.

The scroll boxes let you know where your view of the window's contents is currently. For example, if the scroll box on the horizontal scroll bar is at the far left, there are no more icons or other objects further left.

1. Drag the horizontal scroll box until it is in the middle of the scroll bar and release the mouse button.

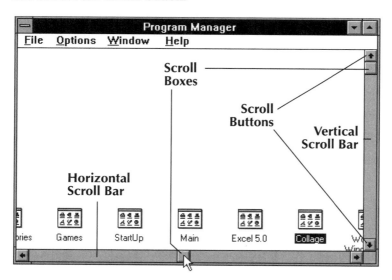

Figure 2.5   *The scroll box in the middle of the scroll bar.*

The scroll box in the middle of the scroll bar tells you that you have scrolled about halfway over in the window. Now, use the scroll button to scroll all the way to the right.

2. Point to the right scroll button and click several times until the scroll box is on the right side of the scroll bar.

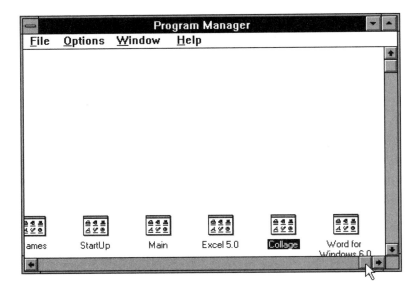

Figure 2.6 *The scroll box at the right side of the scroll bar.*

The contents of the window has shifted to the left so you are viewing what's on the right. Clicking in the scroll bar itself on either side of the scroll box also causes the scroll box to be repositioned.

N O T E You'll find the scroll bar an invaluable tool for navigating large worksheets in Excel and large documents in other applications. If you feel that you need more practice with scroll bars, don't worry, you'll get lots of practice when we get to work in Excel shortly.

Opening and Arranging Windows

The group icons at the bottom of the Program Manager window contain other icons representing programs that can be run in Windows. Icons in a group can also represent documents that are attached to an application.

Before you can run any of the applications represented by icons within the groups, you must first open the group. We'll open the Main group first.

1. Point to the Main group icon and double-click. If you cannot find your Main group icon, you can use one of the other group icons.

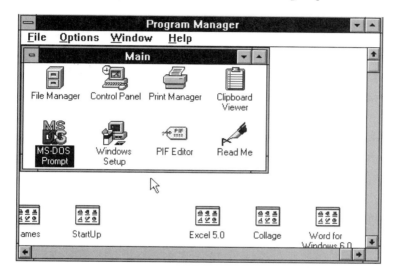

Figure 2.7   *The Main group icon is now a group window.*

N O T E   Technically, a group window is called a *document window*. Typically, document windows contain documents created in applications. You can spot a document window because it has no menus of its own. The application window's menu bar works on the active document window.

You may find it convenient to have several groups opened at once so you can easily refer to the programs you want to use. This can create a problem. With several windows opened, the screen can become a little cluttered. Let's open a couple of additional groups to create the problem and learn how to fix it.

2. Open the **StartUp** and **Games** groups as shown in Figure 2.8. If you can't find your StartUp or Games groups, you can use any other two groups.

Notice that the new opened windows overlap the Main window and the title bar of the Games window is dark, indicating that it is the *active window*, which means it's the window you can work with now. Also notice that although most of the Main and StartUp windows are obscured, a small portion of each is still visible behind the Games window. Windows provides several ways to get at the buried information:

✳ Click on any visible portion of a window to make it the active window.

✳ Move the windows around on the screen to arrange them in a more appropriate fashion.

✳ Move the active window so it doesn't cover as much of the window it's obscuring.

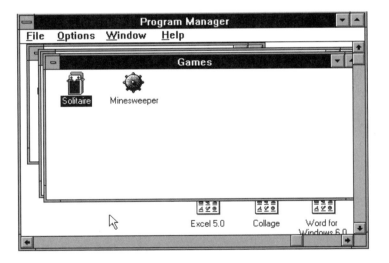

Figure 2.8 *Three group windows cluttering the screen.*

3. Position the pointer in the title bar of the active window and drag it out of the way, as displayed in Figure 2.9.

4. Release the mouse button to complete the repositioning of the window.

You could also resize the windows or drag the icons within the windows to organize things the way you want them. Windows offers a couple of automatic methods for arranging the open windows. *Cascading* the windows stacks one window on top of another, but keeps the title bar of all the windows visible, making it easy to see which windows are available. *Tiling* resizes each window, allocating an equal amount of space for each.

Cascading and tiling give us our first opportunity to use the menus, since the **Cascade** and **Tile** commands are located in the Program Manager's Window menu. Menus are sometimes called *drop-down* menus because, when opened, a list of commands drops down. Menus can be opened with the mouse or the keyboard. To activate a menu command with the mouse, click on the menu that contains the command you want to use. A list of commands drop down so you can click on the command you want to activate.

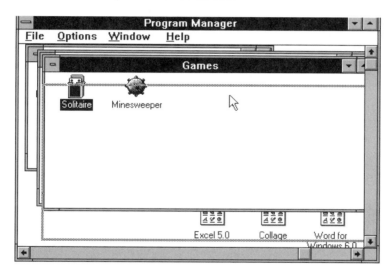

Figure 2.9   *The outline of the Games window.*

Another method is to press the **Alt** key, the underlined letter in the menu's name, and then the underlined letter in the command name. The two methods work equally well. However, once you memorize the keyboard combination (called *hotkey*) for a particular command, you can usually perform the command more quickly from the keyboard. We'll use both the mouse and the keyboard methods in the next few steps. Let's start by cascading the windows.

5. Click on the Window menu.

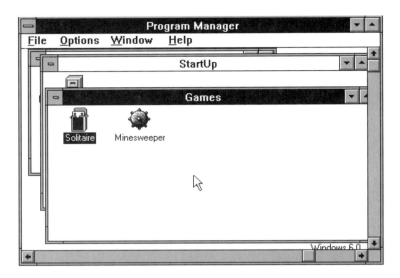

Figure 2.10 *The repositioned Games window.*

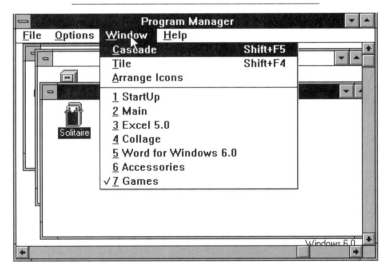

Figure 2.11 *The Window drop-down menu.*

6. Click on the **Cascade** command in the Window drop-down menu.
    Tiling the windows changes the look of the screen.

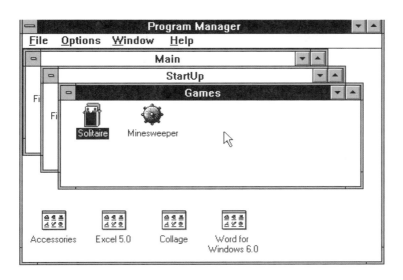

Figure 2.12   *The windows are cascaded with their title bars visible.*

7. This time we'll use the keyboard method to tile the windows.

Press **Alt, W, T** (Press and release the **Alt** key, then **W**, then **T**).

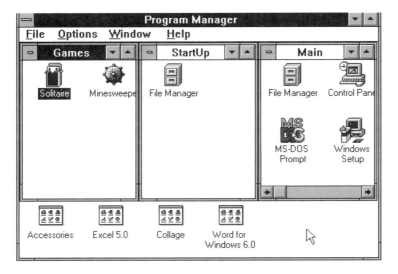

Figure 2.13   *The windows are tiled to give each an appropriate portion of the screen.*

For the remainder of the book, when a step tells you to use a menu command, you'll be instructed to *choose* the command. For example, if you were being told to tile your window, the instruction would look like this: "Choose **Window**, **Tile.**" In this way, the choice of keyboard or mouse access is left to you.

SHORTCUT

Many menu operations that require several mouse or keyboard steps have a shortcut key you can use to perform the action more quickly and directly. Refer to Figure 2.11 and notice that next to the **Cascade** and **Tile** commands there are keyboard shortcuts, **Shift+F5** and **Shift+F4** respectively. This means that you can Cascade your open windows by pressing **Shift+F5** or Tile them by pressing **Shift+F4** without even using the menus.

In most applications, including Excel, most shortcut keys are displayed next to their corresponding menu command. Don't expend a great deal of energy trying to memorize the shortcut keys. If you just notice them on the menus, you will naturally remember the ones for the commands you use regularly.

N O T E

You can manipulate cascaded or tiled windows in just the same manner as you would if they weren't cascaded or tiled. These windows can be moved and sized. You can then cascade or tile them again.

Closing Windows

When you no longer need to work with a window, you may wish to close it to reclaim some screen real estate for the windows you are currently working with.

To close the active window, you open the **Control** menu by clicking on the **Control** menu box in the upper-left corner of the window. Let's close all of the group windows.

1.   Click on the **Control** menu box of the Main group window.
2.   Choose **Close**.

The Main window is closed and represented by its group icon.

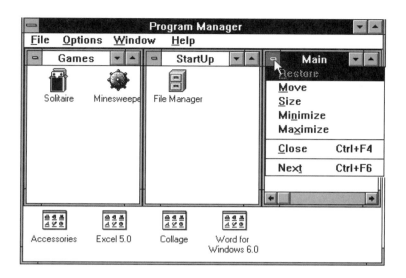

Figure 2.14   *The Control menu.*

SHORTCUT

The fastest way to close a window is by double-clicking on the **Control** menu box.

3. Close the other group windows you have opened.

    Your screen should now look the way it did when you first started Windows.

STARTING EXCEL

The big moment has arrived. It's time to start Excel and get this show on the road. Starting Excel, or any other program in Windows, is done the same way as opening a group window. You can double-click on the program icon or choose **File**, **Open**. Double-clicking is always faster than using the menu access method.

1. Open the Excel group window. If the Microsoft Excel program icon is in another group, open the group that contains the Excel program icon.

2. Double-click on the **Microsoft Excel** icon.

After a few seconds, the main Excel screen appears on your screen, as displayed in Figure 2.15.

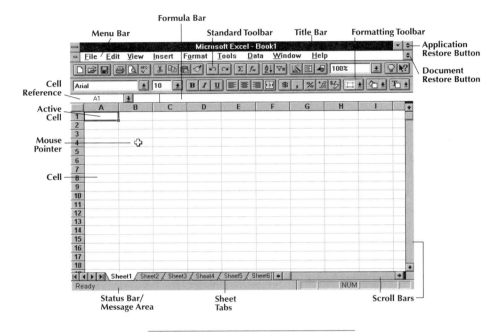

Figure 2.15 *The opening Excel screen.*

A QUICK TOUR OF THE EXCEL SCREEN

Many of the elements in the opening Excel screen should seem familiar to you. The title bar, menu bar, control menu box, and scroll bars all work the same way as they did in the Program Manager. There are also a few new screen elements that are discussed shortly.

When Excel is first started, you see a worksheet called *Sheet1*, that is actually contained in a document window. If the document window is maximized to fill the entire available area, as in Figure 2.15, there is a **Restore** button in the upper-right corner of the worksheet. Clicking on the **Restore** button reduces the size of the window and gives you sizing borders. However, it's often more efficient to work with your worksheet maximized to give you maximum visible area.

The worksheet consists of lettered columns and numbered rows. The intersection of a column and a row is called a *cell* and its name is the column letter followed by the row number. The *active cell* is surrounded by a border and its name is displayed in the cell reference area. The hollow cross on the worksheet is the mouse pointer and it changes shapes as it moves to different parts of the worksheet.

USING DIALOG BOXES

Many Windows applications, including Excel, use dialog boxes to allow more detailed or efficient communication with the program than menus alone can provide. There are many types of dialog boxes providing various kinds of input.

Some dialog boxes appear automatically if you make some sort of mistake or ask Excel to do something that requires confirmation. They appear as a result of choosing a menu command that requires additional input. You can tell which menu commands produce dialog boxes because they are followed by an *ellipsis* (...). Let's examine one of the more complex dialog boxes to see how they work.

1. Choose **Tools** to display the Tools drop-down menu.

    Notice that several of the menu commands have triangles next to them. These commands have sub-menus with additional commands. Sub-menus are used later. Other menu commands are followed by an ellipsis, indicating that choosing that command produces a dialog box.

Figure 2.16   *The Tools drop-down menu.*

2. Choose **Options** to produce the Options dialog box shown in Figure 2.17.

Tabs

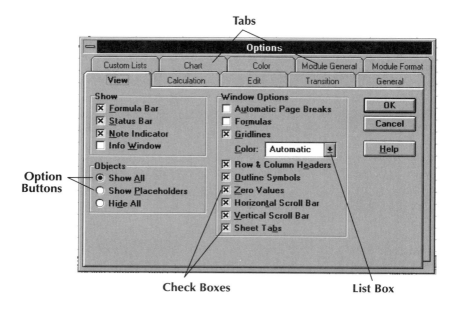

Option Buttons

Check Boxes   List Box

Figure 2.17 *The Options dialog box.*

Most dialog boxes don't have as many options as the Options dialog box. This is a good example of what you encounter in various Excel dialog boxes. *Option* buttons allow you to choose only one of the options in a category. *Check box* categories can have multiple boxes checked. *List boxes* let you select a choice from a list.

Tabbed dialog boxes let you switch among various sets of options by clicking on the tab. As displayed in Figure 2.17, the View tab is highlighted. Let's take a look at another set of options in the same dialog box.

3. Click on the **General** tab.

This set of options includes one more input method—a text box into which you can type information.

4. Click on the **Cancel** button on the right side of the dialog box, or press the **Esc** key to clear the dialog box.

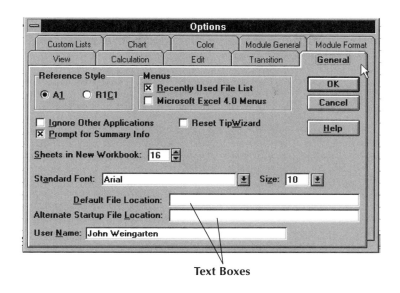

Text Boxes

Figure 2.18 *The Options dialog box with the General tab highlighted.*

USING THE TOOLBARS

You've learned that there are often keyboard shortcuts for accomplishing certain tasks. Excel's toolbars are like shortcut keys that are accessible by clicking on them with the mouse. Another advantage of the toolbars is that they keep the shortcuts visible so they are easier to remember than keyboard shortcuts.

Excel supplies predefined toolbars for a variety of situations. Figure 2.15 displayed the two *default* toolbars that automatically appear when you start Excel. Default refers to the way things are set automatically. The top toolbar is the Standard toolbar and the one on the bottom is the Formatting toolbar.

Each toolbar button is an *icon* (picture) that represents a command or series of commands. Some of the icons are fairly self explanatory, but you may be wondering how you'll be able to figure out what the rest of those cryptic little pictures mean. Never fear. Excel provides an easy way to determine what each of the toolbar buttons does. By simply moving the mouse pointer over one of the buttons, the status bar displays a description of what the button does and a *tool tip* pops up just below the mouse pointer with the button's name. Let's try this out.

1. Without clicking, position the mouse pointer over the Print toolbar button. It's the fourth button from the left on the Standard toolbar.

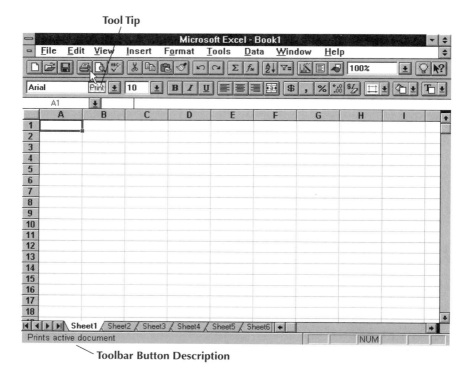

Figure 2.19 *The mouse pointer on the Print toolbar button.*

The tool tip says Print and the status bar tells you that clicking on this would cause the active document to print.

2. Move the pointer over some of the other toolbar buttons. Look at the tool tip and status bar to get an idea of what some of the other buttons can accomplish.

Throughout the book, we'll be working with various toolbars and toolbar buttons. You will learn later how to choose which toolbars you want to appear on screen, how to change their position, and even how to customize them to create special toolbars to meet your own requirements.

NAVIGATING THE WORKSHEET

As you start entering and editing data in worksheets, you need to know how to move about. There are quite a few ways to navigate the worksheet using either the keyboard or the mouse. The simplest method is clicking the mouse pointer on the cell you want to move to, or using the Arrow keys to move to the cell you want to be active.

1. Use the Arrow keys to move to several different cells. The cell reference area tells you what the active cell is.

2. Use the mouse to click on several different cells.

While this method works well for moving short distances, it's very inefficient for moving long distances. Some of the more useful long distance navigation techniques involve keyboard combinations.

Table 2.1   *The most common navigation shortcuts.*

Key	Result
PageUp	Moves up one screen.
Page Down	Moves down one screen.
Alt+PageDown	Moves right one screen.
Alt+PageUp	Moves left one screen.
Ctrl+Backspace	Moves to display the active cell.
Ctrl+Home	Moves to A1.
Ctrl+End	Moves to the last used cell.

You can also move long distances by using the scroll bars. Use the same techniques you learned earlier to scroll to different parts of the worksheet:

✳ Click on the scroll bar buttons to move a row at a time.

✳ Drag the scroll box to move to a distant location.

✳ Click in the scroll bar above or below the scroll box to move one screen up or down.

Using the scroll bars doesn't change the active cell, it only changes the portion of the worksheet you are looking at. Once you've moved to the desired location using the scroll bars, click in the cell you want to become active.

One of the most useful ways to move around is to use the Go To dialog box. With the Go To dialog box. you can enter the cell address you want to move to and, zap! You're there. Let's try it.

3. Choose **Edit**, **Go To** (or press **F5**).

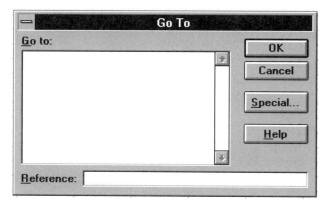

Figure 2.20 *The Go To dialog box.*

As we work through the book, we cover a number of ways to use the Go To dialog box. For now, let's just move to a new cell. Notice the vertical line in the Reference text box. This is called the *insertion point* and indicates that this is where you can start typing. If the insertion point isn't in the Reference text box, just click in the Reference text box and the insertion point is there.

4. Type: **Z45** and click on the **OK** button to make Z45 the active cell.

USING EXCEL'S HELP FACILITIES

One of the most important skills you can learn is how to get yourself unstuck when you run into difficulty. Fortunately, Excel provides some very useful tools for getting help. It even includes electronic demonstrations of many aspects of the program.

Let's explore Help's contents to see what's available.

1.   Choose **Help** to produce the Help drop-down menu.

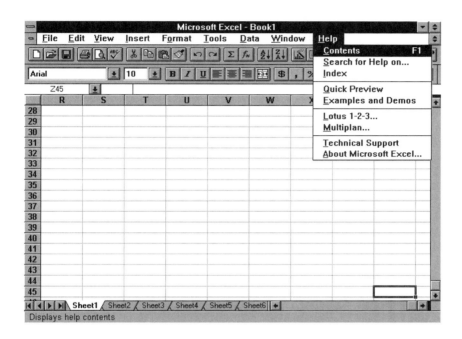

Figure 2.21   *The Help drop-down menu.*

2.   Click on **Contents** to display the Microsoft Excel Help window, as shown in Figure 2.22.

N O T E

The Help window is an application window. You can tell that it is an application window because it has its own menu bar, separate from Excel's menu bar, to control it.

Help is an application, or program, that runs concurrently with Excel. You can keep Help running and switch between the Help window and the Excel window by pressing **Alt+Tab**, or by pressing **Ctrl+Esc** to display the Task List dialog box, clicking on the application you want, and then clicking on the **Switch To** button in the Task List dialog box.

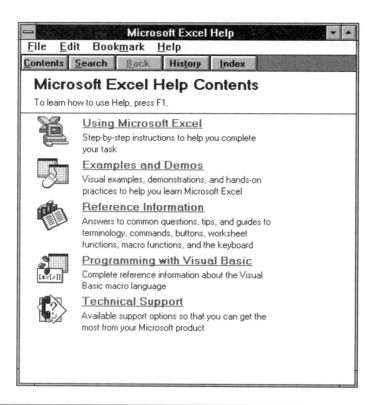

Figure 2.22 *The Microsoft Excel Help window with the contents displayed.*

Help is segmented into logical groups. The first group, *Using Microsoft Excel*, leads you to more sections about using the program. *Example and Demos* provides illustrated mini-tutorials on various aspects of the program. *Reference Information* provides lists and explanations you might need, such as keyboard shortcut guides, installation information, specifications, etc. The *Programming with Visual Basic* section gives you information you'll need when you start delving into the more technical aspects of Excel programming. Finally, *Technical Support* leads you to the many options for obtaining answers to your technical questions.

You can move to any of these sections by moving the mouse pointer over one of the underlined headings (also in green on color screens) and clicking. You can tell when you are positioned over a topic that can be selected because the mouse pointer takes the shape of a hand with a pointing finger.

Let's try moving to one of the help sections now.

3. Position the mouse pointer over the Reference Information heading and click to display the first Reference Information help window, as shown in Figure 2.23.

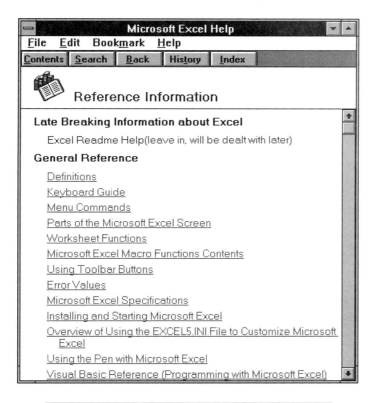

Figure 2.23 *The Reference Information help window.*

We can now choose from a whole new set of categories. Let's move to the Definitions category.

4. Move the mouse pointer over the underlined Definitions category, and click to display a list of items for which we can obtain definitions, as shown in Figure 2.24.

Notice that these items are underlined with dashed underlines. A dashed underline means that you can click on that item to display a definition of the item.

Microsoft Excel Help
File
Edit
Bookmark
Help
Contents
Search
Back
History
Index
Definitions
3-D Walls and Floor
Absolute Cell Reference
Activate
Active Sheet
Add Mode
Add-in
Address
Alternate Startup Directory
Array
Autoformat (for charts)
Autotemplate
Axis
Cell Reference
Changing Cells
Chart
Chart Area
Chart Sheet
Chart Text

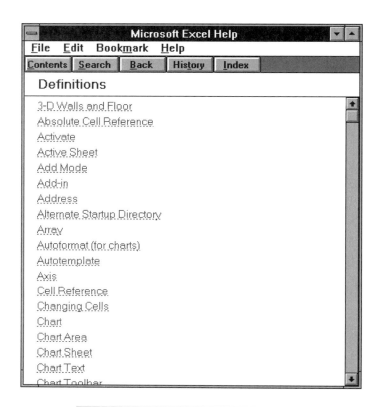

Figure 2.24 *The Definitions help window.*

5. Click on **Chart** to display a definition of a chart, as shown in Figure 2.25.

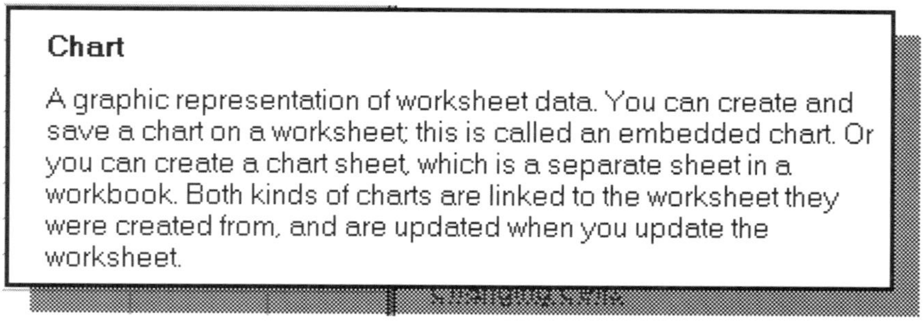

Chart
A graphic representation of worksheet data. You can create and save a chart on a worksheet; this is called an embedded chart. Or you can create a chart sheet, which is a separate sheet in a workbook. Both kinds of charts are linked to the worksheet they were created from, and are updated when you update the worksheet.

Figure 2.25 *The definition of a chart.*

When you have read the definition, you can clear it by clicking the mouse anywhere.

6. Click the mouse to clear the definition.

You can use the buttons just below the menu bar to move to other portions of Help. For example, you can use the Back button to retrace your steps, one screen at a time. The History button displays a dialog box listing all the help screens you've used in the current help session so you can jump back to one directly by double-clicking on it.

7. Click on the **History** button to display the Windows Help History dialog box, as shown in Figure 2.26.

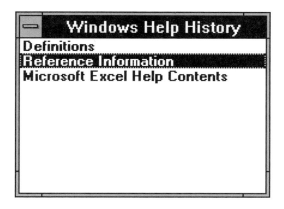

Figure 2.26 *The Windows Help History dialog box.*

The last screen you used is highlighted. Let's jump back to the Reference Information screen.

8. Double-click on **Reference Information** in the History dialog box.

Now that you know how to move around in Help, let's take a look at how you can search for a help screen for a particular topic.

9. Click on the **Search** button to display the Search dialog box, as shown in Figure 2.27.

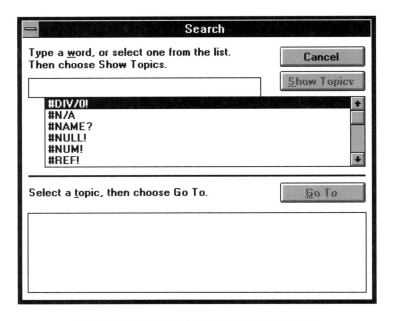

Figure 2.27 *The Search dialog box in Help.*

SHORTCUT

You can go directly to the Search dialog box without having to navigate through the main help window by choosing **Help**, **Search for Help on**, or by double-clicking on the Help toolbar button.

You can either scroll to a category item in the list or just start typing the name of the feature you need help with in the text box above the list. As you type, the category items starting with those letters will appear in the list. When the category item you want is visible, you can click on the **Show Topics** button, or just double-click on the item.

Suppose you can't remember how to specify a print area for your worksheet. Let's try searching for help on print area now.

10. Type: **p** in the text box and notice that the list jumps to the first features that start with the letter p.

11. Type: **rin** and the print area category comes into view. Click on it and then click on the **Show Topics** button to display a list of related help screens you can jump to, as shown in Figure 2.28.

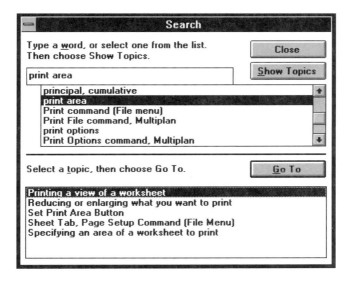

Figure 2.28 *The Search dialog box with the print area topics displayed.*

12. Click on **Specifying an area of a worksheet to print** in the list of topics in the lower portion of the dialog box, and then click on the **Go To** button to display the How To help window shown in Figure 2.29.

    Many help topics appear in How To windows, which offer the advantage of being available for reference as you work in Excel. When you click on the **On Top** button in the How To window, it will remain on top of your worksheet even after you close the main Help window. The How To window can be dragged and sized, just like any other window, so that it is available for reference, but out of the way.

    After you have found the help screen you are looking for and read the information, you can close the Help window by choosing **File**, **Exit**, or double-clicking on the control-menu box. You can close a How To window by clicking on the **Close** button.

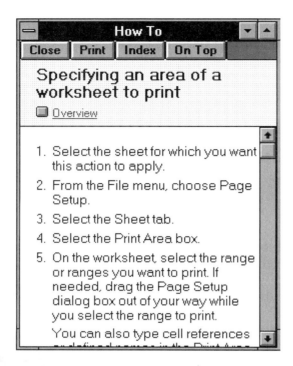

Figure 2.29   *The How To help window for specifying an area of a worksheet to print.*

13. Choose **File**, **Exit** from the main Help window to exit Help.

There may be times when you want help with some object you see on your screen. You could call up Help and search for the appropriate screen, but there's a faster way. By clicking on the **Help toolbar** button, you can simply click on the object for which you want more information. Let's say you want more information about the scroll bars.

14. Click on the **Help toolbar** button, as shown in Figure 2.30.

Notice that the mouse pointer turns into an arrow with a large question mark attached.

15. Position the tip of the pointer inside either the vertical or horizontal scroll bar and click to summon the Scroll Bars help screen.

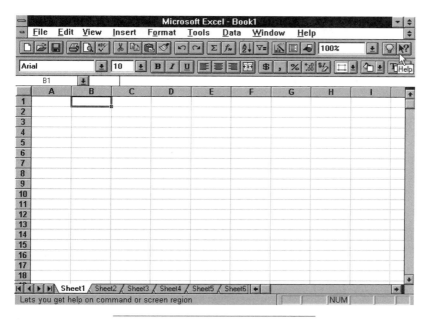

Figure 2.30   *The Help toolbar button.*

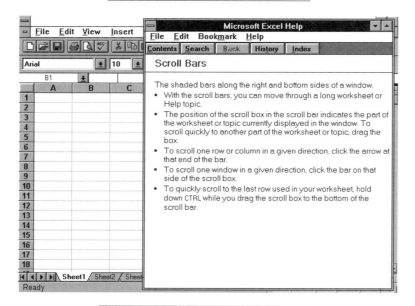

Figure 2.31   *The Scroll Bars help screen.*

Excel also lets you get help on almost any dialog box by clicking the **Help** button in the box, or by pressing the **F1** key.

Using the TipWizard

Not only does Excel make it easy to find and use Help for the topics you are struggling with, the TipWizard can even make suggestions about better ways to perform tasks after you have done them. Excel is a smart program.

When the TipWizard has a suggestion for you, the TipWizard button *lights up*. Lighting up means turning yellow on a color screen or just highlighted if you don't have color.

N O T E   When you start Excel, the TipWizard lights up before you've done anything. This lets you know that it is ready to give you the *tip of the day*, which is a random hint or shortcut for performing some commonly used Excel task.

To display the suggestion the TipWizard has for you, just click on the **TipWizard toolbar** button. To clear the suggestion, click on the **TipWizard** button again. The TipWizard button is lit because, aside from offering us a tip of the day, it has a suggestion for a more efficient way to move to a new cell than the Go To box we used to move to cell Z45 in the last section. Let's take a look at the suggestion, as well as the tip of the day.

1. Click on the **TipWizard toolbar** button to display the tip between the Formatting toolbar and the Formula bar, as shown in Figure 2.32.

    Just to the right of the tip text are up and down arrows for moving to the previous or next tip. There is no next tip, so let's move to the previous tip.

2. Click on the **Up Arrow** to the right of the tip text to display the tip of the day.

    You can leave the TipWizard open to display suggestions automatically, or you can close it and then just open it when you want to see a suggestion. For now, let's leave it open and perform a task in a less-than-optimally-efficient manner. Even though there is nothing in the active cell (Z45), we'll tell Excel that we want to cut (delete) the cell contents using the menu.

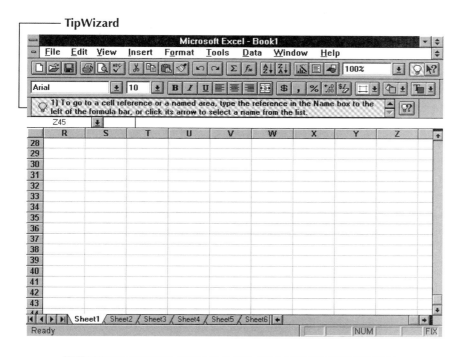

TipWizard

Figure 2.32 *The TipWizard's tip for moving to a different cell.*

3. Choose **Edit**, **Cut** to display a suggestion for cutting using a toolbar button, as displayed in Figure 2.33.

N O T E

Because Excel uses a great deal of intelligence for providing tips, you may see a different tip. Don't worry, Excel is just trying to give you the best suggestion for your particular situation.

You'll also discover that Excel only provides a tip once in an Excel session unless you perform the task inefficiently three more times.

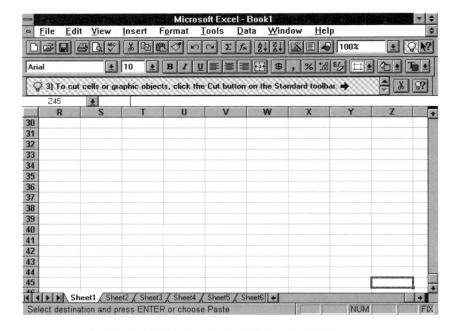

Figure 2.33   *The tip for using the Cut toolbar button.*

If the tip suggests that you use a toolbar button, the button will be displayed to the right of the up and down arrows, as you see for this tip. There is also a Tip Help displayed for tips so that you can jump directly to a help screen for more detailed information about the procedure.

We won't keep the TipWizard displayed for the figures in the remainder of the book, since it does take up some valuable screen real estate. However, don't hesitate to display it as you work through the book to see if there are better ways of accomplishing what you are doing. Of course, just because the TipWizard suggests something, that doesn't mean it's the best approach. It's just giving you a suggestion. Use your own judgment.

   4. Click on the **TipWizard** toolbar button to remove the TipWizard.

EXITING EXCEL

When you are ready to leave Excel, you can do so in the same manner as closing any other window.

1. Choose **File**, **Exit**, or double-click on the control menu box.

    Excel closes and returns to the icon you started from. If you have made changes to a worksheet, Excel is considerate enough to ask you if you want to save the changes. If you see such a message at this point, just click on the **No** button to finish exiting Excel.

A FINAL THOUGHT

The information you've learned in this chapter gives you the tools to *get around* in Windows and Excel. In the next chapter, you finally get a chance to put Excel to work creating worksheets and entering data.

Chapter 3

Creating a Worksheet

PLANNING A WORKSHEET

The worksheet is where you enter the information you want to store and manipulate. Like almost anything you build, a worksheet is more useful, efficient, and understandable if you take the time to plan before you dive in and start entering data willy nilly.

The first step is to decide what the purpose of the worksheet is. For example, if the worksheet is to contain a monthly budget for the next year, then the purpose is to forecast and gain greater control over inflows and outflows for your business.

Give some thought to the level of detail you want to include in the worksheet. Too little detail may render the worksheet useless by omitting critical information required to make decisions based on the analysis of data entered into the worksheet. Too much detail can make the worksheet unwieldy and mask the results, not letting you see the *big picture*.

You may also find it useful to use paper and pencil to sketch out the overall design of your worksheet. This lets you see how the worksheet looks to the user (whether that user is you or someone else) before you take the time to enter a bunch of data.

One more planning tip to keep in mind: Remember that the ultimate result of most worksheets is a printed report of some sort. Many things that seem obvious to you as you create or edit a worksheet can easily be obscured or invisible in the printout. For example, formulas you create to perform calculations can be revealed in the worksheet, but are generally not part of the printed output. The printed report is often only a small portion of the entire worksheet, so the context that might make the worksheet understandable on screen might not be a part of the printout.

Building a Text Framework

The most common, and often the most practical, way to start putting together a worksheet is to enter titles, column and row headings, and any other text elements that provide a structure for your worksheet as you enter the data. There are no hard-and-fast rules for the text framework but, traditionally, columns contain time periods such as hours, days, months, and row headings contain categories such as rent, insurance, cost of goods, and similar headings.

We are going to create a budget worksheet for a small locksmith business that also sells bagels. The Spokane Locks and Bagel Corporation decided to use

Excel to create a budget worksheet to let them compare budgeted amounts with actual figures down the road. Figure 3.1 depicts the initial text framework for this budget worksheet.

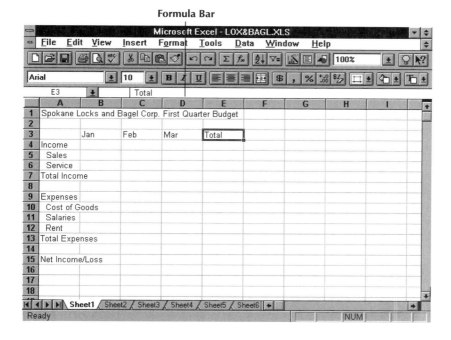

Figure 3.1   *The text framework for the Spokane Locks and Bagel Corporation.*

ENTERING AND EDITING TEXT

To enter text into an Excel worksheet, simply move to the cell in which you want to enter the text and start typing. As you type, the text appears in both the cell and the formula bar. Let's start entering the text as displayed in Figure 3.1.

1.   Start Excel if you don't have it on your screen. Refer to Chapter 2 if you don't remember the steps for starting Excel.

2.   Be sure A1 is the active cell. Check the cell reference area to double-check that you are in the right place.

3.   Type: **Spokane Locks and Bagel Corp. First Quarter Budget**.

As you start typing, notice that a flashing vertical line, called an *insertion point,* appears to the right of the text, as displayed in Figure 3.2. The insertion point lets you know where text is to be entered or deleted. As soon as you start a cell entry, three new icons appear on the left side of the formula bar. From left to right, these icons are the Cancel, Enter, and Function Wizard box.

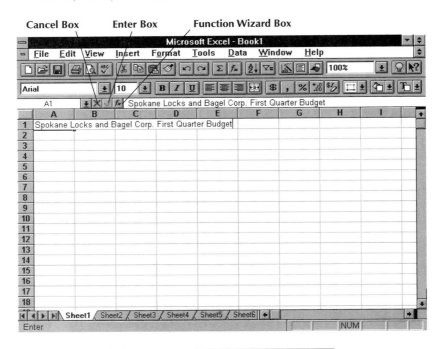

Figure 3.2 *The beginnings of a cell entry.*

If you make a mistake while typing, simply press the **Backspace** key to erase the character to the left of the insertion point. If you've really messed up, you can click on the **Cancel** box or press **Esc**.

NOTE

While you are entering text in a cell, you cannot press the Left Arrow or Right Arrow keys to reposition the insertion point for editing. Pressing an Arrow key causes Excel to complete the cell entry with what you've typed so far and move in the Arrow's direction to the next cell on the worksheet.

The text you typed in cell A1 has apparently spilled over into the adjacent cells in columns B, C, D, and E. But do those other cells really contain part of the information? No. The entire worksheet title is in A1. The cell reference area says you are in A1 and the formula bar displays the whole title. If you were to move to B1, you'd see from the formula bar that B1 contains no data. In fact, it is because B1, C1, D1, and E1 are empty that the contents of A1 are allowed to spill over. If these cells contained data, even a space, the entry in A1 would be truncated.

To see how this works, let's enter something in B1. There are several ways to complete a cell entry, including clicking on the **Enter** box, pressing the **Enter** key, or moving to another cell. The last method is usually the fastest since you often need to make entries in other cells.

4. Press the **Right Arrow** key to move to cell B1. Notice that cell B1 is empty.

5. Press the **Spacebar** and then click on the **Enter** box. The text in A1 is limited to what fits in the current column width. Now let's rid of the space in B1 to restore the title.

6. While B1 is still the active cell, press the **Delete** key to allow the title to flow across the columns.

Column widths can be changed to allow for the amount of text entered in the column. Changing column widths, which is covered in the next chapter, is usually the preferred method for accommodating long text entries.

N O T E

7. Click on cell **B3** to make it the active cell and complete the entry in cell A1.

8. Now that the worksheet title is in place, enter the column headings. In cell B3, type: **Jan**.

Now, you could move to cell C3 and type **Feb** and then type **Mar** in D3, but there's an easier way. In the lower right corner of the box surrounding the active cell is the *fill handle*. The fill handle allows you to perform several copying actions. For now we'll use the fill handle to take advantage of Excel's intelligence. By dragging the fill handle to the right so the outline extends through cell D3, Excel automatically enters **Feb** and **Mar** for you, like magic!

9. Position the mouse over the fill handle until the mouse pointer turns into thin crosshairs. Drag it to the right until the cell outline extends to cell D3, as displayed in Figure 3.3.

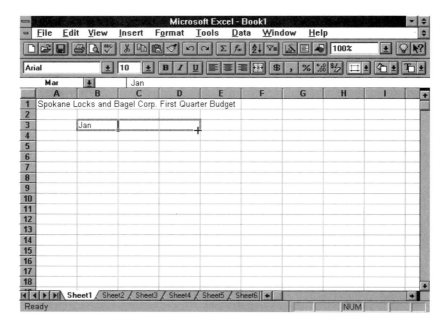

Figure 3.3 *The fill handle being dragged.*

10. Release the mouse button to complete the fill.

N O T E

For example, if a cell contains Mon, dragging the fill handle increments the days of the week as Tue, Wed, Thu, etc. A cell containing text and a number, such as 1st Period, fills as 2nd Period, 3rd Period, etc.

You can use the fill handle to increment a series by dragging to the right or down. If you want to use the fill handle to decrement a series, drag to the left or up. If a cell contained Jan, dragging left or up would fill as Dec, Nov, Oct, etc.

11. Click in cell E3 and type: **Total**.

12. Move to cell A4 and type: **Income**.

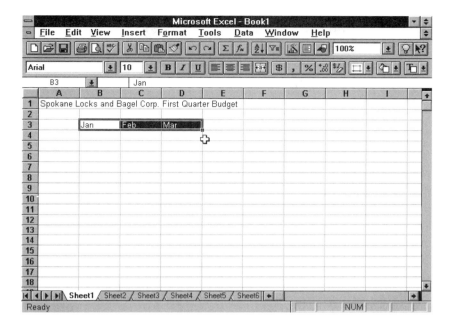

Figure 3.4   *The results of the fill after releasing the mouse button.*

If you're entering several contiguous cells in a column, pressing the **Enter** key is the most efficient way to complete a cell entry since it causes the next cell in the column to become the active cell.

13. Press the **Enter** key to complete the entry and move to the next cell in the column.

    As shown in Figure 3.1, notice that the next two entries in the column are indented just a bit. This was accomplished by preceding the entries with two spaces.

14. Press the **Spacebar** twice and type: **Sales**. Then press **Enter**.

15. Enter the following text:

A6	**Service**
A7	**Total Income**
A9	**Expenses**
A10	**Cost of Goods**
A11	**Salaries**

A12	**Rent**
A13	**Total Expenses**
A15	**Net Income/Loss**

Refer to Figure 3.1 to be sure your screen matches the figure.

ENTERING NUMBERS

Entering numbers is done in the same way as entering text. What you see on screen depends on what sort of number you enter. For example, if you enter 100, the screen displays 100. If you enter 100.43 the screen displays 100.43. But if you enter 100.00, the screen displays 100 without the decimal point or trailing zeros. Here's another example. Suppose you enter 100000000. It is displayed as 1E+08. Hey, what the heck is going on here?

Let me reassure you that Excel isn't actually changing the *number* you enter, just the way it is displayed. The actual number you enter in the cell is used in any calculations Excel performs. Now, here's what's happening. Excel formats numbers using what it calls *General formatting*. General formatting doesn't display trailing zeros after a decimal point and converts very large numbers to scientific notation, which uses exponents.

NOTE   The way numbers (or text, for that matter) are formatted can be changed to suit your taste and requirements. The techniques for changing cell formatting are covered in the next chapter.

Let's start entering the numbers for the budget worksheet that are displayed in Figure 3.5.

1. Move to cell B5 and type: **228000** and press **Enter**.

    The text entries you made earlier were aligned at the left side of the cell. Excel aligns numbers at the right side of the cell. Just like most settings in Excel, these default settings can be changed, and you learn how in the next chapter.

2. Fill in the remaining numbers in the appropriate cells as shown in Figure 3.5.

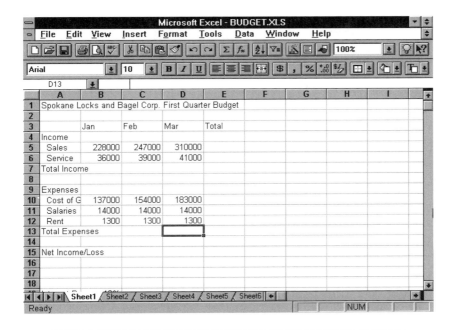

Figure 3.5   *The budget worksheet with its initial numbers entered.*

CREATING FORMULAS

Formulas are a spreadsheet's *raison d'etre*. If all we needed to do was to put text and numbers in rows and columns, just about any word processing program would fill the bill. Formulas allow us to perform calculations using values from any cells and have the result appear in the formula cell.

You build formulas using the four mathematical operators:

✳   The *plus sign* (+).

✳   The *minus sign* (–).

✳   The *asterisk* (*) for multiplication.

✳   The *slash* (/) for division.

You always start a formula by moving to an empty cell where you want the results of the formula to appear, and typing the equal sign (=) which tells Excel to get ready for a formula. For example, you could type the formula **=2*2** in a cell and, after completing the cell entry, the cell would display the result of the formula as 4, but the formula bar displays the formula.

At this point, you know how to use your fancy spreadsheet program like a pocket calculator. Big deal, you say. Well, the real power of formulas comes into play when you use cell referencing. Instead of entering a formula using values, you can enter a formula using cell references, such as **=C12*D14**. If 2 is the value in both C12 and D14, the result is still 4. However, if the values in C12 or D14 change, the result automatically changes as well.

Let's create the formula for January's Total Income in our budget worksheet. The formula adds the values in cells B5 and B6.

1. Move to cell B7 and type: **=B5+B6**, then click the **Enter** box to complete the cell entry while keeping B7 as the active cell.

   If you originally entered the values in B5 and B6 as specified (and I know that you did), cell B7 now displays the value 264000, while the formula bar displays the formula, =B5+B6, as shown in Figure 3.6.

The Formula **The Result of the Formula**

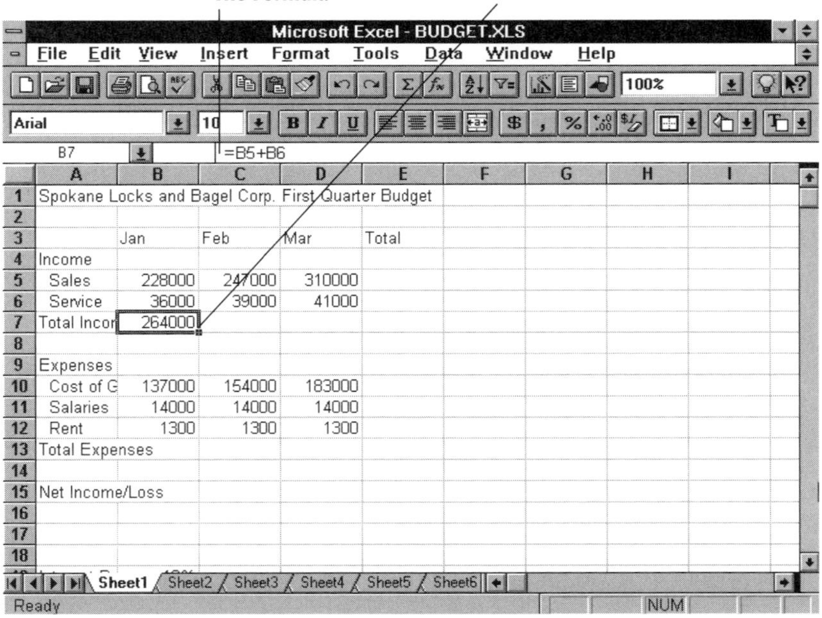

Figure 3.6 *A formula and its result.*

Now, let's try a different method of specifying the cells to be included in a formula. We'll use the pointing method to click on the cells we want to include, thus eliminating any possibility of entering an incorrect cell reference. To create the formula for January's Total Expenses:

2. Move to cell B13 and start the formula by typing: **=** .

3. Click on **B10** to let Excel know that B10 is the first cell you want to include in the formula.

The beginning of the formula (=B10) followed by the insertion point appears in the formula cell and a dashed border appears around B10, as displayed in Figure 3.7.

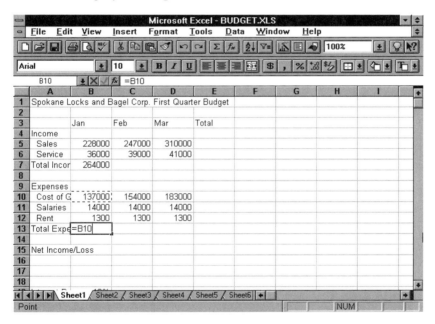

Figure 3.7 *The beginning of a formula using the pointing method.*

4. Type: **+** then click on cell **B11**, type: **+** again and click on **B12**.

5. Click on the **Enter** box or press the **Enter** key to accept the formula.

In this example, pointing may not appear more advantageous than just typing in the cell references, but when dealing with more distant cell references or specifying ranges of cells, pointing can make a substantial difference. I think you'll start to see the advantage of pointing as we create the formula for January's Net Income/Loss.

6. Move to cell B15 and type: **=**.

7. Click on cell **B7** (January's Total Income), then type: **–** (the minus sign). Now click on **B13** (January's Total Expenses) and press **Enter**.

With the three formulas entered, your screen should now look like Figure 3.8.

UNDERSTANDING AND USING FUNCTIONS

Think of functions as predefined formulas. Using just the four mathematical operators, you could duplicate just about any of the supplied Excel functions. It might take a long while to recreate a function with the math operators, particularly for some of the more complicated functions. Just as importantly, you'd have to go through the same process every time you wanted to use the formula.

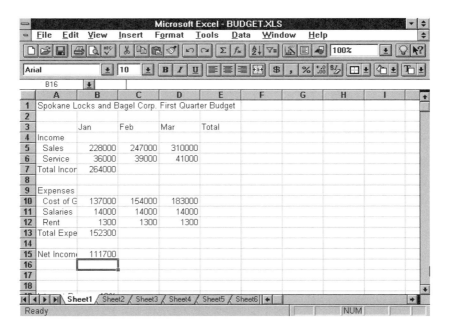

Figure 3.8 *The budget worksheet with the first three formulas entered.*

Perhaps the most common function is the *SUM function*, which adds the values in a range of cells. Most functions require *arguments*, contained within parentheses, which are just pieces of information the function needs to complete the calculation. Only one argument is required for the SUM function—the range of cells to be added.

One advantage of using the SUM function (versus specifying plus signs between each cell reference) is that it's just plain easier. Using the plus signs between each cell reference can become very unwieldy for a large range of cells. For example:

=C2+C3+C4+C5+C6+C7+C8+C9+C10+C11+C12

is much more cumbersome and error-prone than

=SUM(C2:C12), don't you think?

The colon between the two cell references in the argument is the *separator*. It means *through*, as in C2 *through* C12.

Also, using the range argument makes it easier to insert or delete cells in the range without having to modify the function's argument. Let's say you needed to add a row for a new category within the range of C2 through C12. If you had used the SUM function, the new row would automatically be included in the range.

Let's use the SUM function to calculate February's Total Income.

1. Move to cell C7 and type: **=SUM(**

    You are now ready to enter the range of cells to be totaled. Of course we'll use the pointing method to enter the range, and we can do it in one fell swoop.

2. Point to cell C5, drag down to C6 and release the mouse button.

    A dashed border surrounds the range of cells, C5 through C6, and the cell references have been entered after the left parenthesis, as shown in Figure 3.9.

    I know you think the next step is probably to enter the right parenthesis. Not so fast. Excel is so smart, it usually knows when a closing parenthesis is required and enters it for you when you complete the cell entry. Let's try it.

3. Click on the **Enter** box to complete the cell entry.

    The result of the function's calculation appears in cell C7 (286000) and the function with its argument and both parentheses, appear in the formula bar.

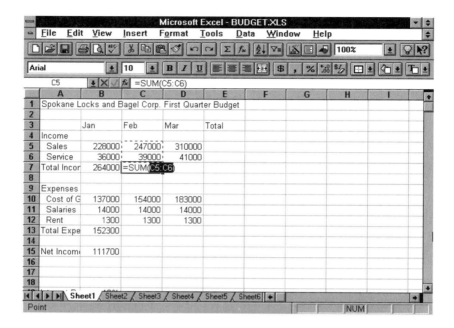

Figure 3.9   *The beginning of the SUM function with its argument.*

Now get ready for some Excel magic. Most of the time, when you want to SUM a range of numbers, you don't even need to enter the function or specify the range. You can put Excel's brains to work and usually figure out the proper range to sum. Let's try to SUM the March Total Income.

4. Click in cell **D7**.

5. Click on the **AutoSum** button on the toolbar.

The SUM function is automatically entered and the closest contiguous range (D5 through D6) is specified as the argument, as shown in Figure 3.10.

6. Press the **Enter** key to complete the entry.

SHORTCUT

If you are sure that Excel will select the correct range for the argument, you can double-click on the **AutoSum** button and the entry is completed for you. This isn't too dangerous, even if the wrong range is selected. You can always delete and start over.

	Microsoft Excel - BUDGET.XLS	
	File **Edit** **View** **Insert** **Format** **Tools** **Data** **Window** **Help**	

Arial ⬍ 10 ⬍ **B** *I* U ≡ ▤AutoSum▤⬍ $, % ⁺.₀₀ ⁰⁄₀ ▦⬍ ⬈⬍ ▥⬍

	D5	⬍✕✓ ƒ₌	=SUM(D5:D6)							
	A	**B**	**C**	**D**	**E**	**F**	**G**	**H**	**I**	
1	Spokane Locks and Bagel Corp. First Quarter Budget									
2										
3		Jan	Feb	Mar	Total					
4	Income									
5	Sales	228000	247000	310000						
6	Service	36000	39000	41000						
7	Total Incor	264000	286000	=SUM(D5:D6)						
8										
9	Expenses									
10	Cost of G	137000	154000	183000						
11	Salaries	14000	14000	14000						
12	Rent	1300	1300	1300						
13	Total Expe	152300								
14										
15	Net Incom	111700								
16										
17										
18										

▐◀▶▶▌\ **Sheet1** / Sheet2 / Sheet3 / Sheet4 / Sheet5 / Sheet6 / ◀ ▶

Inserts SUM function and proposes sum range | | NUM | |

Figure 3.10   *Using the AutoSum button.*

Okay, that was pretty darned easy, but what about all those other functions that are hidden away somewhere in Excel? Don't worry, they aren't too hidden. In the following steps, I'll show you just how easy it is to find just the function you need.

Let's use one of the more complex functions—one that requires several arguments to see what the monthly payments would be for a new piece of equipment the Spokane Locks and Bagel Corporation is thinking of purchasing. It's one of those fancy new combination key-duplicator-and-cream-cheese-spreading machines.

The function we'll use is the PMT function that calculates the payments if we simply supply a few arguments. The information we need to supply is the interest rate per payment period, the number of payment periods, and the present value (the amount of the loan). We'll enter those three pieces of information onto the budget worksheet now.

7. Press the **PageDown** key to move to a new screenful of rows and click in cell **A19** and type: **Interest Rate**.

8. In cell A20 type: **Term**.

9. In cell A21 type: **Loan Amount**.

10. In cell A22 type: **Payment**.

11. In cell B19 type: **10%** and click on the **Enter** box..

Notice that 10% is displayed in the cell, 0.1 (the actual value used in calculations) appears in the formula bar.

12. In cell B20, type: **5** to represent a five-year loan period.

13. Type: **28500** in cell B21, which is the amount the company wants to finance over the five-year period.

We could move to the cell that is to contain the function (B22) and enter the function name and the appropriate arguments, but with three arguments required, it can be difficult to remember what goes where. Never fear! Excel Function Wizard to the rescue. Excel 5 includes several *wizards*—specialized help systems that take you by the hand and step you through some of the more mysterious procedures. Wizards are covered later in the book, but the Function Wizard is one of the most useful.

You can invoke the Function Wizard in a variety of ways. Choosing **Insert, Function** will do it, or you can click on the **Function Wizard** toolbar button, which is what we'll do now.

14. Click in cell **B22** and then click on the **Function Wizard** button on the toolbar.

If the dialog box obscures the values in column B, point to its title bar, drag to the right about an inch, and release the mouse button.

If the function you want is visible in the Function Name list on the right side of the dialog box, you can click on it. Otherwise, click on the category of functions you think your function might be in and then use the scroll bar to find it.

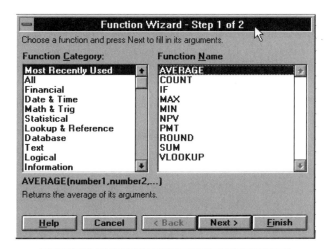

Figure 3.11 *The Function Wizard dialog box.*

We'll go through the steps to find the PMT as though it weren't visible and we didn't know what category to choose.

15. Click on **All** in the Function Category list to display all of the available functions in every category.

16. Click on any of the functions in the Function Name list.

17. Use the scrollbar to scroll down the list until PMT is visible and click on it.

You can type the first letter of the function name and the highlighter jumps to it. Then you only have to search through the functions that start with that letter.

SHORTCUT

With PMT selected, the dialog box displays the proper syntax for the function and, below that, a brief explanation of what the function does, as displayed in Figure 3.12.

If you want to enter the arguments manually, you can click on the **Finish** button, but it's much easier to let the Wizard step you through the argument entry process.

18. Click on the **Next** button to proceed to the Function Wizard dialog box that lets you enter the arguments, as shown in Figure 3.13.

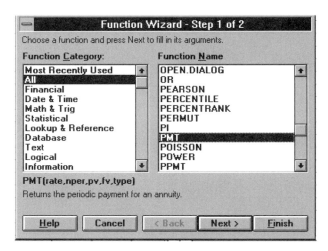

Figure 3.12   *The Function Wizard dialog box with the PMT function selected.*

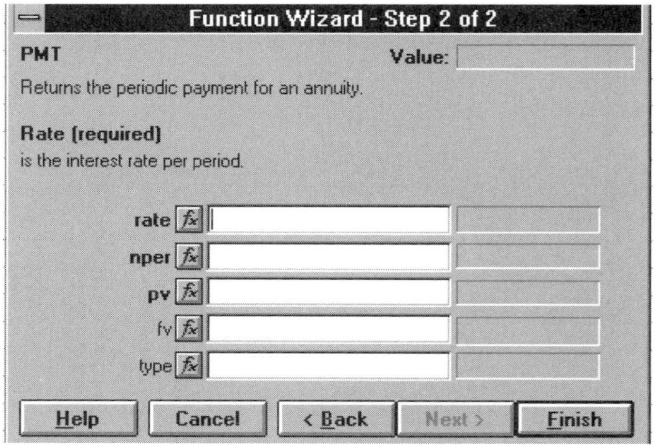

Figure 3.13   *The Function Wizard dialog box for entering arguments.*

The insertion point is in the rate text box. Just above and to the left of the text box, the dialog box lets you know that you are ready to enter the rate per period and that this entry is a required argument.

You could type the cell reference for the rate, but it's easier to point and click.

19. Click on cell **B19** (the interest rate).

    B19 is entered in the rate text box and 0.1 is entered in the box to the right of the text box. We need to make an adjustment here. Remember that the rate the function needs is the rate *per period*. Since we want to determine the monthly payment and 10% is an annual rate, we need to divide it by 12.

20. Type: **/12**.

    Notice that the rate in the box to the right now displays the monthly interest rate, 0.0083333333.

21. Press the **Tab** key to move to the *nper* (number of payment periods) text box and click on cell **B20**.

    Again we need to modify the entry. Cell B20 contains the number of years for the loan and we want the number of months, so we need to multiply by 12.

22. Type: ***12**

    The value to the right of the text box now displays the value 60, which is the correct number of months.

23. Press the Tab key to move to the *pv* (present value) text box and click on cell **B21**.

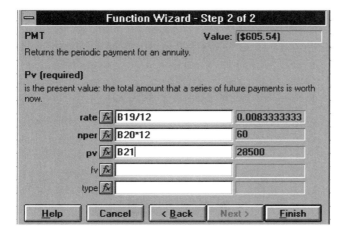

Figure 3.14   *The filled-in dialog box.*

This entry doesn't need to be altered and the dialog box should now look like Figure 3.14. The *fv* (future value) and *type* arguments are optional and we won't use them. With all the required arguments entered, the dialog box displays the value $605.54 in the upper right corner. This is the result of the calculation that appears in cell B22 when we are finished.

24 Click on the **Finish** button to complete the Function Wizard procedure.

The value in cell B22 is in parentheses and in red (if you have a color monitor) to let you know that this is a negative value. The monthly payment is negative because it results in an outflow from the business. If this were money being received, it would be positive.

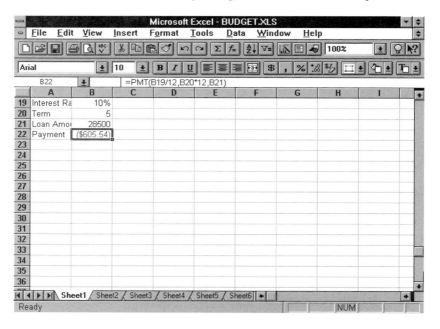

Figure 3.15 *The result of the PMT function.*

SAVING YOUR WORK

Perhaps the most important habit to learn and use is to save your work on a regular basis. Until you save, the data you enter or edit is in your computer's temporary memory called RAM (*Random Access Memory*). Okay, so what's the definition of *regular basis*? Often enough that, if you lost all the work you had done since the last time you saved, you wouldn't be too upset.

Excel stores worksheets in files called *workbooks*. Within a single workbook, you can have many worksheets, all of which are saved to your computer's disk when you save. You don't need to specify which sheet or which portions of a sheet you want to save.

The first time you save a workbook, you are presented with several questions. You need to assign a filename and, if you like, fill in a summary dialog box with more detailed information about the workbook. Filenames can be up to eight characters long, followed optionally with a period and up to three characters for an extension. I recommend skipping the extension and letting Excel assign one for you. The default extension for Excel workbooks is .XLS.

Let's save the workbook that contains the worksheet we've been working on with the name BUDGET. Excel automatically assigns the name BOOK1.XLS to its first blank unnamed workbook, so that's likely the name you see on your title bar now.

1. Choose **File**, **Save As**.

   The Save As dialog box appears, as displayed in Figure 3.16.

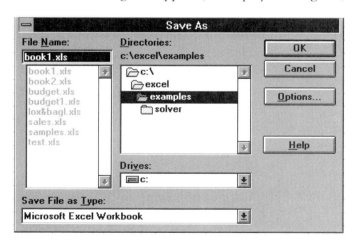

   Figure 3.16   *The Save As dialog box.*

2. In the File Name text box, type: **budget**

The Directories list box tells you which directory your workbook will be saved in. A *directory* is like a file folder on your disk that allows you to organize your files, just as you would in a file cabinet. If you want to save in a directory other than the one specified, double-click on the top level file folder in the list (usually C:\), then scroll to the directory you want to use and double-click on it.

If you want to save to a drive other than the one specified in the Drives drop-down list box, as would be the case if you wanted to save to a floppy disk in drive A or B, click on the list box arrow and then click on the appropriate drive letter from the list.

3. Click on the **OK** button.

The Summary Info dialog box appears, as shown in Figure 3.17, with the author's name already filled in. The author is the name of the registered user of the program.

You can fill in additional information that might help you locate the workbook when you're looking for it later. You can enter any combination of title, subject or comments.

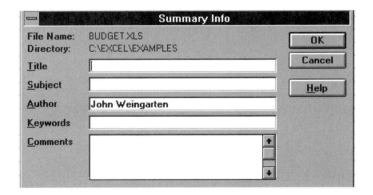

Figure 3.17 *The Summary Info dialog box.*

4. Click on the **OK** button to finish saving your workbook.

As you work in Excel, entering and editing data, you'll want to save often, perhaps every ten or twenty minutes. The fastest way to do this is to click on the **Save** toolbar button. The saved file on your disk is automatically replaced with the updated version and you won't even have to confirm that you want to replace it.

5. Double-click on the document's control menu box to close the document, and then exit Excel if you aren't continuing on to the next chapter immediately.

A FINAL THOUGHT

With what you have learned in this chapter, you already know as much as 80% of the spreadsheet users out there and you are ready to put Excel to productive use. Give yourself a pat on the back.

In the next chapter, you will learn to make some modifications to your worksheet, including inserting and deleting data, and copying formulas.

Chapter 4

Modifying a Worksheet

FINDING AND OPENING AN EXISTING WORKSHEET

One of the biggest fears of new computer users is that they'll put a lot of time and energy into creating a document, dutifully save it to the disk, close the document, and then they'll never be able to find it again. It will be lost forever, as though sucked into a black hole.

Relax! Your document is there and Excel makes it easy to find. You *did* save it, didn't you?

Let's explore some of the ways to open a document.

1. Start Excel, if it isn't running.

   Unless you've been doing some work with Excel behind my back, the last workbook you had on your screen was BUDGET.XLS. Even if you were working on a few other documents since working with BUDGET, Excel displays BUDGET along with the three other recently opened files at the bottom of the File menu.

2. Choose **File**.

   Notice the group of four file names at the bottom of the menu, just above the Exit command, in Figure 4.1. Your File menu may only display one or two file names, if those are the only files you've worked with.

File	
New...	**Ctrl+N**
Open...	Ctrl+O
Close	
Save	Ctrl+S
Save As...	
Save Workspace...	
Find File...	
Summary Info...	
Print Report...	
Page Setup...	
Print Preview	
Print...	Ctrl+P
1 EXAMPLES\BUDGET.XLS	
2 EXAMPLES\BOOK1.XLS	
3 EXAMPLES\BOOK2.XLS	
4 EXAMPLES\BUDGET1.XLS	
Exit	

Figure 4.1   *The File menu with the four most recently opened files displayed.*

You could open the BUDGET workbook by clicking on it or pressing the underlined number in front of its name. Instead, let's examine some other methods for finding and opening the file.

3. Click on any cell outside the menu to clear the menu, or press the **Esc** key twice.

4. Click on the **Open** toolbar button.

Choosing the **Open** toolbar button is the same as choosing **File**, **Open**, and calls up the Open dialog box, as displayed in Figure 4.2.

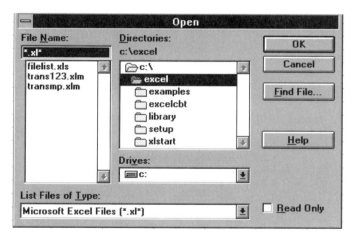

Figure 4.2 *The Open dialog box.*

5. If BUDGET.XLS isn't displayed in the File Name list box, use the Directories list box, as described in the Saving Your Work section of Chapter 3, to move to the directory that contains the file.

I know you're anxious to open the file, but there's one more method we're going to take a look at first. Bear with me for just a few more minutes.

6. Click on the **Cancel** button or press **Esc** to clear the dialog box without opening a file.

The first two methods for opening a file are fine if the file you want to open was one of the last four you worked with, or if you know its name and the directory where it is located. But suppose you haven't worked on the file recently. In fact, it's been so long that you've forgotten its name and even the directory where you saved it. Hey, it happens to the best of us.

It's *still* easy to find the file using Excel's magnificent Find File facilities. As long as you know *something* about the file, such as the approximate date when it was saved last, some information you entered into the Summary Info dialog box, or even some unique text that is contained anywhere in the file, Excel does the legwork and finds the long lost file for you.

7. Choose **File**, **Find File**.

The first time you use Find File, the Search dialog box appears on the screen, as displayed in Figure 4.3. If the Find File dialog box appears, it means that Excel executed a search the last time Find File was used, so click on the **Search** button to summon the Search dialog box.

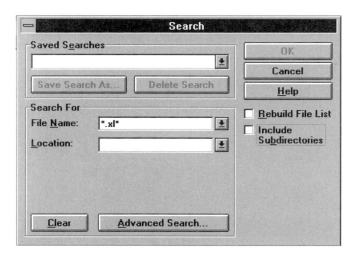

Figure 4.3 *The Search dialog box.*

This dialog box lets us search for files based on their file name or location, but, we could have done that in the Open dialog box. Let's get to the more sophisticated search features.

8. Click on the **Advanced Search** button.

The Advanced Search dialog box with three tabs appears, as displayed in Figure 4.4.

9. Click on the **Location** tab if it isn't highlighted.

The location portion of the dialog box lets you specify more detailed instructions about where to search for the file.

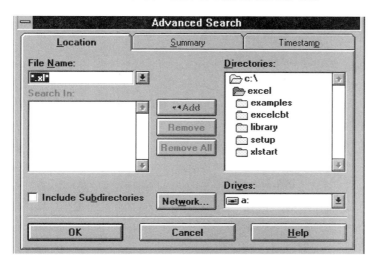

Figure 4.4   *The Advanced Search dialog box with the Location tab highlighted.*

10. Click on the **Timestamp** tab.

The Timestamp portion of the dialog box appears, as displayed in Figure 4.5, and lets you specify a date or range of dates (as well as the author) from which to search.

11. Click on the **Summary** tab.

The Summary portion of the Advanced Search dialog box, as shown in Figure 4.6, is where you can specify information you entered in the Summary Info dialog box, or that little bit of text you're sure is contained somewhere in the file. This is the portion of the dialog box used to locate and then open the BUDGET workbook. Wait. Forget I said that. We're pretending that we forgot the name of the file, so forget that you know the name of the file is BUDGET.

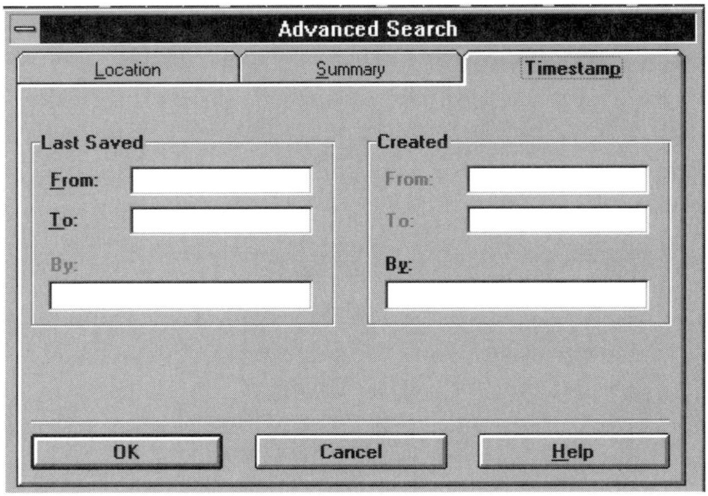

Figure 4.5 *The Timestamp portion of the Advanced Search dialog box.*

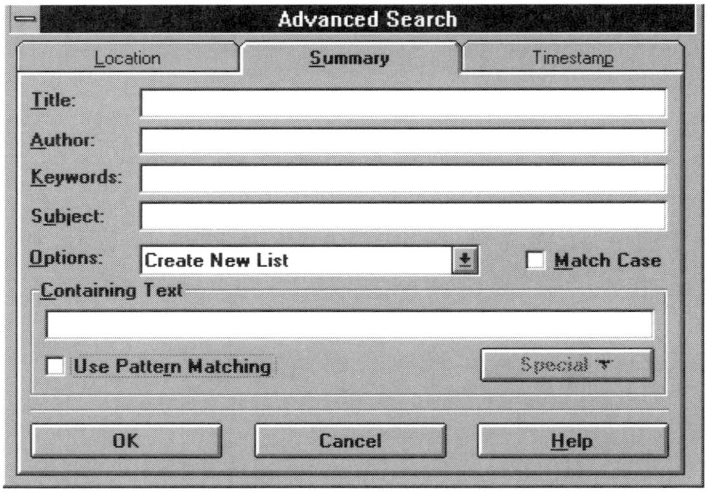

Figure 4.6 *The Summary portion of the Advanced Search dialog box.*

Perhaps the only information you remember that is in the file is a portion of the title. Maybe all you remember is that the title has the words *locks and* in it. Good enough. That's all you need to know.

12. Click in the Containing Text box and type: **locks and**, then click on **OK**.

You are returned to the Search dialog box to complete the information Excel needs to execute the search. We need to specify a location, but we don't need to be any more specific than the drive to search.

You can only search one drive at a time. If you have more than one hard drive and you don't know which drive contains the file you're looking for, you may need to perform separate searches on each **N O T E** drive.

13. Click on the Arrow for the Location drop-down list and click on the drive you wish to search, (usually C:).

14. Click in the Include Subdirectories checkbox so Excel searches the entire drive for your file.

Using the Include Subdirectories option can dramatically increase the amount of time required for your computer to complete the search. The amount of time depends on the size and speed of the hard disk, the **WARNING** number of files it contains, and the overall speed of your computer. If you know where your file is located, you save time by specifying a directory in the Location portion of the Advanced Search dialog box.

The Search dialog box is displayed in Figure 4.7.

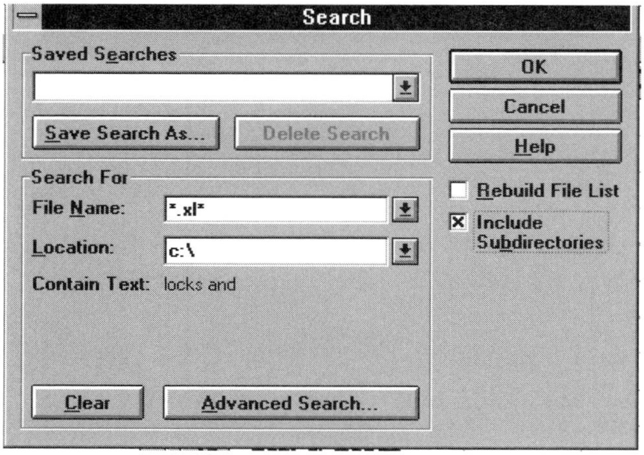

Figure 4.7 *The filled-in Search dialog box.*

15. Click on **OK** to begin the search.

You'll see dialog boxes indicating that Excel is searching the directories and building the file list. When the search is completed, the Find File dialog box displays the files containing the text in the Listed Files list. The highlighted file, probably *budget.xls*, is previewed in the Preview portion of the dialog box, as displayed in Figure 4.8. Your list may include more or fewer files than the list in the figure.

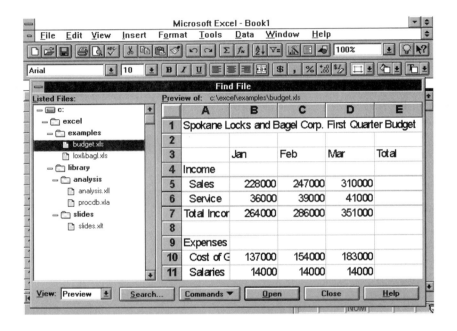

Figure 4.8 *The Find File dialog box with the found files.*

16. If budget.xls isn't highlighted in Listed Files, then click on it. Click on the **Open** button to open the file. The file opens, with the active cell where it was when you last saved it.

COPYING FORMULAS AND FUNCTIONS

In the last chapter, you learned how to create formulas and use functions to perform calculations. Often, you need to apply the same formula or function to several cells.

Before we copy any formulas or functions, let's use the AutoSum button to add the calculations for February and March Total Expenses.

1. Make C13 the active cell.

2. Double click on the **AutoSum** toolbar button.

3. Move to D13 and, once again, double-click on the **AutoSum** button.

    With all the Total Income and Total Expenses calculations in place, we're ready to add the formulas for calculating the Net Income/Loss for February and March. Instead of creating separate formulas, we'll copy the formula for January's Net Income/Loss to February and March.

4. Move to cell B15.

    If you look in the formula bar, the formula *appears* to be =B7-B13. Well, appearances can be deceiving. Excel and other spreadsheets employ a type of cell referencing called *relative reference*. By using relative references, cells containing text, values or even formulas or functions can be copied and they are automatically adjusted to perform properly in their new location.

    Relative reference logic sees the formula in B15 as, "subtract the value in the cell that is two rows up from the value in the cell that is eight rows up." When you copy a formula, the logic of the formula (not the actual formula) is copied, so the formula works in its new location.

    Let's use the fill handle that we used in the last chapter to create a series to copy the formula to cells C15 and D15.

5. Position the mouse pointer over the fill handle and drag two cells to the right, as shown in Figure 4.9.

6. Release the mouse button and then press the **Right Arrow** key to make C15 the active cell.

    Take a look at the formula bar to assure yourself that the logic of the formula was correctly copied. You can check out cell D15 for further proof.

Selecting Ranges

So far, other than copying formulas to several cells, we've been manipulating one cell at a time. Excel lets you select a range of cells on which you want to perform some action.

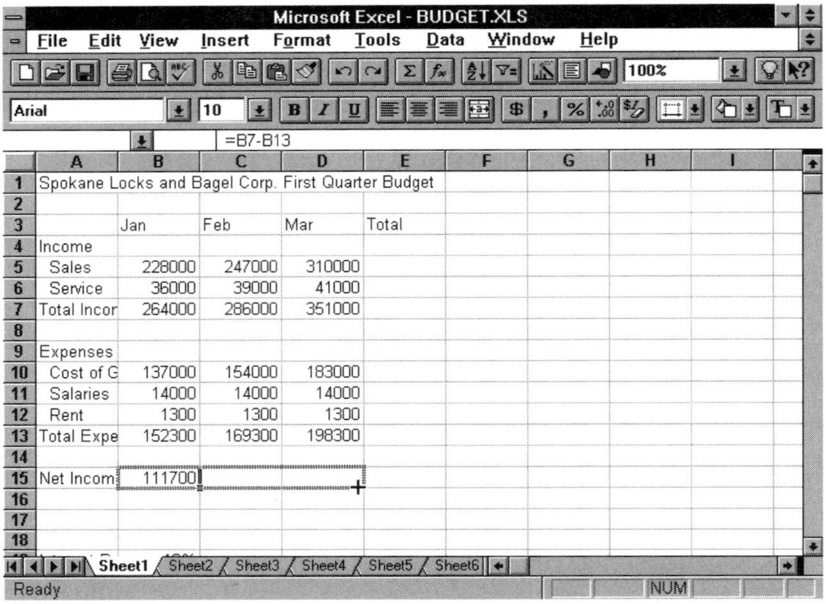

Figure 4.9 Copying a formula with the fill handle.

The easiest way to select cells is to simply drag the mouse over the cells you want to select. Let's select E5 through E7 and use the AutoSum function to calculate the quarter total income.

1. Position the mouse pointer in E5 and drag down to E7 and release the mouse button.

   The selected range is highlighted and the cell you started with is the active cell, as shown in Figure 4.10.

2. Double-click on **AutoSum** to add the function to all the selected cells at once.

   There may be times when you want to select non-contiguous ranges of cells. For example, suppose you wanted the sum for the quarter totals of the expenses and the net income/loss at the same time. No problem. Just use the **Ctrl** key to add to a selection.

3. Position the mouse pointer in cell E10, drag down to E13 and release the mouse button.

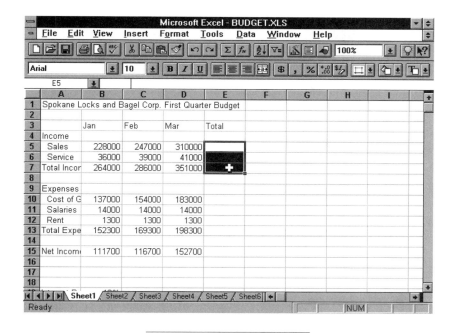

Figure 4.10 *A selected range.*

4. Hold down the **Ctrl** key and click on cell **E15**.

   E10 through E13 and cell E15 are selected, as displayed in Figure 4.11. The last cell, E15, is the active cell.

5. Double-click on **AutoSum** to add the function to the selected cells.

SHORTCUT

If you need to select a rectangular range, the **Shift** key can make the task more efficient. Just click on one corner of the range you want to select, then hold down the **Shift** key and click on the opposite corner of the range. You can also use the Go To dialog box to select a range. Instead of typing a single cell address in the Reference text box, you can enter two cell addresses separated by a colon. When you click on **OK**, the range is selected.

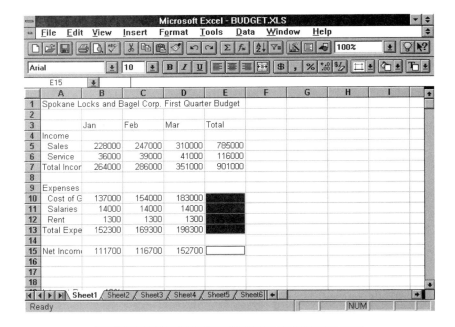

Figure 4.11   *Two non-contiguous selected ranges.*

DEFINING NAMES

So far, we've only referred to cells by their addresses. Naming ranges can make your worksheets much easier to understand. Using names in formulas instead of ranges of cell addresses can make it instantly clear what the formula does. For example, B7-B13 is meaningless until you look at the worksheet and determine what these cell addresses represent. However, if the formula read Total Income-Total Expenses, you'd know exactly what was going on.

You can name individual cells or ranges of cells. You can also specify the name you want to assign, or let Excel do it for you. Generally, an appropriate name is already adjacent to the cell or range of cells you want to name. If this is the case, you can include the name with the range and let Excel use it.

Let's create names for the income and expense categories, including total income and total expenses.

1. Select the ranges **A5** through **D7** and **A10** through **D13**, as displayed in Figure 4.12. Remember to use the **Ctrl** key to select non-contiguous ranges.

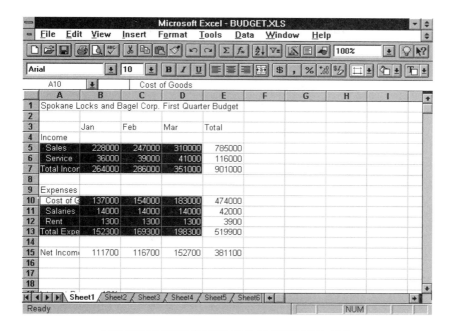

Figure 4.12 *The selected ranges to be named.*

2. Choose **Insert**, **Name**, **Create**.

The Insert Names dialog box appears, as displayed in Figure 4.13 with the Create Names in Left Column check box checked.

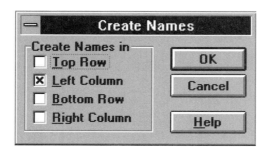

Figure 4.13 *The Create Names dialog box.*

3. Click on **OK**.

Although Excel uses the names in the left column, they aren't included as part of the range. You can use the Define Name dialog box to see which ranges each name is applied to, but the easiest way—and a good shortcut for selecting a named range—is the *name list* in the cell reference area. Let's use this method to select the Service range.

4. Click on the **Arrow** for the name list, just to the right of the cell reference area.

    The drop-down list, as shown in Figure 4.14, displays the names that are contained in the worksheet.

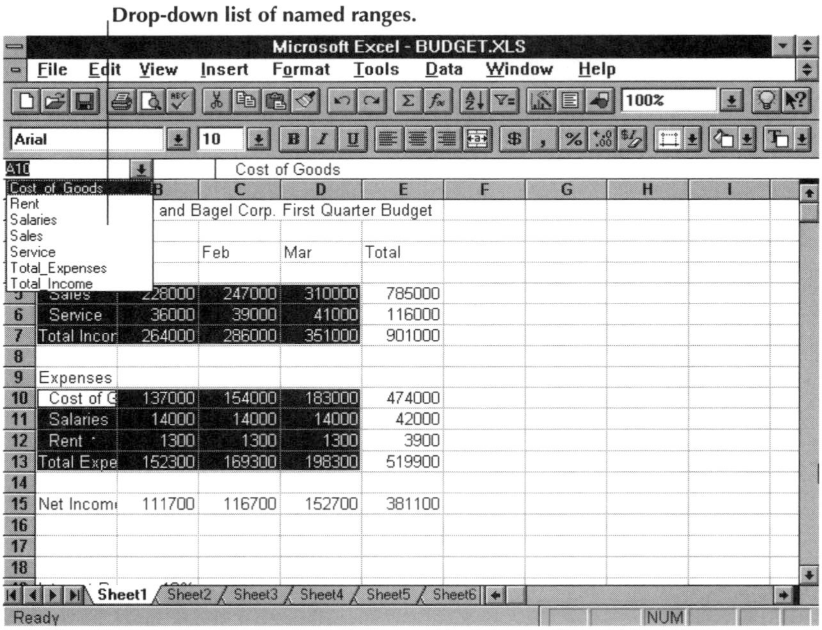

Figure 4.14 *The worksheet's named ranges.*

5. Click on **Service** in the list to select the range B6 through D6.

    Now let's make the formulas in the worksheet more understandable by substituting the range addresses with the range names. To have Excel automatically apply range names, we first need to select the cells that contain formulas or functions. To make sure we don't miss any, we'll select the whole worksheet. A shortcut for selecting the entire worksheet is to click on the **Select All** box (the rectangle in the upper-left corner of the worksheet where the row and column heading intersect).

6. Click on the **Select All** box.

7. Choose **Insert**, **Name**, **Apply**.

The Apply Names dialog box, with all the range names highlighted, is shown in Figure 4.15. If some of the names aren't highlighted, click on each of them.

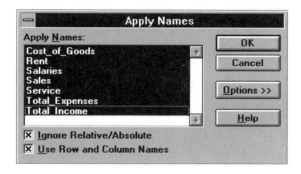

Figure 4.15   *The Apply Names dialog box.*

8. Click on **OK** to apply the names to all the formulas and functions that refer to those ranges.

The formula in B7 used to read, =B5+B6. Let's take a look at how it's changed.

9. Click on cell **B7** and look at the formula bar.

The new formula is =Sales+Service. Click on some of the other cells containing formulas or functions to see how the names have been applied.

INSERTING AND DELETING ROWS AND COLUMNS

As you create and edit worksheets, you frequently need to insert or delete rows and columns. Perhaps you want to add or remove categories or time periods.

Let's insert a row to add a new category, income, to our budget worksheet, showing interest income for the company's investments.

WARNING

Inserting or deleting rows or columns can be very dangerous. You could inadvertently interfere with some data that you can't see on the screen. You could have data off to the side, or above or below the portion of the worksheet that is currently visible.

When inserting or deleting rows or columns, be sure to take into account the effect these actions could have on all portions of your worksheet.

Even though Excel provides an Undo feature to get you out of sticky situations, it's always a good idea to save your work just before making any sort of change that could wreak havoc on your worksheet.

1. Move to cell A6. Actually, any cell in row 6 will do.

2. Choose **Insert**, **Rows**.

   A new row has been inserted and named ranges have been adjusted to reflect their new locations, as have cells containing formulas and functions.

3. Enter the data for the new row, as shown in Figure 4.16.

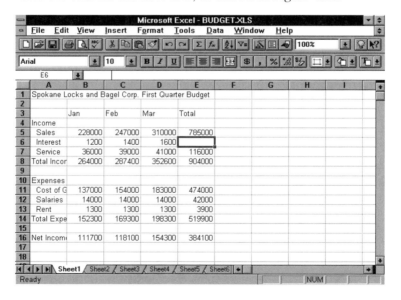

Figure 4.16 *The Budget worksheet with the data entered for the newly inserted row.*

Notice that the January Total Income calculation didn't adjust to accommodate the new cell, but February and March did. What happened? January used a formula that added two specific cells, while February and March used the SUM function to add a range of cells. When we inserted a row, the new row was included in the **SUM** function's range, but was not automatically added to the formula.

We fix this by replacing the formula with the **SUM** function. We also use **AutoSum** to add the calculation for the quarter total interest.

4. Move to cell B8 and double-click on the **AutoSum** toolbar button.

5. Move to cell E6 and double-click on the **AutoSum** button.

One way to reduce expenses would be to get rid of the rent. Let's delete row 13 to improve the company's profit picture.

6. Move to any cell in row 13 and choose **Edit**, **Delete**.

The Delete dialog box, as displayed in Figure 4.17.

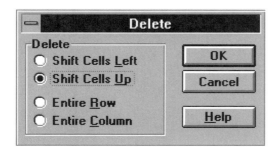

Figure 4.17   *The Delete dialog box.*

Because only a single cell is selected, Excel suggests shifting the cells below the active cell. This is not what we had in mind. We want to get rid of the entire row.

7. Click in the **Entire** Row option button and click on **OK**.

N O T E   If you see a dialog box telling you that Excel can't resolve the circular reference, click on **OK**. A circular reference usually means that the formula in the formula cell refers to itself. For example, the formula =B4+B5+B6 in cell B6 would be a circular reference.

Okay, that got rid of our rent, but wait a minute. Maybe we need to pay rent after all, so we'll have a place to operate our business. We'll use the Excel's Undo feature to reverse the deletion.

8. Choose **Edit**, **Undo** or click on the Undo toolbar button to restore the rent row.

CHANGING COLUMN WIDTHS

Finally, what you've been waiting for. When text entries are too long and they are truncated or numbers show up as pound signs (#), your column is probably too narrow and needs to be adjusted.

I'll bet you've been anxiously looking at column A since we first entered the numbers and lost part to the text. Well, the time has come to fix the problem and adjust the column.

You can change the column width by entering a new value in the Column Width dialog box by choosing **Format**, **Column**, **Width**, but there's an even easier, more visual way. You can position the mouse pointer over the right border of the column heading and drag it to the left to reduce the width, or to the right to increase the width. Let's use the dragging method to increase the width of column A.

1. Position the mouse pointer over the right border of the column heading, and drag to the right about 1/2", as shown in Figure 4.18.

2. Release the mouse button to complete the adjustment.

   The column is now wide enough to display all the text in *most* of the cells. The disadvantage of the dragging method is that you may need to make several stabs at the proper adjustment before you get it right. Also, if there are long cell entries below what you can see, you won't know if you have it right until you scroll down, or print the worksheet and it's too late.

   There is an even better way. When you double-click on the right border of the column heading, Excel adjusts the column so it is wide enough to accommodate the longest cell entry.

   But wait a minute. If the column is adjusted for the longest entry, it will be wide enough for the title in cell A1, which would make the column much too wide for the remaining entries.

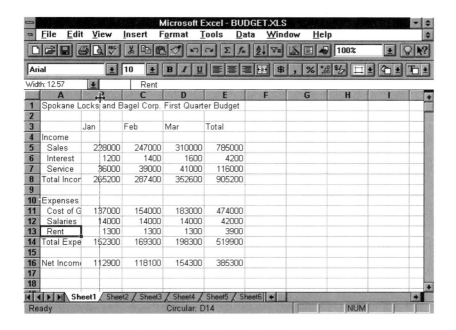

Figure 4.18   *The column width being adjusted.*

3. Select the range **A4** through **A16** and choose **Format**, **Column**, **AutoFit Selection**. Now the column width is adjusted properly.

4. Save your work and exit Excel if you're not continuing on to the next chapter at this time.

A FINAL THOUGHT

Now you know that you will always be able to find your worksheets, and this worksheet is starting to shape up nicely. The columns are finally adjusted to accommodate the cell entries, and the range names make the worksheet clearer.

In the next chapter, you learn some ways to make the worksheet look snazzier. You also learn how to add notes to further clarify the worksheet, and how to protect portions of the worksheet.

Chapter 5

Enhancing and Annotating Your Worksheet

* ALIGNING CELL CONTENTS
* FORMATTING NUMBERS
* CHANGING FONTS
* ADDING BORDERS AND SHADING
* USING AUTOFORMAT
* ADDING NOTES
* PROTECTING DATA

87

This chapter concentrates on aesthetics, adding those nice little touches that make the worksheet more attractive, readable and, perhaps most importantly, persuasive.

Most worksheets are prepared to persuade someone else to come to a particular conclusion. In the case of a budget or forecast, perhaps you're trying to convince your boss, or the board of directors, to go along with your assumptions. If you're preparing a business plan, maybe you need to sell your plan so a banker or venture capitalist will provide the needed funds for your new startup or to expand your existing business.

Whatever your worksheet's purpose, the way it looks and how well it's documented does matter and should be given as much consideration as the underlying data. Don't worry if you think you don't have an eye for good design. Excel even has the ability to format your worksheet for you.

ALIGNING CELL CONTENTS

Choosing the appropriate alignment for the contents of your cells can have an immediate impact on the look of the worksheet. You have seen that, by default, numbers are right-aligned and text is aligned on the left. A variety of alignment options can be applied to a single cell or a range of cells.

Let's align the column headings so they are centered over the numbers. Aligning cells falls in the general category of *cell formatting*. You can reach the cell formatting options through the Format menu, but there is a shortcut.

1. Select cells **B3** through **E3**.

2. Right-click (click the right mouse button) anywhere inside the selected range to display the Shortcut menu, as displayed in Figure 5.1.

SHORTCUT

There are Shortcut menus for almost every screen or worksheet element. You can display the shortcut menu by right-clicking on the object you want to manipulate. If you aren't sure what sort of manipulation you can perform on an object, the Shortcut menu lets you know. We'll be using shortcut menus for many tasks as the book proceeds.

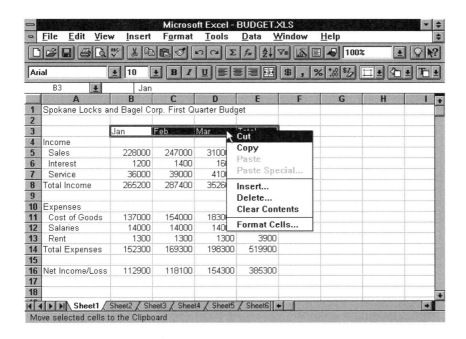

Figure 5.1   *The Shortcut menu for the selected cells.*

3. Choose **Format Cells** in the Shortcut menu.

   The Format Cells dialog box appears, as shown in Figure 5.2.

   The tabs in the dialog box let you specify what sort of formatting you want to do. We want to get to the Alignment portion of the dialog box.

4. If it isn't already highlighted, click on the **Alignment** tab to display the Alignment portion of the dialog box.

   This dialog box lets you specify the type of horizontal and vertical alignment you want, the orientation of the text in the cells, and if you want long text entries wrapped (split into several lines).

   The two alignment types that might need a bit of explanation are Justify and Fill. If the **Wrap** check box is checked, the Justify option forces the cell entry to spread out so the left and right edges are even, like the text in this book. The Fill option repeats the cell entry until the cell is filled.

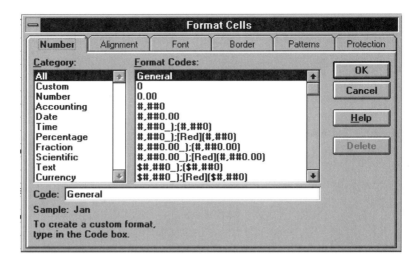

Figure 5.2 *The Format Cells dialog box Number portion.*

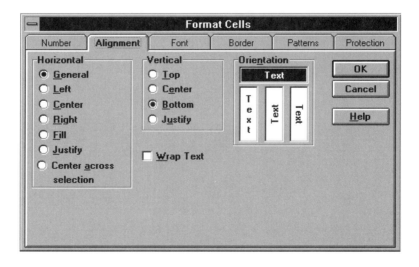

Figure 5.3 *The Format Cells dialog box Alignment portion.*

5. Click on the **Center** option button in the Horizontal portion of the dialog box and click on **OK**.

The toolbar has buttons for some of the more common cell formatting options, including these alignment options. Instead of using the dialog box, you can simply click on the appropriate toolbar button. In the previous step, you would click on the Center button on the Formatting toolbar.

SHORTCUT

Each column heading is now centered over its column, as displayed in Figure 5.4.

	A	B	C	D	E	F	G	H	I
1	Spokane Locks and Bagel Corp. First Quarter Budget								
2									
3		Jan	Feb	Mar	Total				
4	Income								
5	Sales	228000	247000	310000	785000				
6	Interest	1200	1400	1600	4200				
7	Service	36000	39000	41000	116000				
8	Total Income	265200	287400	352600	905200				
9									
10	Expenses								
11	Cost of Goods	137000	154000	183000	474000				
12	Salaries	14000	14000	14000	42000				
13	Rent	1300	1300	1300	3900				
14	Total Expenses	152300	169300	198300	519900				
15									
16	Net Income/Loss	112900	118100	154300	385300				
17									
18									

Figure 5.4 *The center-aligned column headings.*

The title in cell A1 would look better if it were centered over all the columns in the worksheet. We can't just center it in the cell. It's already longer than the column width of column A. What can we do? One of the alignment options is to center across a selection. That's the option we'll use for the title.

6. Select cells **A1** through **E1**, choose **Format Cells** and click on the **Center Across Columns** toolbar button.

The title is now centered between columns A and E.

FORMATTING NUMBERS

In addition to changing cell alignment, you may also choose to alter the format of the numbers in your worksheet. All of the numbers have been entered using Excel's default formatting. The numbers would look better if they were formatted with commas separating thousands and a decimal point with two decimal places.

1. Select **B5** through **E16** and click on the **Comma Style** button on the Formatting toolbar.

The number format has been changed as shown in Figure 5.5, but some of the numbers have been replaced by pound signs. Uh oh! What does this mean? It means some of the numbers, with their new commas and decimal places, are now too wide for the column width. Don't worry, we can fix that.

2. Choose **Format, Column, AutoFit Selection**.

The column widths have been adjusted to accommodate the new number format, as shown in Figure 5.6.

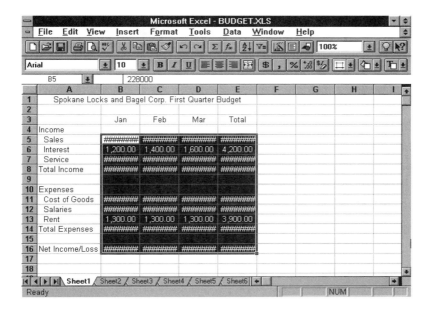

Figure 5.5   *The numbers with the comma format.*

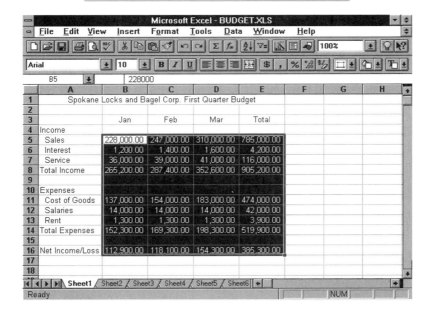

Figure 5.6   *The adjusted column widths.*

The totals might look better if they were formatted with dollar signs, so let's take care of that little detail now.

3. Select the ranges **B8** through **E8**, **E5** through **E7**, **B16** through **E16**, and **E11** through **E14**. Remember to use the **Ctrl** key to select non-contiguous ranges.

4. Click on the **Currency Style** button on the Formatting toolbar.

5. Once again choose **Format**, **Column**, **AutoFit Selection** to adjust the column widths to accommodate the dollar signs.

    Your screen should now look like Figure 5.7.

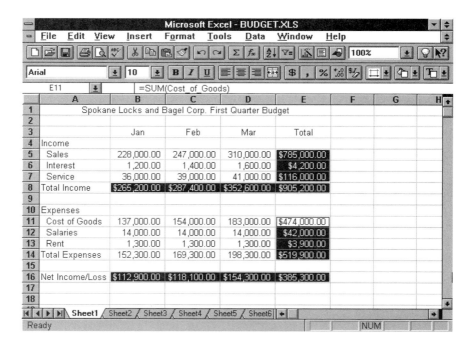

Figure 5.7 *The totals are formatted with the currency style.*

There are many other number formatting options available through the Cell Formatting dialog box, which can be displayed through the Shortcut menu or the Format menu.

N O T E

CHANGING FONTS

In Excel, a font is a particular typeface. Windows 3.1 includes several typefaces from which you can choose to add impact to your documents. You can also purchase additional fonts that work with almost any Windows program. Choosing the correct font for the situation can do more to help or hinder your cause than just about any other type of formatting you can do to your worksheet, so choose carefully.

There are many good books available to help you choose and use fonts well. If one of your goals is to produce the most professional looking and persuasive worksheets possible, learning more about fonts is a worthwhile investment of your time and money.

N O T E

In addition to changing the font, you can change the style (bold, italic, underline) and the size of the font. Font sizes are specified in *points* because most fonts these days are *proportional fonts.*

The fonts used on a typewriter (and even some that are still used on computers) were fixed-width or monospaced, where each character took up the same amount of horizontal space. In proportional fonts, some characters are wider or narrower than others. For this reason, using the old method of measurement, based on the number of characters per inch (pitch) no longer works. Points measure the font's height. One point is roughly 1/72nd of an inch.

Typical font sizes for the main body of the worksheet are between 9 and 12-points. Anything smaller than 9-point type is considered fine print. Larger than 12-point type is considered large type.

With the introduction of Windows 3.1, a new font technology called *TrueType* fonts, became available. TrueType fonts have several advantages over other font technologies. They are scalable to just about any point size you choose and have corresponding screen

N O T E

fonts so they display very accurately. They work with just about every Windows program in existence.

Unless you are a real font connoisseur, you'll likely find the quality of TrueType fonts more than adequate. Keep in mind that TrueType is not a brand of fonts, but rather a *type* of font technology. You can buy TrueType fonts from a variety of manufacturers and the quality can vary.

Let's change the font, style and size of the title so that it really stands out.

1. Click on cell **A1**.

2. Click on the **Arrow** for the font drop-down list on the Formatting toolbar to display the list of available fonts, as displayed in Figure 5.8.

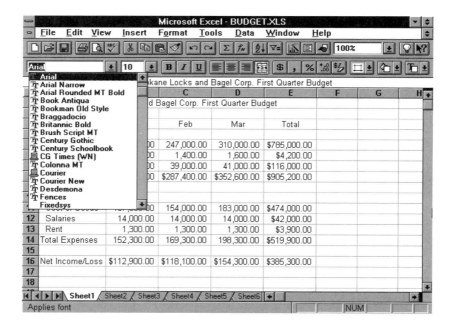

Figure 5.8   *The Formatting toolbar's drop-down font list.*

The fonts in your list may differ from those in the figure. Only those fonts that are installed and available on your system appear on your list.

Also, notice that some of the fonts have TT in front of them signifying that they are TrueType fonts.

Let's use a slightly more ornate font called Times New Roman, which is currently out of view near the bottom of the list.

3. Use the scroll bar to scroll down until Times New Roman comes into view and then click on **Times New Roman**.

Notice that the typeface of the title has changed. Since this is a title, it should also be larger, so we'll change the size. The current size, as you can see from the Font Size box on the Formatting toolbar, is 10 points. Let's change it to 18 points.

4. Click on the **Font Size** arrow on the Formatting toolbar to reveal the list of font sizes, as shown in Figure 5.9.

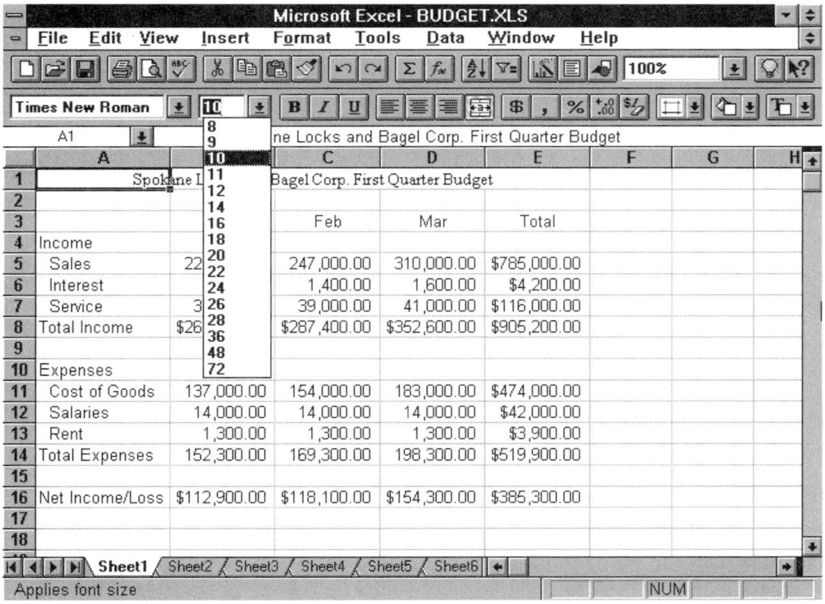

Figure 5.9   *The Font Size drop-down list.*

Unlike the list of fonts, the Font Size list only lists the more common sizes. However, you are not limited to these sizes. You can type in the size you wanted, say 19 points, and the font would change to that size.

5. Click on **18** to enlarge the title, as displayed in Figure 5.10.

	A	B	C	D	E	F	G	H
1	kane Locks and Bagel Corp. First Quarter Budget							
2								
3		Jan	Feb	Mar	Total			
4	Income							
5	Sales	228,000.00	247,000.00	310,000.00	$785,000.00			
6	Interest	1,200.00	1,400.00	1,600.00	$4,200.00			
7	Service	36,000.00	39,000.00	41,000.00	$116,000.00			
8	Total Income	$265,200.00	$287,400.00	$352,600.00	$905,200.00			
9								
10	Expenses							
11	Cost of Goods	137,000.00	154,000.00	183,000.00	$474,000.00			
12	Salaries	14,000.00	14,000.00	14,000.00	$42,000.00			
13	Rent	1,300.00	1,300.00	1,300.00	$3,900.00			
14	Total Expenses	152,300.00	169,300.00	198,300.00	$519,900.00			
15								
16	Net Income/Loss	$112,900.00	$118,100.00	$154,300.00	$385,300.00			
17								

Figure 5.10   *The 18-point type.*

Notice that the row height automatically adjusted for the larger size. We do have one small problem here. Because the title is centered over columns A through E, the left portion of the text is cut off. Change the title back to left alignment to fix that problem.

6. Click on the **Align Left** button on the Formatting toolbar.

Now you can see the entire title again. We'll add one more embellishment before we're done. Let's make the title bold.

7. Click on the **Bold** toolbar button.

Your worksheet should look like Figure 5.11.

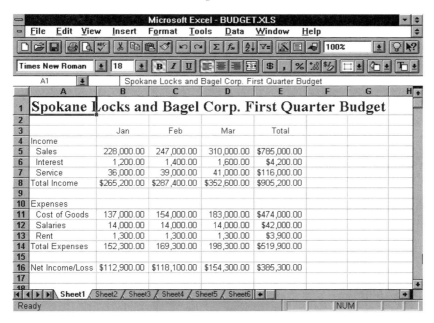

Figure 5.11 *The bold title completely visible.*

N O T E

Although the fastest way to change fonts is from the toolbar, it may be advantageous to use the Font portion of the Format Cells dialog box, particularly if you aren't familiar with the way the different fonts look. The dialog box provides a preview of the font, including size and style, so you can see what the font looks like before you apply it.

ADDING BORDERS AND SHADING

To further embellish your worksheet, you can surround cells with borders and fill them with shading. Just like fonts, you need to use appropriate borders and shading or these elements can detract from the look of the worksheet.

Let's add a border and some shading to the column headings.

1. Select **B3** through **E3**.
2. Click on the **Arrow** for the Border drop-down box on the Formatting toolbar.

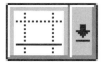

The Border drop-down box is displayed, as shown in Figure 5.12.

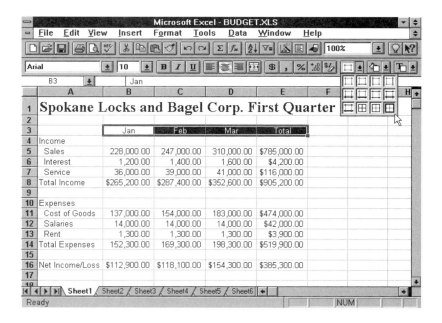

Figure 5.12 *The Border drop-down list.*

3. Click on the border style of your choice in the lower-right corner on the drop-down box. (It is the one the mouse pointer is pointing to in the figure.)

4. Click outside the selection so you can see the border surrounding the column headings, as shown in Figure 5.13.

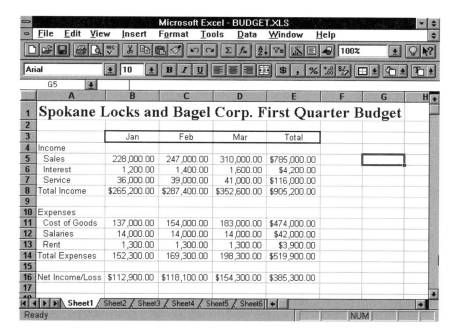

Figure 5.13   *The column headings surrounded by a border.*

Now let's add some shading to the titles.

5. Select **B3** through **E3** again and right-click in the selection area to display the shortcut menu.

6. Click on **Format Cells** to display the Format Cells dialog box and then click on the **Patterns** tab to see the Patterns portion of the dialog box, as shown in Figure 5.14.

7. Click on the **Arrow** next to the Patterns box to display the available shading patterns.

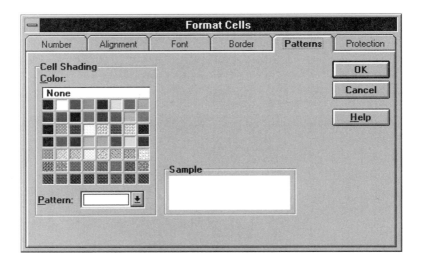

Figure 5.14   *The Format Cells dialog box Patterns portion.*

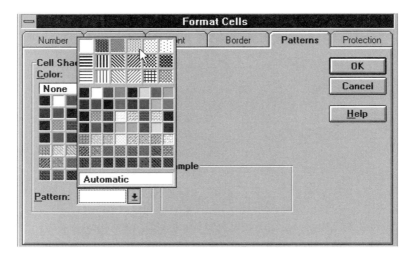

Figure 5.15   *The available patterns.*

8.   Click on the fourth pattern from the left on the top row. (It's the one the mouse pointer is pointing at in the figure.)

The sample area in the dialog box displays the pattern you have chosen.

9. Click **OK** and then click outside the selected area so you can see the pattern's effect.

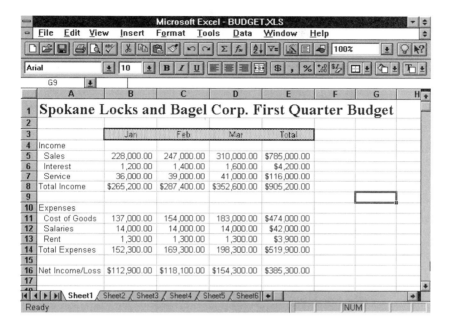

	A	B	C	D	E	F	G	H
1	Spokane Locks and Bagel Corp. First Quarter Budget							
2								
3		Jan	Feb	Mar	Total			
4	Income							
5	Sales	228,000.00	247,000.00	310,000.00	$785,000.00			
6	Interest	1,200.00	1,400.00	1,600.00	$4,200.00			
7	Service	36,000.00	39,000.00	41,000.00	$116,000.00			
8	Total Income	$265,200.00	$287,400.00	$352,600.00	$905,200.00			
9								
10	Expenses							
11	Cost of Goods	137,000.00	154,000.00	183,000.00	$474,000.00			
12	Salaries	14,000.00	14,000.00	14,000.00	$42,000.00			
13	Rent	1,300.00	1,300.00	1,300.00	$3,900.00			
14	Total Expenses	152,300.00	169,300.00	198,300.00	$519,900.00			
15								
16	Net Income/Loss	$112,900.00	$118,100.00	$154,300.00	$385,300.00			
17								

Figure 5.16 *The column headings with a border and shading.*

Graphic elements, such as shading, can look very different on the printed page than they do on the screen. Don't decide that a pattern is too dark or light until you print.

N O T E

USING AUTOFORMAT

Suppose you have as little design sense as I have—which is very little. Excel's AutoFormat feature automatically turns your shabby old unformatted worksheet into a work of art.

All you have to do is select the portion of the worksheet you want automatically formatted and choose the most pleasing format style from the list in the AutoFormat dialog box. Let's try it out.

1. Select the range **A3** through **E16** and choose **Format**, **AutoFormat**, to display the AutoFormat dialog box, as shown in Figure 5.17.

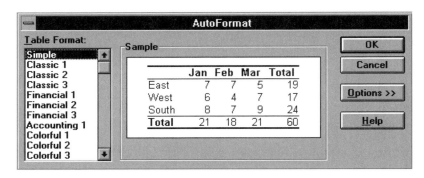

Figure 5.17   *The AutoFormat dialog box.*

The Simple Table Format is highlighted and you can see what that style looks like in the Sample area. The easiest way to check out the various options is with the down arrow key. Each time you press the **Down Arrow** key, you see another format style in the sample area.

We'll use the Classic 1 style. It's simple, yet elegant. We don't want to use anything too overpowering, do we?

2. Click on **Classic 1**, then **OK,** and then click outside the selected area so you can behold the beauty of the newly formatted worksheet, as displayed in Figure 5.18.

Adding Notes

As hard as you try to make your worksheet understandable and self explanatory to anyone who reads it, some entries just need more detailed explanations than the surrounding cells provide. Wouldn't it be great if you could write some explanatory text on one of those yellow sticky notes and attach it to a cell so your readers could see exactly what you had in mind?

Excel actually has a better system for attaching notes to cells than yellow stickies. To attach a cell note, just move to the cell you want to attach the note to and choose **Insert Note**.

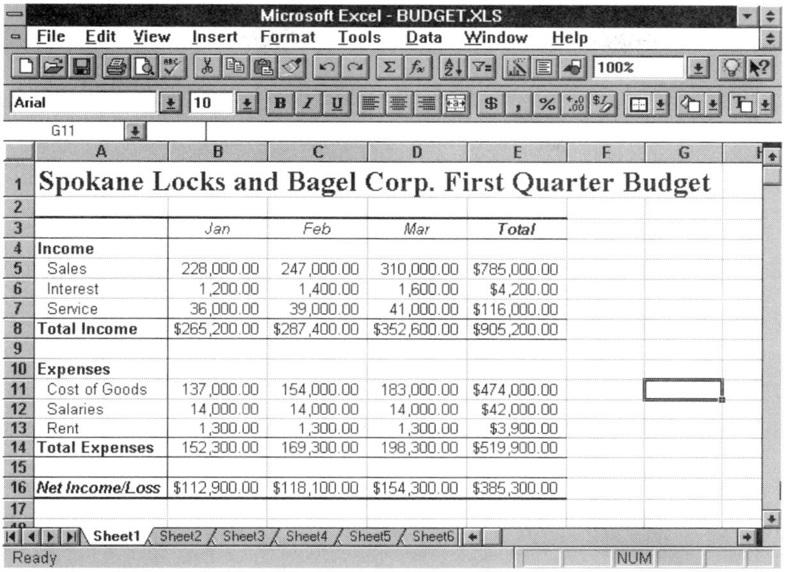

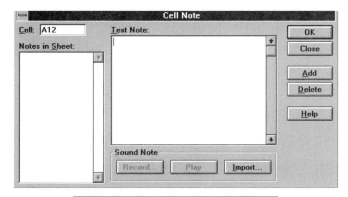

Figure 5.18   *The worksheet formatted with the Classic 1 style.*

Let's attach a note to cell A12 to explain our assumptions for the salaries figures.

1. Move to cell A12 and choose **Insert**, **Note**.

    The Cell Note dialog box appears, as displayed in Figure 5.19, with the insertion point in the Text Note area.

Figure 5.19   *The Cell Note dialog box.*

2. Type the following text: **The salary figures assume a 6% raise for Sally and Joe, and an 8% increase for Mary**.

3. Click on **OK** to attach the note to the cell.

A red dot appears in the upper-right corner of the cell indicating that there is a note attached. The red dots do not print when you print the worksheet, although you can print the notes if you wish.

When you want to display a note that is attached to a cell, you follow pretty much the same procedures as for attaching a note. Let's display the note in cell A12.

4. Choose **Insert**, **Note**.

The note appears in the Cell Note dialog box, as shown in Figure 5.20. Any other notes are listed in the Notes in Sheet list and you can display those by clicking on them.

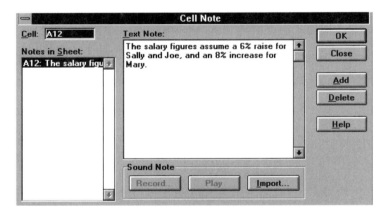

Figure 5.20 *The Cell Note dialog box with the note displayed.*

N O T E If your computer is equipped with sound recording capabilities, you can attach sound notes to a cell. In this way you can explain what you mean, or give instructions to the user, verbally. To attach a sound note, you call up the Cell Note dialog box and click on the **Record** button. You then see the Record dialog box where you can make your recording. To play the note, call up the Cell Note dialog box and click on **Play**.

PROTECTING DATA

If you want to ensure that certain cells in the worksheet can't be accidentally altered (or even seen at all) you can lock or hide them. It's often a good idea to lock cells containing formulas so someone cannot accidentally delete them or enter something over them.

If your worksheet contains confidential information, you may want to hide portions of it. You can also require that a password be used to remove the protection you've specified.

Let's protect the formulas in column E.

1. Select cells **E5** through **E16** and right-click in the selected area to display the shortcut menu.

2. Choose **Format Cells** and click on the **Protection** tab to display the Protection portion of the Format Cells dialog box, as displayed in Figure 5.21.

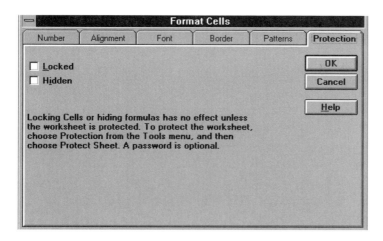

Figure 5.21   *The Format Cells dialog box Protection portion.*

3. Click in the **Locked** check box, unless it is already checked, and then click on **OK**.

Before the protection takes effect, you must turn on the protection facility.

4. Choose **Tools**, **Protection**, **Protect Sheet** to display the Protect Sheet dialog box, as displayed in Figure 5.22.

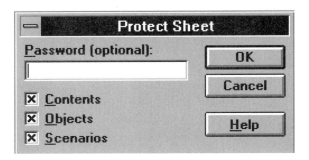

Figure 5.22   *The Protect Sheet dialog box.*

5. After making sure all three check boxes are checked, click on **OK**. (We won't add a password.)

   Now, let's see if the protection is really working.

6. Press the **Delete** key to try to delete the contents of the selected cells.

   The message dialog box, as shown in Figure 5.23, lets you know that you cannot mess with locked cells. It works!

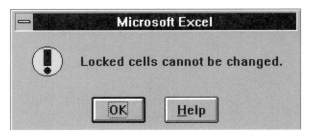

Figure 5.23   *The message dialog box showing that a cell is locked.*

7. Click on **OK** to clear the dialog box.

8. Choose **Tools**, **Protection**, **Unprotect Sheet** to remove protection from this sheet.

9. Save your work and exit Excel if you are not continuing on to the next chapter.

A FINAL THOUGHT

You now know how to put together a worksheet so that it is presentable, fully documented, and protected. In the next chapter you learn how to transfer your masterpiece to the printed page.

Chapter 6

Printing Worksheets

* CHOOSING A PRINTER
* SETTING UP THE PAGE

Because the printed page is ultimately how the information in most worksheets is communicated, printing may be the most important task you can learn in Excel. The options for what portion of your workbook (or worksheets) you want to print, and how you want them printed, are almost limitless.

CHOOSING A PRINTER

Windows makes life easy by allowing all your Windows programs to share the same printer files without having to install your printer for each program, as you do with non-Windows programs. If you already have one or more printers installed in Windows, they are automatically available to Excel. If you don't have a printer installed, refer to your Windows documentation for instructions.

If you have more than one printer installed, you need to choose the printer you want to use from the Printer Setup dialog box to be sure Excel uses the right one.

1. Start Excel and open the **Budget** workbook if it isn't already on your screen.

2. Choose **File**, **Print**.

    The Print dialog box appears, as shown in Figure 6.1.

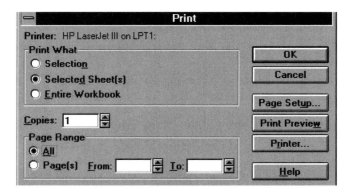

Figure 6.1 *The Print dialog box.*

When we are ready to print the worksheet in a little while, we'll take a look at the various options in the Print dialog box.

3. Click on the **Pr̲inter** button to display the Printer Setup dialog box, as shown in Figure 6.2.

   If the highlighted printer is the printer you want to use, you are all set. Otherwise you need to select the printer you want to use from the list.

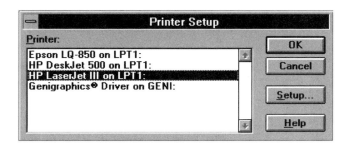

Figure 6.2   *The Printer Setup dialog box.*

4. Click on the printer you want to use from the list of available printers, then click on **OK**.

   If your chosen printer is already selected click on **OK**.

N O T E   The list of printers you see in the Printer Setup dialog box most likely differs from the list in the figure. Your list reflects the printers that have been installed in Windows. If only one printer is connected to your computer, your list probably only has that one printer's name in the list.

WARNING   If you select a different printer in another Windows program, Excel uses that printer the next time you print in Excel. If you are switching between printers in other applications, be sure to check the Printer Setup dialog box before printing in Excel.

You could click on the **OK** button to print the active worksheet according to default settings, but we're going to explore some of the other printing options before sending the worksheet to the printer.

SETTING UP PAGES

Excel needs some information about how you want your pages printed before you start printing. If you don't provide this information, Excel prints using its current settings, which may not be what you want to use.

Let's take a look at the settings in the Print dialog box on your screen. Refer to Figure 6.1. The Print dialog box lets you opt to print the Selection (if you've selected a portion of your worksheet), the Selected Sheet(s), or the entire workbook. You'll see how to specify specific ranges to print in a little while.

You can also choose how many copies you want to print and whether you want to print all the pages or, if not, which specific pages. Let's call up the Page Setup dialog box now to start giving Excel some more details.

1. Click on the **Page Setup** button to display the Page Setup dialog box, as shown in Figure 6.3. If the Sheet portion of the dialog box isn't visible, click on the **Sheet** tab.

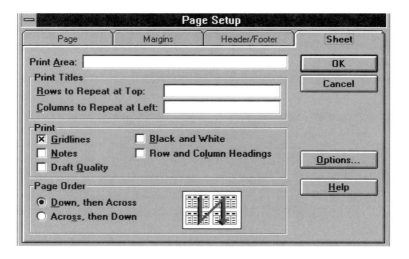

Figure 6.3 *The Page Setup dialog box Sheet portion.*

In the Print Area text box, you can specify a range of cells to print. Let's specify the range A1 through G16.

2. Click in the Print Area text box and type: **A1:G16**

The reason we need to go all the way over to column G is to make sure the entire title is printed. Even though the title is actually in cell A1, the print area specifies an actual rectangular area on the worksheet. If we only printed over to column E, for example, we'd end up cutting off the last word and a half of the title.

SHORTCUT

You can use the pointing method to specify a print area. Simply point to one corner of the rectangular area you want to print and then drag to the opposite corner and release the mouse button. The range automatically is entered in the Print Area text box.

This method can be a little tricky because the Page Setup dialog box usually obscures the range you want to print. You can drag over the dialog box, but that's kind of like flying blind, so, whether typing the range or pointing and dragging, it's a good idea to know what range you want to print before you display the Page Setup dialog box.

The **Rows to Repeat at Top** and the **Columns to Repeat at Left** text boxes let you specify one or more rows and columns to repeat on each page of multiple-page printouts. This can be useful for keeping track of which column and row headings a particular cell entry belongs to. We don't have a multiple-page worksheet to print, so we won't use these options.

The check boxes in the Print area of the dialog box provide several options for customizing the way your pages print.

* **Gridlines** chooses whether to print the lines you see on your worksheet separating rows and columns.

* **Notes** prints any cell notes you have attached to your worksheet.

* **Draft Quality** causes Excel to omit any charts or other graphic objects, as well as gridlines, from your printout. Draft Quality often causes your pages to print faster.

* **Black and White** is chosen if you have used any colors for text or graphics on your worksheet and are printing on a black and white printer. This option may also cause your pages to print faster on a color printer since color printers often print slower in color than black and white.

* **Row and Column Heading** causes the row numbers and the column letters to print. This can make it easier to determine which cell a particular entry is in, but it can also detract from the look of the page.

✳ **Print Order** specifies how multiple pages print. This won't affect our single-page printout.

3. With the Print Area text box filled in and only the Gridlines check box checked, click on the **Page** tab to display the Page portion of the Page Setup dialog box, as shown in Figure 6.4.

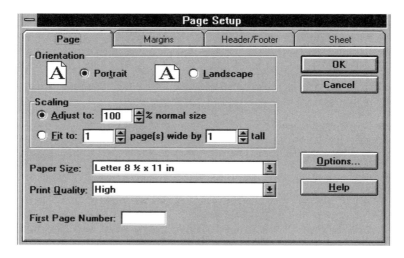

Figure 6.4   *The Page Setup dialog box Page portion.*

✳ **Orientation** determines whether you want the information printed on the page in the normal upright (*portrait*) orientation, or sideways (*landscape*). Portrait orientation allows you to print more rows but fewer columns on a page. Landscape accommodates more columns but fewer rows. We'll keep portrait as our orientation option.

✳ **Scaling** adjusts the size of the document you are about to print. The Adjust to option button lets you print at 100% (normal size) or a smaller or larger percentage. For example, if you adjust to 200%, all the data, including text, numbers, and graphics prints at twice their normal size. This means that each page only holds half as much data. You can scale pages up to 400% and down to 10%.

✳ **Fit to** lets you force the information you want to print to fit on a specified number of pages. This can be useful for shoehorning your data into fewer pages than it might otherwise require. This option does not enlarge the data on the worksheet to fit on the specified pages.

WARNING

Be careful with this option. You could end up with such small print that you cannot read it. Actually, come to think of it, for some worksheets, that might be an advantage!

✳ **Paper Size** lets you choose the paper size you are using in your printer. Some printers are only able to use one or two sizes of paper and the list reflects your printer's capabilities.

✳ **Print Quality** selects the quality of print for your document. The trade-off here is that choosing a higher quality generally results in slower print speeds. You may want to print with a lower print quality for drafts and a higher quality of final prints.

N O T E

Some printers don't have print quality options. For others, a change in print quality only affects graphics. The latter is true of laser printers. On a laser printer, the worksheet's text and numbers print at the same quality regardless of your print quality choice in Excel.

✳ **First Page Number** specifies the starting number that is printed on the first page of a worksheet. For example, if you enter 3 as the First Page Number for a three-page worksheet you are about to print, the pages are numbered 3, 4, and 5. This option has no effect if you choose not to have page numbers printed on your pages.

We won't be changing any of the options on the Page portion of the dialog box, so let's take a look at the Margins portion of the dialog box.

4. Click on the **Margins** tab to display the Margins portion of the dialog box, as displayed in Figure 6.5.

Changing the margin setting lets you determine where your document appears on the printed page. The default top, bottom, left, and right margins are generally adequate. You may wish to reduce the margins so you can fit more data on a page or you may want to increase the margins so you have more breathing room (white space) around your data.

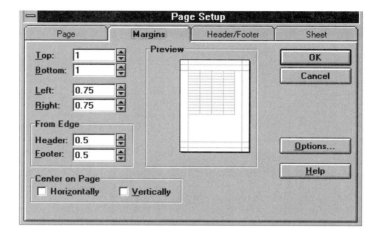

Figure 6.5   *The Page Setup dialog box Margins portion.*

You can also specify how far from the edge of the page your headers and footers appear. You learn more about headers and footers in just a bit.

We use a couple of the options on this dialog box to center the data both vertically and horizontally on the printed page.

5. Click both the **Horizontally** and **Vertically** check boxes in the Center on Page area of the dialog box.

Notice that the Preview area now shows a representation of the data as centered on the page.

Before we finish setting up the pages, let's take a look at headers and footers.

6. Click on the **Header/Footer** tab to display the Header/Footer portion of the Page Setup dialog box, as shown in Figure 6.6.

Headers and footers are text elements that appear at the top and bottom of your printed documents. There is no difference between a header and a footer except that a header appears at the top of the printed page and a footer appears at the bottom.

Excel prints default headers and footers unless you specify different ones, or specify none at all. The default header simply prints the sheet name. The sheet name is Sheet1, Sheet2, and so forth, unless you've changed the name to something else. The default footer is Page 1 for the first page, Page 2 for the second page, and so on.

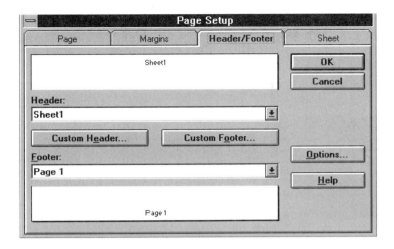

Figure 6.6 *The Page Setup dialog box Header/Footer portion.*

Excel also provides a variety of predefined headers and footers that you can use. Figure 6.7 displays some of the predefined headers (the predefined footers are the same) that can be seen by clicking on the **Arrow** for the Header drop-down list.

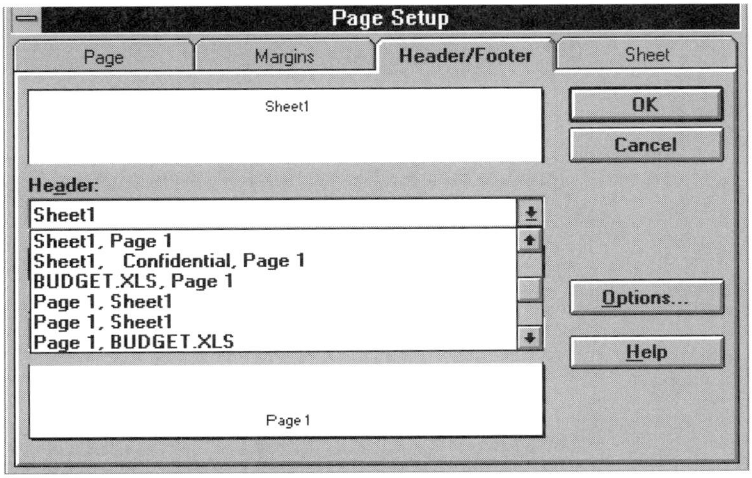

Figure 6.7 *The Header drop-down list.*

Instead of using one of the predefined headers, let's create a custom header.

7. Click on the **Custom Header** button to display the Header dialog box, as shown in Figure 6.8.

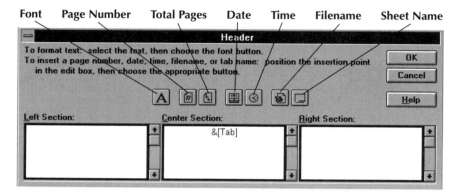

Figure 6.8 The Header dialog box.*

The dialog box displays the current header. But wait a minute. That thing in the middle box doesn't look like the header we saw in the previous dialog box. The default header is the sheet name centered between the left and right margins. What you see in the Header dialog box is the *code* for the sheet name. In addition to the sheet name, when creating a custom header (or footer) you can insert codes for the page number, the total number of pages, the date and time, and the filename by clicking on the appropriate icon. There's even an icon to allow you to change the font you're using for the header or footer.

Let's type some text in the Left Section.

8. Click in the Left Section box and type: **Prepared by Saul Salmon**.

9. Click in the Center Section box and press **Backspace** until all the text is deleted, then click on the **Date** icon. (Refer to Figure 6.8)

10. Click in the Right Section box and then click on the filename icon.

Your screen should now look like Figure 6.9.

11. Click on **OK** to accept the custom header and return to the Header/Footer section of the Page Setup dialog box, where you see what your new header actually looks like.

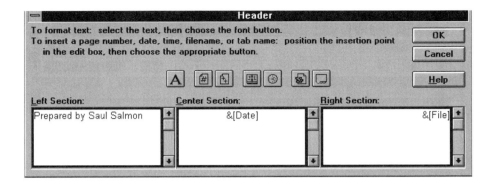

Figure 6.9   *The Header dialog box with the custom header filled in.*

12. Click on **OK** to accept the header and footer and return to the Print dialog box.

    We're just about ready to print, but first we'll preview the page. It's almost always a good idea to preview before sending a document to the printer. It can save time and paper by letting you ensure that everything is just the way you want it.

13. Click on **Print Preview** to display a reasonable facsimile of what your printed pages will look like when they emerge from the printer.

    Because you're looking at a full page, it's hard to see the detail of the worksheet (unless you have a very large screen). Notice that as you move the mouse pointer over the representation of the page, the pointer turns into a magnifying glass. By clicking on a portion of the page, you can zoom in on that portion.

    Let's zoom in on the January column heading (where the mouse pointer is in Figure 6.10).

14. Point to **Jan** and click.

    You can zoom out by clicking anywhere on the page or clicking on the **Zoom** button at the top of the Preview screen. The **Next** and **Previous** buttons let you preview the next and previous pages in multi-page documents. The **Setup** button takes you back to the Page Setup dialog box.

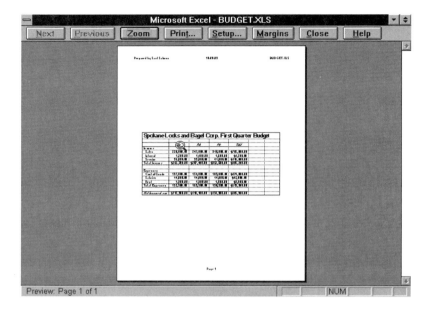

Figure 6.10 *The Print Preview screen.*

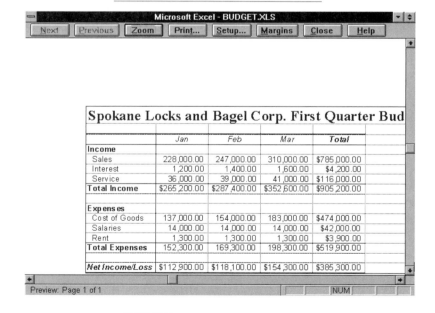

Figure 6.11 *The zoomed preview.*

The one button in preview that does something a bit unique is the **Margins** button. I know, we already looked at the Margins portion of the Page Setup dialog box. But clicking on the **Margins** button in Print Preview lets you change margins by dragging margin and column markers so you can see the result prior to printing.

15. Click on the **Margins** button.

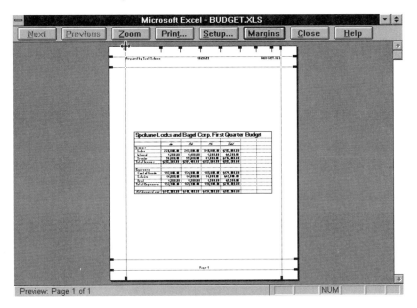

Figure 6.12   *The margin markers displayed in Print Preview.*

By moving the mouse pointer over one of the markers until it turns into crosshairs, as shown in Figure 6.12, you can reposition any of the margins or columns by dragging. The status bar displays information about which margin you are changing and its position as you drag.

We won't change any of the margins here. It's time to print. Be sure your printer is properly connected, has paper, is turned on, on line, and ready to print.

16. Click on the **Print** button to send the worksheet to the printer.

You see a message dialog box informing you that you are printing to the printer you have selected. In a few seconds, your printed worksheet should appear.

The next time you want to print using the same settings, simply click on the **Print** button on the toolbar.

To go directly to Print Preview, click on **Print Preview** on the toolbar.

17. Save your work so the print setting is retained for the next time you want to print and exit Excel if you are not moving on to the next chapter.

A FINAL THOUGHT

The process of setting up your pages for printing and sending them to your printer should be a piece of cake by now. In the next chapter you learn how to turn your worksheet's text and numbers into beautiful charts and graphs.

Chapter 7

Creating a Chart

As the saying goes, a picture is worth a thousand words. If you've ever thought of a chart as *a nice little extra*, or even a *waste of time and energy*, think again!

If the purpose of your worksheet is to increase your readers' understanding of the numerical data and to persuade them to accept your point of view, then adding a chart is much more than a frill. It is an integral part of the information package. A chart can enhance clarity and add strength to your message.

Until now we've been working strictly with numerical data. I won't deny the importance of numbers—just try sending a bunch of pictures to the IRS and see how far you get! But often, numeric data is just a means to an end. A chart can enable you to direct your reader's focus and make your points with pizzazz.

CHART FUNDAMENTALS

Before we start creating charts, we need to understand some fundamental chart concepts and terminology. After all, the world of charts is very different from the worksheet world we have been working with until now. We are really charting new territory here. Sorry about that. I just couldn't help myself.

If some of the terminology we are about to cover seems a bit murky and arcane, don't worry. As we progress through the steps in this chapter, the fog lifts. Excel makes preparing charts automatic enough that you do not need to master all the details of charting to be able to create good looking charts. However, a basic understanding of charting basics increases your comfort level and allows you to prepare even more powerful charts.

A chart is a graphical representation of the numeric data in a worksheet. Each cell (piece of data) represented in the chart is called a *data point*. Data points are represented on the chart by bars, columns, lines, or some other graphical device. A group of related data points is called a *data series*. For example, if we were charting the quarter's monthly income compared with expenses, each month's income or expense figure would be a data point. The January, February, and March income figures are one data series, and the January, February, and March expense figures are another data series.

Typically, values are plotted along the vertical plane (*y-axis*) and categories are plotted along the horizontal plane (*x-axis*). *Labels* that run horizontally under the various data series and display the categories represented are *x-axis labels*. Labels running vertically and listing the value increments are the *y-axis labels*.

Most charts include a title, a legend to help clarify what each data series represents, a y-axis title and an x-axis title. Many other elements can be added to a chart and all of the chart elements can be customized to suit your requirements, but these are the most common elements you'll find in a chart.

Figure 7.1 shows a typical chart with the data series represented by columns. This is called a *column chart.*

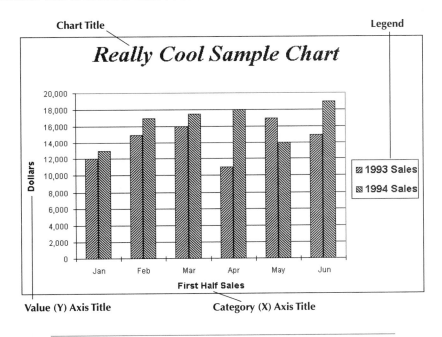

Figure 7.1 *A typical column chart with the basic chart elements.*

You use Excel's ChartWizard to step you through the chart creation process. You can create charts that are embedded in the worksheet or place charts on their own chart sheets. It makes sense to place charts on their own chart sheets if you want to print charts on separate pages from the worksheet data so you can use them for handouts. You might want to incorporate chart files in a presentation graphics program such as Microsoft PowerPoint. *Embedded charts* are placed on the same worksheet as the data they represent. Using an embedded chart, you can see the chart and numerical data at the same time.

Whether a chart is embedded or on a chart sheet, it is linked to the data it represents. This means that, if the numbers change, the chart changes to reflect the new numbers.

CREATING EMBEDDED CHARTS

Let's start by creating an embedded chart next to the numbers in our Spokane Locks and Bagel Corp. First Quarter Budget numbers. We create a chart that compares the first quarter's total income to total expenses over the three month period.

1. Start Excel and open the **BUDGET** workbook if it isn't already on your screen.

   The first step in the chart creation process is to select the data you want included in the chart.

2. Select the ranges **A3** through **D3**, **A8** through **D8** and **A14** through **D14**. Don't forget to use the **Ctrl** key to select non-contiguous ranges.

   The reason we included the empty cell A3 in the first range is that the ChartWizard understands how to deal with selections if each spans the same number of columns.

3. Click on the **ChartWizard** button on the toolbar and then, without clicking, position the mouse pointer (which is now a crosshair with a chart icon attached) in the upper-left corner of cell G3, as shown in Figure 7.2.

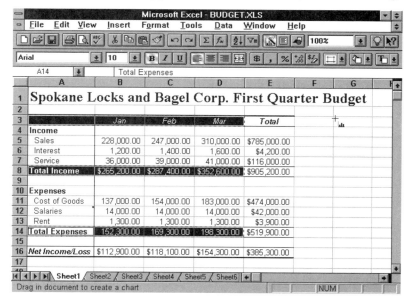

Figure 7.2 *The selected ranges for the chart and the ChartWizard mouse pointer.*

You could just click the mouse and let Excel choose the size of the chart for you, but let's drag the mouse pointer to the lower-right corner of our desired chart size to create a larger chart that is easier to work with. You can, of course, change the size of a chart after it's created, and you learn how to do that later.

4. Drag down to row 16 and over to column M, as shown in Figure 7.3. The screen automatically scrolls as you drag the mouse pointer to the right edge of the screen.

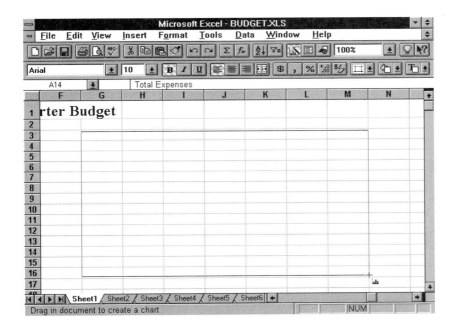

Figure 7.3 *The outline of the chart we are about to create.*

5. Release the mouse button.

The first ChartWizard dialog box appears, as shown in Figure 7.4.

The Range textbox displays the ranges you selected in step two. The dollar sign ($) in front of each column letter and row number indicates that these are absolute references, which means that the references won't change if the data is moved or copied.

Since the ranges are correct, we move on to the next dialog box.

Figure 7.4   *The ChartWizard dialog boxes—Step 1 of 5.*

6. Click on the **Next** button to move to the next ChartWizard dialog box, as displayed in Figure 7.5.

N O T E

If you want to go back to the previous ChartWizard dialog box to make different choices, you can click on the **Back** button. Click on the **Finish** button to have the ChartWizard complete your chart based on the defaults for the following ChartWizard dialog boxes.

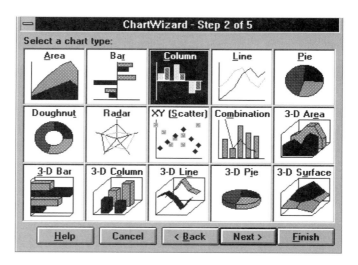

Figure 7.5   *The ChartWizard dialog box—Step 2 of 5.*

This dialog box lets you choose from among fifteen available categories. The default is the Column chart, which is a fine choice for the type of data we are charting. To choose a different chart type, you simply click on the chart type of your choice.

Each chart type has its strengths and weaknesses. Carefully consider the kind of data you are charting and how it could be most powerfully presented before choosing the chart type.

N O T E   For example, the column chart works well for comparing related data at a point in time. Pie charts are better for highlighting proportional relationships between data. Line and area charts are good for showing changes over time.

There is no one correct choice when choosing chart types. Fortunately, Excel makes it easy to experiment with various chart types, even after you've created the chart, to see how your data is best presented. You may choose to present the same data with more than one chart type to draw attention to different aspects of the data.

7. Click on the **Next** button to move to the third ChartWizard dialog box, as shown in Figure 7.6.

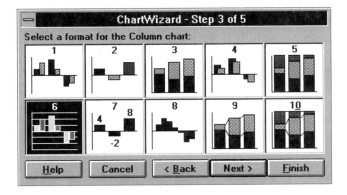

Figure 7.6   *The ChartWizard dialog box—Step 3 of 5.*

The third ChartWizard dialog box lets you choose from a variety of sub-categories of the chart type you have chosen. Once again, stick with the default, although most of the other choices would do nicely too.

Notice that choices 3, 5, 9 and 10 are different from the others. They are known as stacked column charts and are good for displaying how much one piece of data in a series contributes to the overall series. Since this is not what we are doing here, these would not be appropriate choices.

8. Click on the **Next** button to display the fourth ChartWizard dialog box, as displayed in Figure 7.7.

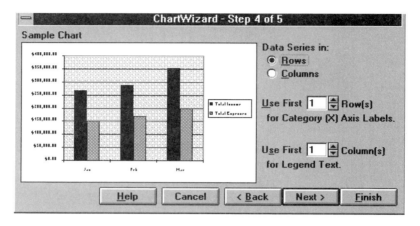

Figure 7.7   *The ChartWizard dialog box—Step 4 of 5.*

This is where we get to see a preview of the chart we are creating and to make sure Excel is charting the data the way we intend. On the right side of the dialog box, the first thing the ChartWizard wants to know is whether the data series are in rows (the default) or columns. Our data series are indeed in rows, so we do not need to change this option.

The next piece of information the ChartWizard wants to know is which row or rows to use for the Category axis (x axis) labels. The first row we selected to chart was row 3, which included the column headings Jan, Feb and Mar—our category labels—so we don't have to change anything here. If you squint, you can see Jan, Feb, and Mar under the columns in the sample chart.

The ChartWizard wants to be sure that the first column contains the text for the legend. The labels for our data series, Total Income and Total Expenses, are in column A, which is the first column we selected, so we are all set here as well. The legend (on the right side of the sample chart) displays the text and the color/pattern keys for our chart.

There's nothing in this dialog box to change, so let's move on.

9. Click on the **Next** button to move to the fifth and final ChartWizard dialog box, as shown in Figure 7.8.

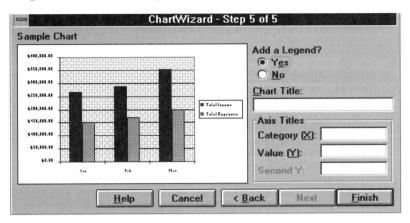

Figure 7.8   *The ChartWizard dialog box—Step 5 of 5.*

The first option in this dialog box is to add a legend. Without a legend, it would be difficult to tell which columns belong to which data series, so leave the **Yes** option button selected. Next, we have the option of adding a chart title. Let's add one.

10. Click in the **Chart Title** text box and type: **1st Quarter Income vs. Expenses**.

As you type the title, the Sample Chart portion of the dialog box is updated to display the title. We can also add titles to the category (x) axis and the value (y) axis. Let's add a value axis title to show that the numbers indicate dollars, which will be helpful when we remove those distracting dollar signs later.

11. Click in the **Value (Y)** text box and type: **Dollars**.

Before we finish, be sure your dialog box looks like Figure 7.9.

12. Click on the **Finish** button and then scroll right until the entire chart is visible, as shown in Figure 7.10.

The embedded chart is now part of the worksheet. Upon placing the chart in the worksheet, Excel automatically displays the Chart toolbar near the chart. If the Chart toolbar obstructs the chart elements you want to manipulate, you can position the mouse pointer over its title bar and drag it out of the way. You can also remove the Chart toolbar from the screen by clicking in the close box in its upper-left corner. Keep the Chart toolbar around for a while to help us manipulate some of the chart's properties.

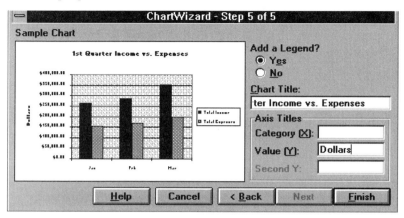

Figure 7.9 *The filled-in final dialog box.*

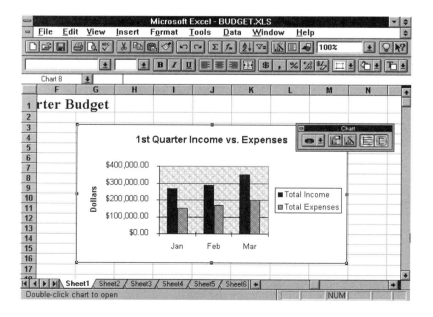

Figure 7.10 *The embedded chart.*

N O T E

If you want to add a new data series to a chart, you can take advantage of an interesting new feature called *drag and plot*. Simply select the new data series in your worksheet and drag it onto the chart and release the mouse button. The new series is automatically added to the chart. Even the data series label is added to the legend if you include the label in the selection.

Keep in mind that Excel makes a best guess as to how you want the new data series applied to the chart. If it guesses incorrectly, you may need to make some modifications manually.

The data series—columns in this example—are filled with solid colors, unlike the example in Figure 7.1, where the columns are filled with patterns. The properties of any of the chart elements can be customized and you have a chance to change some chart elements later in the chapter.

Notice the handles on each corner and the sides of the chart. These handles indicate that the chart is selected, which means it can be sized and moved and that the overall chart properties can be manipulated. But the individual chart elements cannot be directly manipulated unless the chart is active.

To make an embedded chart active, double-click on it. Observe that the status bar in Figure 7.10 displays the message "Double-click chart to open." Let's activate the chart and examine some of the ways we can customize the chart.

13. Double-click anywhere in the chart to activate it.

    The chart's border changes to indicate that it is active. With the chart active, you can right-click on a chart element to use its shortcut menu, or you can double-click on it to display a dialog box to format that element. You can also click on a chart element to select it so you can move or resize it.

    We added the value (y) axis title because we knew we wanted to get rid of the dollar signs on the numbers along the y-axis. Let's take care of that detail now.

14. Double-click on one of the numbers along the y-axis to display the Format Axis dialog box, as shown in Figure 7.12. Click on the **Number** tab if it isn't highlighted.

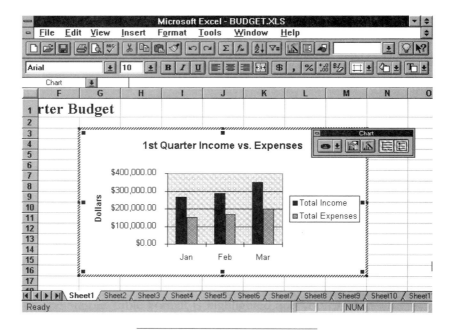

Figure 7.11   *The activated chart.*

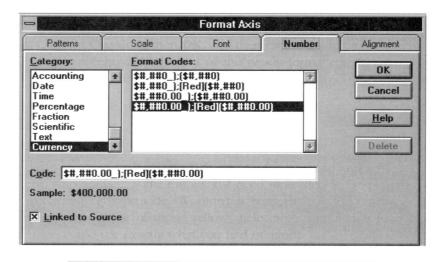

Figure 7.12   *The Format Axis dialog box Number portion.*

This dialog box should look familiar to you. It's almost the same as the number portion of the Format Cells dialog box used earlier in the book. The check box in the lower-left corner of the dialog box tells you that the formatting for the numbers along the value axis is linked to the source.

This means that whatever formatting was applied to the data series being represented is being used here. While this is often a good assumption, we want to make a change here. We do not need to uncheck the Linked to Source check box because, as soon as we choose another number format, Excel understands that the formatting is no longer linked to the source and removes the check mark.

15. In the Category list, scroll up until the Number category is visible and click on it.

16. In the Format Codes list, click on the third code from the top (**#,##0**) and then click on **OK** to change the format of the y-axis numbers, as displayed in Figure 7.13.

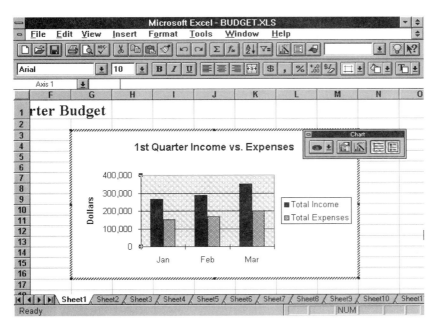

Figure 7.13 *The chart with the reformatted y-axis numbers.*

Next change the chart title's font.

17. Double-click on the chart title, **1st Quarter Income vs. Expenses** to display the Format Title dialog box, as shown in Figure 7.14. Click on **Font** tab if it isn't highlighted.

This is the same as the Font portion of the Format Cells dialog box used in Chapter 5 so its options should be familiar. The default font is Arial, its style is bold and its size is 12 point. Let's change to Times New Roman, Bold Italic, 18 point.

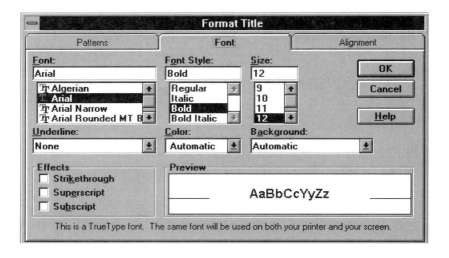

Figure 7.14   *The Format Title dialog box Font portion.*

18. Scroll down the Font list and click on **Times New Roman**. Click on **Bold Italic** in the Font Style list, and then click on **18** in the Size list. Finally, click on **OK** to change the title, as shown in Figure 7.15.

Just to see how easy it is to change chart types, let's use the Chart toolbar to display our data as a line chart.

19. Click on **Chart Type** on the Chart toolbar to display the drop-down chart type list, as shown in Figure 7.16.

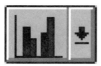

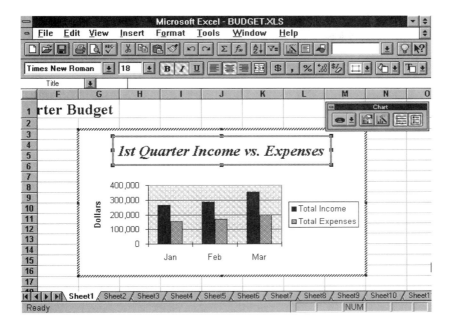

Figure 7.15   *The chart with its newly formatted title.*

20. Click on the **Line Chart** button in the drop-down list of chart types. (The one the mouse pointer is pointing to in Figure 7.16.)

    This line chart doesn't show the comparison between income and expenses as clearly as the column chart, so let's change it back.

21. Choose **Edit**, **Undo Chart Type** to reverse the chart type change you just made.

    To prove that the chart really is linked to the worksheet data, let's change some of the worksheet data and see how the chart is affected.

22. Click on any of the worksheet cells outside the chart area to deactivate it and scroll left until the column A is visible.

While the chart is active, the scroll bars are hidden. They reappear when the chart is deactivated.

N O T E

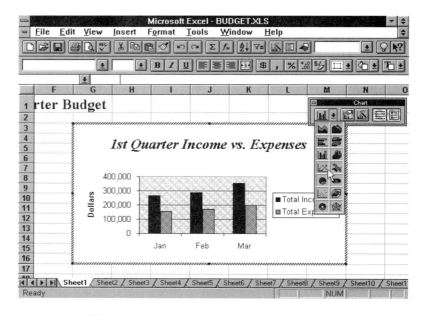

Figure 7.16   *The Chart drop-down chart types.*

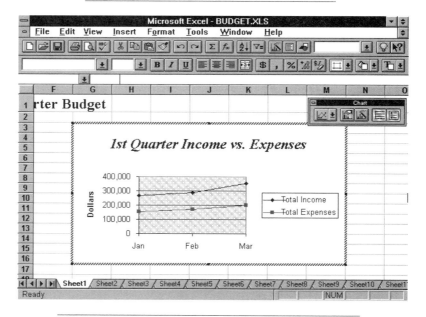

Figure 7.17   *The chart has been changed to a line chart.*

The Chart toolbar is automatically removed from the screen when the chart isn't selected. Let's change the Sales figure in cell D5 to reflect a more optimistic forecast.

23. Enter **500000** in cell D5 (the March sales figure), then scroll right until the chart is visible again and observe the change in the March Total Income column, as displayed in Figure 7.18.

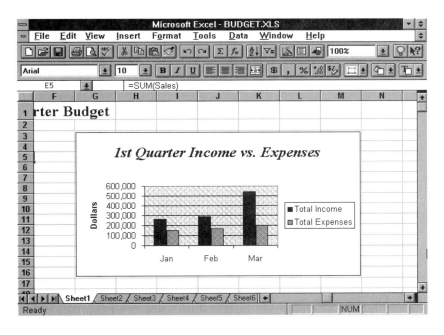

Figure 7.18   *The chart reflecting the new data.*

USING EXCEL'S DRAWING TOOLS

Before we're finished with this chart, let's add a few more touches with Excel's drawing tools. In addition to the standard chart elements we've discussed, Excel provides a wide variety of drawing tools for adding lines, arrows, circles, and even additional text that isn't one of the normal chart title elements.

The drawing tools aren't just for use with charts. You can add any of these graphic elements to any part of the worksheet. For example, you might want to draw an arrow pointing to a portion of the worksheet you want the reader to notice and perhaps draw a circle around that portion as well. These graphic elements are used the same way whether you are adding them to a chart or the worksheet.

To use the drawing tools you must display the Drawing toolbar, so let's do that now.

1. Click on the **Drawing** button on the Standard toolbar to display the Drawing toolbar, as shown in Figure 7.19.

Figure 7.19   *The Drawing toolbar.*

To use one of the drawing tools to create a graphic element, just click on the button and then drag it to where you want the shape. Add an arrow pointing to the March income column.

SHORTCUT

If you want to use a drawing tool several times in succession, just double-click on it and you won't have to reselect it the next time. When you're through using that tool, just click on it again.

2. Click on the **Arrow** button on the Drawing toolbar. Position the mouse pointer, which is now a crosshair, above and to the left of the March income column, as displayed in Figure 7.20.

Drag the crosshair toward the top left corner of the column and release the mouse button to create the arrow, as shown in Figure 7.21.

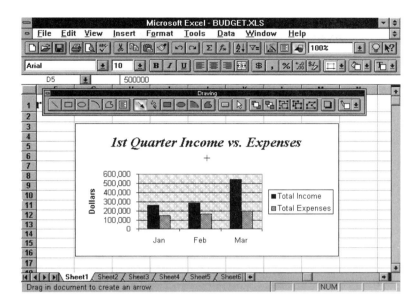

Figure 7.20   *The crosshair mouse pointer ready to draw an arrow.*

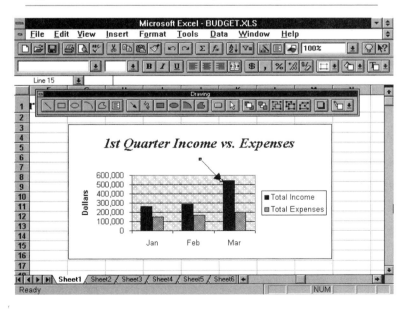

Figure 7.21   *The completed arrow.*

The handles on the ends of the arrow indicate that it is selected and can be moved or sized. You can also format the arrow, or any other graphic object, by double-clicking on it. Sound familiar? Let's take a look at how we can change the format of the arrow.

3. Double-click on the **Arrow** to summon the Format Object dialog box, as displayed in Figure 7.22. Click on the **Patterns** tab if it isn't already highlighted.

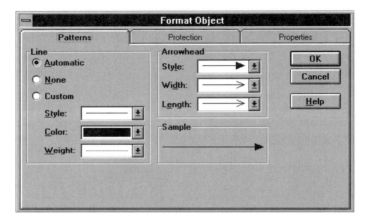

Figure 7.22   *The Format Object dialog box Patterns portion.*

The dialog box is specific to the type of object you are formatting. In this case, you can change the type of arrowhead or its line. Let's make the line a bit thicker by changing its weight.

4. Click on the **Arrow** next to the Weight drop-down list to display the available options, as shown in Figure 7.23.

5. Click on the thickest line at the bottom. (The mouse pointer is pointing to it.)

The Sample area of the dialog box displays a sample arrow with the selected line weight.

6. Click on **OK** to accept the changes.

Let's draw an ellipse around Mar to further highlight it.

7. Click on the **Ellipse** button on the Drawing toolbar, drag the crosshair around Mar and release the mouse button to create an ellipse, as shown in Figure 7.24.

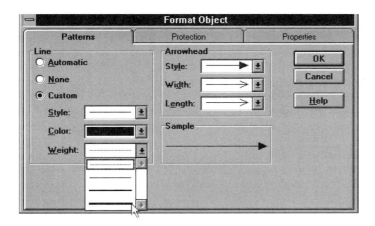

Figure 7.23   *The available line weight choices.*

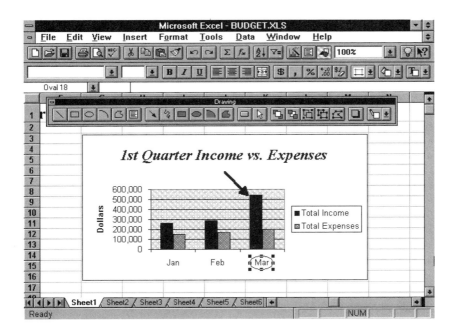

Figure 7.24   *The selected ellipse around Mar.*

NOTE

If you want to draw a perfectly round circle instead of an ellipse, hold down the **Shift** key while using the ellipse tool. The same trick works with the Rectangle tool to create perfect squares.

8. Click on the **Drawing** button on the Standard toolbar (or click on the Drawing toolbar's close box) to remove the Drawing toolbar from the screen.

CREATING CHARTS IN CHART SHEETS

The steps for creating a chart in a chart sheet are essentially the same as for creating an embedded chart. The first difference is that you need to start from the Insert menu and not the ChartWizard button on the toolbar.

You can perform the same manipulations on a chart in a chart sheet as in an embedded chart. The only difference is that you can't see the data the chart is based on while the chart is on screen.

Let's create a chart comparing the company's Net Income/Loss for the quarter.

1. Select the ranges **A3** through **D3** and **A16** through **D16** and then choose **Insert**, **Chart**, **As New Sheet** to begin the chart sheet creation process.

   The first ChartWizard dialog box appears, just as it did when creating an embedded chart.

2. Click on the **Next** button to accept the selected ranges and move to the second ChartWizard dialog box.

   Since this chart only has one data series and we are comparing how much each month contributes to the quarter, a pie chart would work well here.

3. Click on the **Pie** which is the last one on the top row of choices in the dialog box, and then click on the **Next** button to proceed.

4. In the third and fourth ChartWizard dialog boxes, click on the **Next** buttons to accept the default options.

5. In the fifth ChartWizard dialog box, click in the **No** option button under Add a Legend.

   We do not need a legend here because the pie format the ChartWizard selects places the month labels next to each wedge of the pie.

6. In the Title text box, type: **Pie in the Sky Projection** and click on the **Finish** button.

> The finished pie chart appears in a chart sheet, as shown in Figure 7.25, that is inserted in front of the worksheet containing the data it is based on. If you look at the sheet tabs above the status bar you see the highlighted Chart1 tab to the left of the Sheet1 tab.

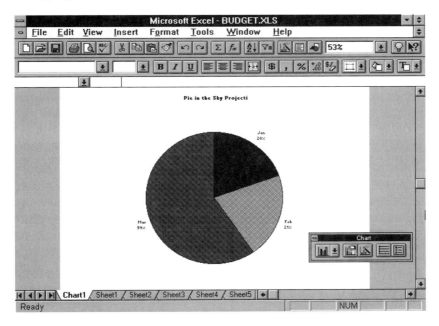

Figure 7.25   *The pie chart in its chart sheet.*

Use exactly the same techniques to format any of the chart elements in a chart sheet that you use with an embedded chart. The only step you can omit is double-clicking on the chart to activate it. When a chart sheet is visible, the chart is active and you can manipulate the chart elements.

PRINTING CHARTS

You print embedded charts in exactly the same way as the other portions of the worksheet. Just include the embedded chart in the print range and you are all set to go.

Printing a chart on a chart sheet is even easier than printing an embedded chart since there is no range to select. It is, of course, still a good idea to use **Print Preview** before printing to be sure you are printing what you think you'll be printing.

1. Click on the **Print Preview** toolbar button to display a preview of the printed page, as displayed in Figure 7.26.

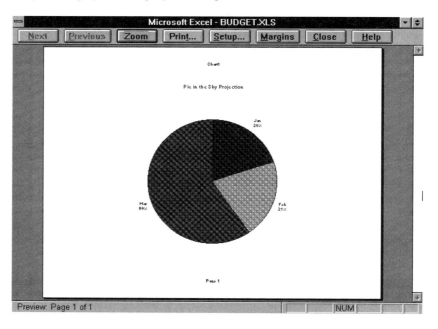

Figure 7.26 *The Print Preview screen for the chart sheet.*

2. When you are ready to print the chart, check to make sure your printer is turned on, is on line, and has paper loaded. Then click on the **Print** button.

3. Click on the **Sheet1** tab to move back to the worksheet containing your data.

4. Save your work and exit Excel if you're not continuing on to the next chapter.

NOTE

When you save your work, you are saving the entire workbook, so you do not need to save the chart sheet separately from the worksheet.

A FINAL THOUGHT

You have learned to turn numbers into dazzling charts that are sure to add punch to your presentations and help you persuade the most skeptical. In the next chapter you will learn to put Excel's database capabilities to work.

Chapter 8

Managing Data

- ✳ DATABASE BASICS
- ✳ SETTING UP A DATABASE
- ✳ ENTERING DATA
- ✳ SEARCHING THE DATABASE
- ✳ DELETING AND EDITING RECORDS
- ✳ SORTING THE DATABASE
- ✳ FILTERING THE DATABASE

151

DATABASE BASICS

In addition to the worksheet and charting capabilities we've worked with in the beginning chapters of this book, Excel provides a powerful facility for creating and manipulating databases.

So what is a database? A database is a collection of information (data) organized to make it easy to find and use the data you are looking for. An example of a database you use every day is the phone book. The white pages of the phone book contain several categories of data: Last Name, First Name, Address, and Phone Number.

In database terms, each of these categories is called *a field*. All the field entries for one person make up a *record*. On one page of the phone book, there are four fields and perhaps several hundred records. The phone book makes it easy for you to find the data you want by sorting the records into alphabetical order. With Excel databases, you can sort and search the data in a wide variety of ways. You can even perform calculations on the data in an Excel database, just as you can with any worksheet data.

SETTING UP A DATABASE

To create a database, you first enter *field names* in the first row you want to use for your list. Each row below the field name or *header row*, is a record. There can't be any blank rows between records, and all the cells in a field should be formatted the same way to facilitate sorting and database manipulation.

There are a few rules to follow when choosing a field name. Every field name must be unique. For example, if you were creating a name and address list in which you needed two fields for the address to accommodate suite and apartment numbers, they couldn't both be called ADDRESS. You could solve this situation by calling the first field ADDRESS1 and the second field ADDRESS2.

N O T E   It's best to keep field names as short as possible, yet descriptive enough that you know what should be entered in the field. If you need to use a field name that is longer than the column width, consider formatting the text to wrap so it occupies multiple lines instead of requiring an inordinately wide column. To wrap text, choose **Format Cell** from the cell's shortcut menu and click in the **Wrap Text** check box.

The field names do not need to be capitalized or formatted in any special way. Using all uppercase letters (assuming the data you enter is in lower or mixed case) tells Excel that the first row is the header, or field name row.

Let's start creating a partial inventory list database for the Spokane Locks and Bagel Corp.

1. Start Excel and open the BUDGET workbook if it isn't already on your screen.

2. Click on **Sheet2** at the bottom of the worksheet to move to a clean worksheet in the same workbook.

<table>
<tr><td>N O T E</td><td>Keeping related worksheets in the same workbook is one of the reasons Excel uses workbooks in the first place. We could put the inventory list in a new workbook, but then when we want to work with our various data from Spokane Locks and Bagel, we'd have to open two workbooks instead of one.</td></tr>
</table>

3. Enter the field names and data for the first record in the appropriate cells, as displayed in Table 8.1.

    The formula in E2 multiplies the item's cost by the quantity.

Table 8.1 *The field names and the data for the first record of our inventory database.*

	A	B	C	D	E
1	ITEM	TYPE	COST	QTY	TOTAL
2	Small Padlock	Hardware	4.33	42	=C2*D2

The fastest way to enter the data in this range is to select the entire range first (A1 through E2) and press **Enter** after each cell entry to move to the next cell in the selection.

N O T E

Next we'll format the cells containing the field names as center-aligned and first record cells to display the numbers properly.

4. Select the range **A1** through **E1** and format the cells as center-aligned. You can right-click on the selection to display the shortcut menu, then choose **Format Cells**, click-on the **Alignment** tab, and select the **Center** option button in the Horizontal portion of the dialog box.

5. Format cell C2 with the number format #,##0.00. The number formats are found in Number portion of the Format Cells dialog box.

6. Format cell E2 with the currency format $#,##0.00_):($#,##0.00).

7. Double-click on the right border of each of the column headings to adjust the column widths to accommodate the cell entries.

   You'll need to do this again after entering data that is wider than the current column widths. Your screen should now look like Figure 8.1.

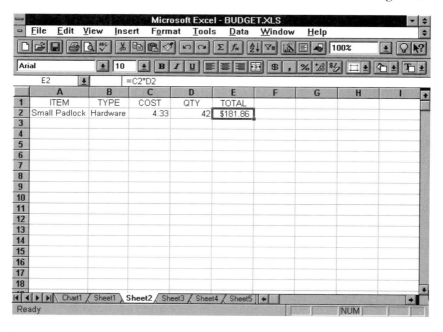

Figure 8.1   *The field names and first record of the database.*

ENTERING DATA

You already entered data in a database when you entered the first record. You can enter data directly into the database in the same way to add as many records as needed. However, Excel provides an even slicker method for entering data in a database—the *data form*.

Once you've started the database, you can use the data form, which includes text boxes for the fields requiring data entry and also displays the results of calculated fields.

N O T E   There's no right or wrong way to enter data in an Excel database. You may decide that entering data directly into the database and bypassing the data form is the easiest method for you. One advantage of using the data form to enter data is that the cell formatting for the previous record automatically applies to the next record, thus eliminating the need to format more than one record.

Let's enter the next record using the data form.

1. Be sure one of the cells in the database is active and choose **Data**, **F**__o__**rm** to display the data form dialog box, as displayed in Figure 8.2.

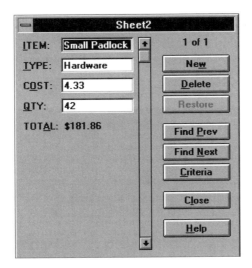

Figure 8.2   *The Sheet 2 data form dialog box.*

The title bar in the dialog box displays the name of the sheet where the database is, in this case Sheet2. If the sheet were renamed something more relevant to the database, such as INVENTORY, that name would be displayed in the title bar.

The data for the first record is displayed in the text boxes for each field. Notice that the data for the TOTAL field isn't in a text box since, being a calculated field, it can't be edited. The scroll bar to the right of the text boxes is used if you have more fields than can be displayed in the dialog box at one time. The dialog box also displays the number of the record you are currently viewing and the total number of records in the database in the upper-right corner of the dialog box.

Let's add the next record in the data form now.

2. Click on the **New** button to clear the text boxes for the new record entry.

As you enter new records, the dialog box displays the text *New Record* in the upper-right corner.

3. Type: **Bagel Dogs, Food, 1.27, 375** in the ITEM, TYPE, COST, and QTY text boxes. You can press the **Tab** key to move the insertion point from one text box to the next.

If you need to correct a typo in a text box you've already done, you can click in the text box you need to edit, or press **Shift+Tab** until the field you need to edit is highlighted and type the correct data.

N O T E

---

4. Click on the **New** button to add this record to the bottom of the database and clear the text boxes for the next record.

The new record is added and you'll notice that the cell formatting was copied from the first record. If the dialog box is obscuring too much of the database, you can drag it out of the way by its title bar.

Next, we'll enter the remaining records for the inventory database.

5. Enter the data for the records, displayed in Table 8.2.

When you finish entering the data for the last field in a record, the fastest way to confirm the entry and clear the text boxes for the next record is to press the **Enter** key. This way you don't need to move your hands from the keyboard as you enter a series of records.

SHORTCUT

ITEM	TYPE	COST	QTY
Plain bagels	Food	.22	456
8 oz. Cream Cheese	Food	1.33	78
BMW keys	Hardware	.87	26
Mercedes keys	Hardware	.47	73
Ferrari keys	Hardware	.56	37
Garlic bagels	Food	.25	133
Jalapeno bagels	Food	.27	277
Chocolate bagels	Food	.32	76
Large padlock	Hardware	3.42	44

6. Click on the **Close** button to clear the dialog box from the screen and readjust the column width of column A to accommodate the new entries.

Your screen displays all the records, as shown in Figure 8.3.

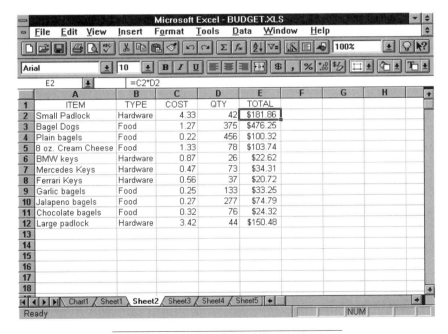

Figure 8.3 *All the records in the database.*

SEARCHING THE DATABASE

In the database we have created, there is no need to use any fancy searching techniques because there are so few entries and all of them are visible at the same time. However, as the number of records increases to hundreds or thousands, it can be difficult, if not impossible, to find the records you want by visually scanning the list.

Excel provides a couple of ways to find records that meet certain criteria. Later in the chapter you learn to use Excel's filtering system to display the records that meet your specifications. But, the most straightforward way to find records you are looking for is to use the data form dialog box.

Using the data form dialog box does not change the database in any way. As you perform the search, the dialog box displays the records in the database that meet the search criteria, one at a time. Let's use the data form dialog box to search for some records.

1. Be sure one of the cells in the database is still active, and choose **Data**, **Form**.

    The data form dialog box displays 1 of 11 in the upper-right corner, indicating that the data for the first of eleven records is presented.

    The three dialog box buttons used for searching the database are: **Find Prev**, **Find Next**, and **Criteria**. If you don't specify any criteria, the Find Prev and Find Next buttons display the data for the previous or next record in the list. Using the Criteria button, you can tell Excel which records to search for, and then the Find Prev and Find Next buttons display the previous or next records that meet your criteria.

    Let's use the Criteria button to provide Excel with search specifications.

2. Click on the **Criteria** button.

    The upper-right corner of the dialog box now displays Criteria indicating that you can enter search conditions called *comparison criteria* in the text boxes. When you perform the search, Excel compares the comparison criteria with the records in the list and displays the first one that matches.

    The other difference between this and the normal data form dialog box is that even the calculated TOTAL field has a text box. This is because you can specify search criteria on any field, including calculated fields.

Let's enter criteria to search for the BMW keys.

3. In the ITEM text box, type: **bmw** and then click on the **Find Next** button.

 The comparison criteria are not case sensitive, which means that you can type your conditions in uppercase or lowercase and it won't affect the outcome of the search.

N O T E

The data form now displays the data for the BMW keys record and, in the upper-right corner, displays 1 of 1 indicating that this is the only record matching the comparison criteria. If you click on the **Find Next** button, your computer is likely to beep at you and won't display any other records.

Now, let's try finding records that match the multiple criteria.

4. Click on the **Criteria** button again so you can enter new criteria.

The ITEM text box is highlighted so you can start typing to enter new criteria for the ITEM field, or delete what's there. We delete it since we won't be using the ITEM field as part of our next search.

The first comparison criterion we use is HARDWARE to locate only records that have HARDWARE entered in the TYPE field.

5. Press the **Delete** key to delete the highlighted text, then press the **Tab** key to move the insertion point into the TYPE text box and type: **HARDWARE**

If you enter comparison criteria in more than one text box, the record must meet both conditions. We search for records that fall into the Hardware category and also have a total value more than $100.00.

6. Click in the **TOTAL** text box and type: **>100**

The > (greater than) symbol is one of Excel's *comparison operators* that can be used to compare values. The other comparison operators are:

✴ **=** (equal to)

✴ **<** (less than)

✴ **>=** (greater than or equal to)

✳ <= (less than or equal to)

✳ <> (not equal to)

These operators can only be used with numeric values, not text data.

7. Click on the **Find Next** button to display the first record that meets both of the comparison criteria.

Only two records match both criteria. You can click on **Find Prev** to display the other match.

Deleting and Editing Records

As with any other data on a worksheet, you can delete and edit records directly. If you wanted to delete a record directly, you could select a cell in its row and choose **Edit**, **Delete**, **Entire Row**. Editing a record's data directly is simply a matter of moving to the cell you want to edit and making the change, just as you would in any cell.

Another way to edit and delete records is with the data form dialog box. An advantage of using the dialog box is that you can combine editing and deleting with the search capabilities we covered in the previous section. For example, if you wanted to edit all the records that matched certain comparison criteria, you could specify the criteria, click on the **Find Next** button, perform the edits in the text boxes and click on **Find Next** to display the next record you want to edit.

Let's delete one of the records using he data form dialog box now.

1. Click on **Find Next** or **Find Prev** until the Small Padlock record is displayed in the data form dialog box.

2. Click on the **Delete** button.

The message box, as shown in Figure 8.4, is displayed to let you know that what you are about to do can't be undone.

WARNING

Excel isn't kidding. When you click on the **Delete** button, the record is removed permanently. There's no way to get it back. Don't let the grayed-out Restore button in the data form dialog box fool you either. That only works for restoring an *edited* record to its original state prior to confirming the edit. So be careful before deleting a record in this way.

There is one safety measure you can take before doing something dangerous like deleting a record—save your work. If you save your work just before deleting the record, you can always close the workbook without saving changes and then open the saved version to get back to where you were before the deletion.

Figure 8.4 *The warning message box.*

3. Click on **OK** to proceed with the deletion.

   The Small Padlock record is deleted and the other records are moved up to fill in the void left be the deleted record.

4. Click on the **Close** button to clear the data form dialog box.

SORTING THE DATABASE

At the beginning of the chapter, I discussed how the phone book makes it easy to find a particular entry. The records are sorted in alphabetical order. When you add records to the database list, you don't need to worry a bit about entering them in the correct order. Excel makes it easy to sort the list in a variety of ways.

N O T E

Your list doesn't even have to be a database for Excel to sort it. Any rectangular area consisting of rows and columns of related data can be sorted in the same manner as database data.

One sorting concept that is important to understand is the *sort key*. The key is the basis for the sort and you can sort by up to three keys. In the phone book example, the first sort key is the last name. A second sort key (the first name) is used as a tie breaker. If there is more than one entry of a particular last name, those last names are sorted by first names.

Let's perform a simple sort on the inventory database. First we sort the list in alphabetical order by the ITEM field. This is so easy you won't believe it.

1. Make any cell in the database in column A (the ITEM field) the active cell.

2. Click on the **Sort Ascending** toolbar button.

Voila! The list is instantly sorted, as displayed in Figure 8.5.

	A	B	C	D	E	F	G	H
1	ITEM	TYPE	COST	QTY	TOTAL			
2	8 oz. Cream Cheese	Food	1.33	78	$103.74			
3	Bagel Dogs	Food	1.27	375	$476.25			
4	BMW keys	Hardware	0.87	26	$22.62			
5	Chocolate bagels	Food	0.32	76	$24.32			
6	Ferrari Keys	Hardware	0.56	37	$20.72			
7	Garlic bagels	Food	0.25	133	$33.25			
8	Jalapeno bagels	Food	0.27	277	$74.79			
9	Large padlock	Hardware	3.42	44	$150.48			
10	Mercedes Keys	Hardware	0.47	73	$34.31			
11	Plain bagels	Food	0.22	456	$100.32			

Figure 8.5 *The Sorted Database.*

The *Ascending* in *Sort Ascending* means from lower to higher. For an alphabetical sort such as this, it means A through Z. For a numerical sort, ascending would be 1 through 100. The toolbar button to the right of the Sort Ascending button is the *Sort Descending* button which performs a sort from higher to lower.

It's a good idea to save your work before performing a sort so you can get back to the original sort order later if you need to.

If you perform a sort and want to return the list to its original order, you can choose **Edit**, **Undo Sort** before taking any other actions in Excel.

A trick you can use if you think you will need to return to the original sort order more than once is to add a field for record numbers. In one column in the database, type **1**, and then use the fill handle with the **Ctrl** key to increase the numbers in ascending order down the column. With the records numbered, you can get back to the original order any time you want by performing a sort by the column containing the record numbers.

Let's sort the list in descending order by the COST field.

3. Move to any cell in the database range in column C and click on the **Sort Descending** toolbar button.

Finally, we sort the database by two sort keys. Sorting by two fields isn't quite as easy as clicking on a toolbar button. But it is still pretty easy.

We use the TYPE field as the first sort key, which groups the food and hardware items separately. Because there are several records for each of the two types of items, we have Excel use the ITEM field as the second sort key.

4. Be sure that any cell in the database is the active cell and then choose **Data**, **Sort** to display the Sort dialog box, as shown in Figure 8.6.

Notice that the entire list is selected, excluding the column headings and the field name in the Sort By list box is ITEM, which is the first column in the database. This isn't what we want to use for the first Sort By, so we change it now.

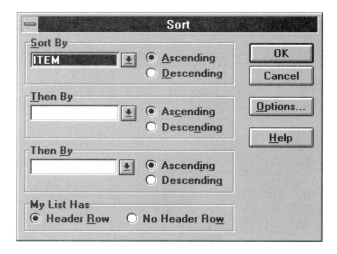

Figure 8.6 *The Sort dialog box.*

5. Click on the **Arrow** next to the Sort By drop-down list to display all the field names in the database, as shown in Figure 8.7.

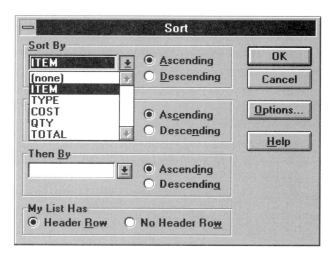

Figure 8.7 *The Sort dialog box displaying the drop-down list of field names.*

6. Click on **TYPE** in the drop-down list to select it as the first field to sort by.

Each field we choose to sort by can be sorted in ascending (the default) or descending order. We accept ascending for both of our sort keys.

7. Click on the **Arrow** next to the Then By drop-down list and click on **ITEM**.

Since there are no duplicate item names, there is no need for a third sort key, so we leave the bottom Then By list blank.

8. Click on the **OK** button to perform the sort.

The list is sorted with all the food items at the top and the item names alphabetized within the food group. Next, the hardware item names are alphabetized within the hardware group, as shown in Figure 8.8.

	A	B	C	D	E	F	G	H
1	ITEM	TYPE	COST	QTY	TOTAL			
2	8 oz. Cream Cheese	Food	1.33	78	$103.74			
3	Bagel Dogs	Food	1.27	375	$476.25			
4	Chocolate bagels	Food	0.32	76	$24.32			
5	Garlic bagels	Food	0.25	133	$33.25			
6	Jalapeno bagels	Food	0.27	277	$74.79			
7	Plain bagels	Food	0.22	456	$100.32			
8	BMW keys	Hardware	0.87	26	$22.62			
9	Ferrari Keys	Hardware	0.56	37	$20.72			
10	Large padlock	Hardware	3.42	44	$150.48			
11	Mercedes Keys	Hardware	0.47	73	$34.31			

Figure 8.8 *The list sorted by two sort keys.*

N O T E — Excel can only use three sort keys, which could be a serious limitation for some complex lists. However, as with most limitations in Excel, there is a way around it. If your sort requires more than three sort keys, simply sort multiple times. Specify the first three keys for the first sort, and then choose up to three more and perform a second sort.

FILTERING THE DATABASE

The major limitation to using the data form to find records that meet certain criteria is that you can only display one record at a time. There may be times when you want to be able to view and manipulate a subset of the list. Excel's filter capability permits you to do just that.

By filtering the database, Excel automatically hides all the records that do not meet your specifications, leaving only the records you want to see displayed on your screen. Just as in sorting, you can have multiple criteria for filtering the database.

Let's use Excel's AutoFilter feature to display only the food records.

1. With one of the cells in the database as the active cell, choose **Data**, **Filter**, **AutoFilter**.

    Drop-down Arrows appear next to each field name at the top of each column, as shown in Figure 8.9.

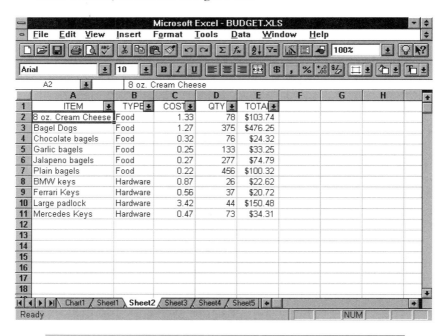

Figure 8.9 *The list with the AutoFilter drop-down arrows displayed.*

2. Click on the drop-down **Arrow** next to the TYPE field name.

    The drop-down list provided by the AutoFilter Arrows display all the unique entries for that field, as shown in Figure 8.10.

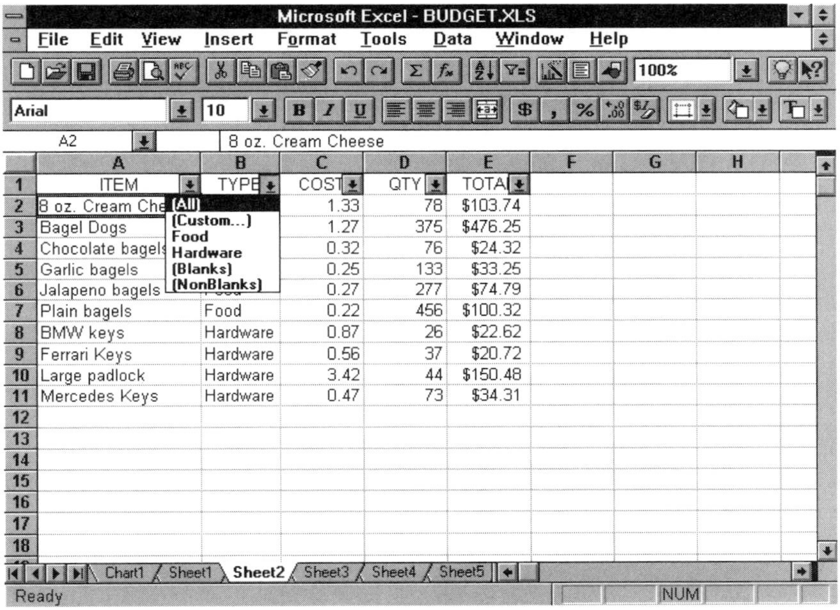

Figure 8.10   *An AutoFilter drop-down list.*

You would select All in the drop-down list to cancel a filter selection for that field. Selecting custom lets you specify more complex filter specifications, including the use of the comparison operators we use in the data form dialog box. The Blanks choice tells Excel you want to display all records that have no entry in that field. NonBlanks excludes records with no entry in that field.

3. Click on **Food** in the drop-down list.

    Instantly, all the records that don't meet the food criterion are hidden, as shown in Figure 8.11.

    You cannot tell from the figure, but if you look at your screen, you'll notice that the arrow next to the TYPE heading is blue. This indicates that a filter criterion has been specified for this field. If you display the list again and choose **All**, the hidden records reappear and the arrow loses the blues.

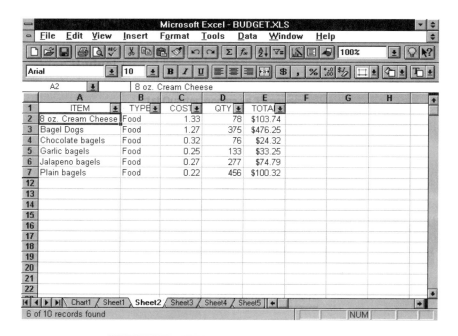

Figure 8.11   *The list with just the food items.*

If you have a very long list of field entries from which to choose, you can move to the desired field quickly by typing the first few letters of its name.

SHORTCUT

Let's specify a filter criterion for another field. This time we only allow Excel to display records from the filtered list that have quantities of greater than 100 and less than 400.

4. Click on the drop-down **Arrow** next to the QTY column heading.

    We need to create a custom filter for this field to specify the range of acceptable values.

5. Click on **Custom** to display the Custom AutoFilter dialog box, as shown in Figure 8.12.

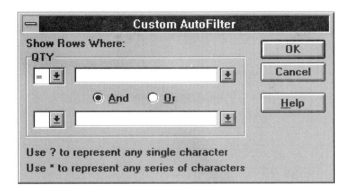

Figure 8.12 *The Custom AutoFilter dialog box.*

The comparison operators must be chosen from their own drop-down list in the dialog box, instead of being typed in the text box as we did in the data form dialog box.

6. Click on the drop-down **Arrow** next to the box with = in it, (just below QTY) in the dialog box to display the list of comparison operators, as shown in Figure 8.13.

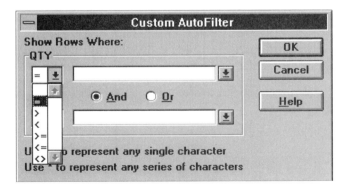

Figure 8.13 *The drop-down list of comparison operators.*

7. Click on the > (greater than symbol) in the drop down list and then click in the text box to the right of the comparison operator list and type: **100**

8. Leave the And option button selected and then choose the < (less than symbol) from the bottom drop-down list of comparison operators and type: **400** in the bottom text box.

9. When the Custom AutoFilter dialog box is displayed as in Figure 8.14, click on **OK**.

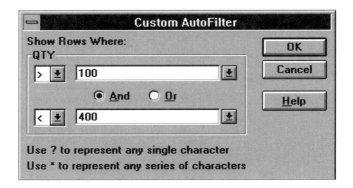

Figure 8.14   *The Custom AutoFilter with the filter specifications entered.*

Your screen as displayed in Figure 8.15, should now have three records matching the two filter criteria.

We are finished with the filtered list, so let's turn off AutoFilter and redisplay all the records.

10. Choose **Data**, **Filter**, **AutoFilter** to remove the check mark in front of the AutoFilter and reveal the hidden records.

11. **Save** your work and exit Excel if you aren't moving on to the next chapter now.

A FINAL THOUGHT

As you work with Excel, you will find yourself using the database creation and manipulation techniques you have learned in this chapter more frequently than you can imagine. You will also discover that many of these database concepts also apply to the full-featured database programs used for larger database applications.

In the next chapter you learn to use some of Excel's worksheet, data proofing and analysis tools.

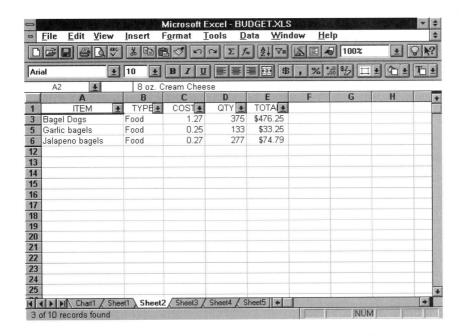

Figure 8.15 *The list after entering the two filter criteria.*

Chapter 9

Proofing and Analyzing Worksheet Data

* USING THE SPELL CHECKER
* WORKING WITH PIVOTTABLE WIZARD
* USING SCENARIO MANAGER

173

You should be sure that the final version of any document is as error-free as possible and presents the data you want to present, whether from a spreadsheet program, a word processor or a database. Excel provides several tools for making sure your worksheet is accurate and for looking at the data in various ways to find the best one for your purpose.

USING THE SPELL CHECKER

The most obvious place to start ensuring accuracy is with Excel's spell checker. Spelling errors can contribute to a perception that your entire worksheet and even the logic you used to prepare it, is sloppy. If you want to convince your readers that the data in your worksheet is accurate and your conclusions are correct, you want to be absolutely sure any spelling errors (and typos) are corrected.

Many cells in a worksheet contain only values or formulas. You may be wondering how the spell checker deals with these cells. That's easy. Excel ignores the contents of these cells.

So far, we've been entering only correctly spelled data into our worksheets, so we should not have to worry about checking the spelling. Of course, it is still a good idea to check the spelling just in case there are some typos. Just to be sure we have something to correct, let's edit one of the cell entries so that it is intentionally misspelled.

1. Start Excel and open the BUDGET workbook if it is not already on your screen and make sure Sheet2 (the database sheet) is active. If it isn't, click on the **Sheet2** tab.

2. Edit the contents of cell B2 from Food to **Foood**.

3. Click on **Spelling** in the toolbar to start the spell check process.

The Spelling dialog box appears, as shown in Figure 9.1, with the cell value of the first misspelled word displayed in the lower-left portion of the dialog box above the two check boxes.

Because the **Always Suggest** check box is checked, the dialog box offers suggestions for correcting the misspelled word. The word in the

Change To box is the suggestion Excel thinks is most likely the correct spelling of the word you had in mind. In this case, the Change To box does, in fact, contain the correct spelling. If the spelling of the mis-spelled word had been too badly mangled, Excel might not have been able to make a correct guess. In such a case you could click on one of the other suggestions in the Suggestion list, or edit the word in the Change To box.

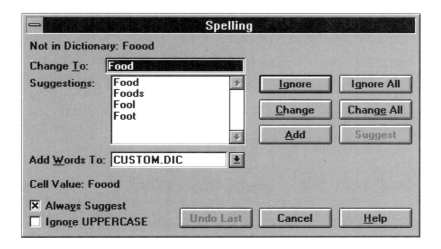

Figure 9.1   *The Spelling dialog box.*

N O T E

Having Excel make suggestions every time it stops at a misspelled word can slow down the process, so you might consider clicking in the **Always Suggest** check box to remove the check mark. If Excel stops on a particular word and you want suggestions, you can click on the **Suggest** button.

If you find that eliminating suggestions does not improve the speed noticeably, it might be more convenient to have Excel always provide you with suggestions.

You may also want to use the Ignore UPPERCASE check box to have the spell checker ignore any word that is in all uppercase letters. This option might be useful if, for example, you had a list of names or other words that would not be in the dictionary, in all uppercase.

The Add Words To box displays the name of the custom dictionary where you can add the word if it is correctly spelled, but isn't a word in the normal dictionary. The default dictionary for adding words is CUSTOM.DIC, but you can create other dictionaries for use with various types of documents. If you add a word to the dictionary, the spell checker won't stop on that word as a misspelled word in other documents. Examples of the kinds of names you might want to add to the dictionary are your name, your company's name or other special names or terms you use in your business.

4. Click on the **Change** button to replace the cell contents with the word in the Change To box.

Excel stops next on Jalapeno, which is spelled correctly but is not in the regular dictionary. We have several appropriate choices. The Add button would add the word to the custom dictionary. If you are sure the word is correctly spelled, this might be the best choice. The Ignore button would leave the word as it is. Ignore All would leave the word as it is and also ignore any other occurrences of the word in this document.

5. Click on the **Ignore** button.

Excel continues checking the spelling until it reaches the bottom of the worksheet and then displays the message dialog box, as shown in Figure 9.2, asking if you want to continue checking from the beginning of the sheet.

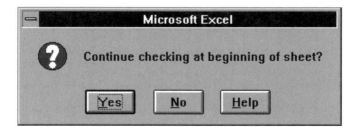

Figure 9.2 *A spelling message dialog box.*

6. Click on **Yes**.

If there are no typos in your document, Excel displays the message dialog box, as shown in Figure 9.3.

Figure 9.3 *The end of spell check message.*

7. Correct any other spelling errors Excel finds and then click on **OK** in the message box to end the spell check session.

WARNING

A common error some people make is to assume that if the spell checker doesn't find any errors, everything is spelled correctly. Wrong! What the spell checker does is to make sure each word in your worksheet matches a word in its regular or custom dictionary.

If there is a word in your document that is a correctly spelled word, but just not the word you mean, the spell checker won't catch it as a misspelled word. For example, if you type the word *pane* but you meant *pain*, the spell checker won't catch your error.

The moral of this warning is that, even when you use the spell checker, you still need to proofread your document. Better yet, have someone else do it. It's hard to spot your own errors.

WORKING WITH PIVOTTABLE WIZARD

The PivotTable command lets you analyze the data in a list or database. We want to get a quick summary of the total of the food items and the total of the hardware items in our list. PivotTable makes this a snap. Let's create this simple PivotTable now.

1. With one of the cells in the list as the active cell, choose **Data, PivotTable** to display the first of the PivotTable Wizard dialog boxes, as shown in Figure 9.4.

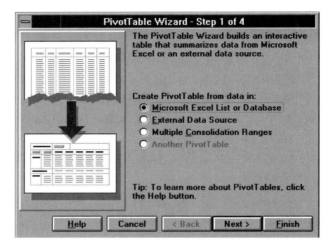

Figure 9.4   *The PivotTable Wizard dialog box.*

Figure 9.4 shows Microsoft Excel List or Database in, selected. That is exactly what we want to do, so we move on to the next step.

2. Click on the **Next** button to display the next dialog box.

    The PivotTable Wizard places a dashed line around the data it thinks you want to use for the PivotTable and asks you to confirm (or modify) the range here.

3. Click on the **Next** button to confirm the range and display the third dialog box, as displayed in Figure 9.6.

    You can place field names in the ROW or COLUMN portion of the dialog box to determine which data is summarized and place a field name in the DATA portion to determine how the data is summarized. This is accomplished by dragging the field name buttons to the position you want.

    We want to summarize the data by type and have the totals of the types of fields summarized.

4. Drag the TYPE field name button (on the right side of the dialog box) into the ROW portion of the dialog box.

5. Drag the TOTAL field name button into the DATA portion of the dialog box. (It becomes a Sum of TOTAL button).

6. When your dialog box is displayed, as shown in Figure 9.7, click on the **Next** button.

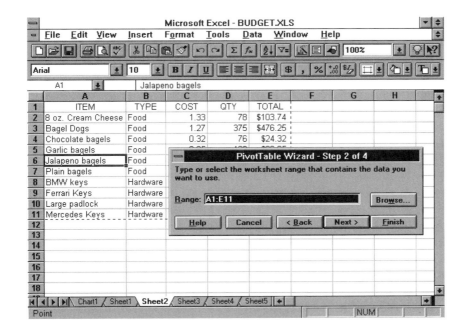

Figure 9.5 *The Pivot Table Wizard dialog box.*

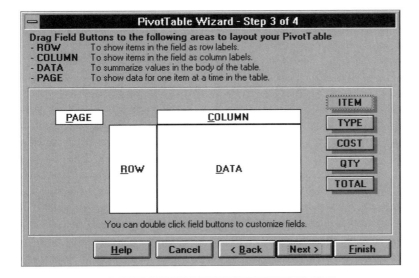

Figure 9.6 *The PivotTable Wizard dialog box.*

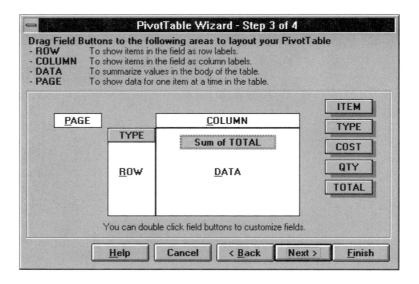

Figure 9.7 *The field buttons in place for the PivotTable Wizard.*

Figure 9.8 *The PivotTable Wizard dialog box.*

7. In the PivotTable Starting Cell text box, type: **A13** to have the PivotTable placed a couple of rows below our list.

If you do not specify a starting cell in this dialog box, the PivotTable replaces the database, which may not be what you have in mind.

WARNING

8. Click on the **Finish** button to accept the PivotTable specifications and have it placed on the worksheet, as shown in Figure 9.9.

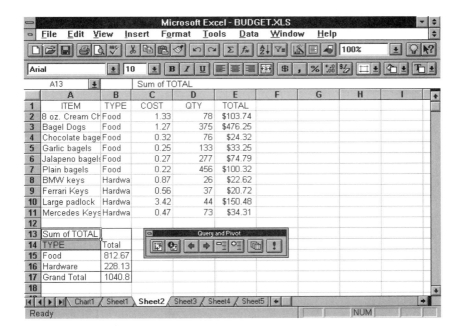

Figure 9.9 *The PivotTable displayed below the list.*

The Query and Pivot toolbar also appears with the PivotTable so you can work with the PivotTable more conveniently. You may want to drag the Query and Pivot toolbar to a new location if it obscures part of the PivotTable or is too far away from the PivotTable.

The PivotTable we have created displays the food total, the hardware total, and the grand total for both.

9. Save your work before proceeding with the next section.

USING SCENARIO MANAGER

Playing "what if" is one of the spreadsheet's most useful facilities. You can change values in various cells of the worksheet to see the effect the changes will have. For example, what would happen if January sales increased by $100,000? You could just enter the new value in the January sales cell. But you'd have to re-enter the original value, then the new value to switch between the scenarios.

Excel's Scenario Manager makes switching between various what-if scenarios a breeze by letting you name the scenarios and then choosing the one you want to see from a list in a dialog box.

Let's create scenarios for our budget worksheet to allow us to switch among a couple of sales possibilities.

1. Click on the **Sheet1** tab to make the budget worksheet data visible and then choose **Tools**, **Scenarios** to display the Scenario Manager dialog box, as shown in Figure 9.10.

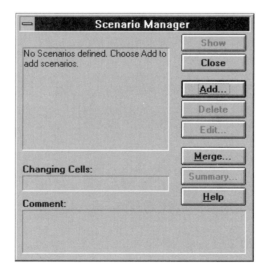

Figure 9.10 *The Scenario Manager dialog box.*

2. We do not have any scenarios defined yet, so click on the **Add** button to add a scenario.

The Add Scenario dialog box appears, as shown in Figure 9.11.

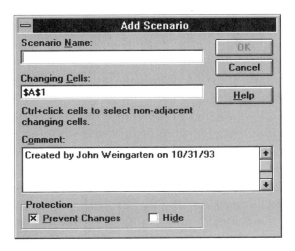

Figure 9.11 *The Add Scenario dialog box.*

3. In the Scenario Name text box, type: **Best Guess**.

4. Drag the I-beam mouse pointer across the entire comment that says "Created by Your Name on MM/DD/YY" and type: **This is what I expect sales to be**.

5. Drag the dialog box by its title bar down far enough so cells B5, C5 and D5 are visible, then double-click in the **Changing Cells** text box.

   This is where we define which cells will have different values for the scenario.

N O T E The cells you specify as the Changing Cells should not contain formulas, but rather be cells containing values that formulas depend on. For example, B5 is the cell containing the January sales value, but several formulas in the worksheet depend on this value for their results. Therefore, B5 is a good choice for a Changing Cell.

6. Click on cell B5, then hold down the **Ctrl** key while you click on **C5** and then **D5**.

7. When the dialog box is displayed, as shown in Figure 9.12, click on **OK**.

   The Scenario Values dialog box appears, as shown in Figure 9.13, where you can enter the values for this scenario. For our Best Guess scenario, we leave the values as they are.

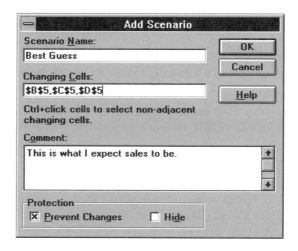

Figure 9.12   The completed Add Scenario dialog box.

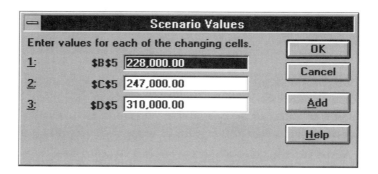

Figure 9.13   The Scenario Values dialog box.

8.   Click on the **Add** button to display the Add Scenario dialog box and try another scenario.

9.   In the Scenario Name text box, type: **Wishful Thinking**, and edit the Comment box so the comment is **Not a chance**, then click on **OK**.

10.   Edit the values in the Scenario Values dialog box so the values are 328,000 for B5, 347,000 for C5 and 410,000 for D5, then click on **Add** button again so we can add one more scenario.

11. In the Scenario Name text box, type: **The Sky Is Falling**! and edit the Comment box so the comment is **We're in big trouble**. Then click on **OK**.

12. Edit the values in the Scenario Values dialog box so the values are **128,000** for $B#5, 147,000 for C5 and 210,000 for D5, then click on **OK**.

   The Scenario Manager dialog box appears once again, this time with the three scenarios listed. You can now click on any of the scenario names in the Scenarios list. Click on the **Show** button and the worksheet changes to values for that scenario. You can switch among the scenarios while still in the dialog box and view the changes on the worksheet. When you close the dialog box the worksheet displays the values from the last chosen scenario.

   As you switch among the three scenarios, notice that the numbers in cells E5, B13 through E13, and B16 through E16 change.

13. When you are finished experimenting with the scenarios, switch to the Best Guess scenario to return to our original numbers and then click on **Close** to clear the Scenario Manager dialog box.

14. Save your work and exit Excel if you're not continuing on to the next chapter now.

Your scenarios are saved with the workbook so they are available whenever you are working with this worksheet in the workbook.

N O T E

A FINAL THOUGHT

In this chapter, you learned to use just a few of Excel's tools for proofing and analyzing your worksheet data. You now know how to ensure that your data is free of spelling errors and how to view the data in a variety of ways using PivotTable and Scenario Manager.

In the next chapter you learn about one of the biggest time savers in Excel—Macros.

Chapter 10

Automating Your Work with Macros

* UNDERSTANDING MACROS
* RECORDING A MACRO
* RUNNING A MACRO
* ASSIGNING MACROS TO MENUS, SHORTCUT KEYS AND BUTTONS

UNDERSTANDING MACROS

Without a program, your computer is nothing more than a big, expensive paper-weight. A program is a set of instructions, in a language your computer can understand, which allows your computer to perform useful (or so one would hope) tasks. Excel is a big computer program that tells your computer what to do. A *macro* is nothing more than a little program (in this case, inside Excel) that tells Excel what to do.

Don't let the word *program* scare you. You can use Excel macros to cut time-consuming, repetitive tasks down to size without knowing the first thing about programming. Excel lets you *record* any series of Excel actions for later use, just as you would record a series of sounds on a tape recorder for future playback.

Suppose you routinely format groups of selected cells in some particular ways—perhaps centering their contents, surrounding them with a border, and adjusting the column width to accommodate the longest entry. To do this manu-ally, you have to perform three separate tasks requiring many mouse actions or keystrokes. However, if you record these tasks as a macro, you can perform all these tasks at once with a couple of mouse clicks or keystrokes to run (*play*) the macro. You even learn a few tricks for assigning macros to menus, buttons, and shortcut keys so they are even easier to use.

Another common use for a macro is to automate the typing of frequently entered text, such as your name, address, or company name. Recording fre-quently entered text as macros saves time and eliminates typos—assuming you typed it correctly while recording the macro.

This cell formatting example is a very simple example of what you can do with macros. Literally any series of tasks can be consolidated into a single macro. No series of tasks is too simple or too complex to be turned into a macro. Consider the toolbar buttons. You have likely noticed that they are short-cuts for performing tasks with just the click of a mouse.

Some buttons, such as the Open button, do not save you much time. Instead of clicking on the Open button, you could simply choose **File**, **Open**. It may hardly seem worth the effort to use a button to save one keystroke or mouse click. However, because opening files is something that is repeated many times during a typical Excel session, the button can accumulate a savings in time that is worthwhile.

Let's discuss the issue of programming. You don't need to know anything about programming to make good use of macros. However, if you take the time to learn a little about Excel's programming language, you can extend your macros' potential flexibility and complexity enormously.

Even if you don't do any programming and just use Excel's macro recorder, you are actually programming. Huh? Let me explain. When you turn on the macro recorder and perform the tasks you want included in the macro, Excel creates a computer program for you and runs the program when you run the macro.

N O T E The programming language Excel uses to create your macro is called *VBA* (Visual Basic for Applications). This language is an extension of the ubiquitous BASIC programming language that comes with many computers. In fact, you may already have some familiarity with BASIC. If you already know a little about any version of BASIC, you won't have any trouble adapting to VBA. If you have no clue about the ins and outs of programming, but have some healthy curiosity, you can quickly learn some simple VBA programming from the documentation that is included with Excel.

RECORDING A MACRO

To start recording, simply choose **Tools**, **Record Macro**, **Record New Macro** and then enter a macro name, description, and perform the tasks you want included. There are a couple of things to take into account before you start recording. The first is planning.

When you record a macro, everything you do including mistakes, is recorded in the macro and turned into program code. If you start recording a macro while in one worksheet and then realize that you want to use the macro on another worksheet, you switch to the other worksheet and start performing the tasks you want to be part of the macro. The problem is, whenever you run the macro, the first thing it does is switch to a different worksheet, which probably isn't what you want to do at that point. Recording a macro with a lot of mistakes can also slow down the execution of the macro.

If you want the macro to manipulate some selected cells, you want to perform the macro recording tasks on a single active cell in the worksheet. Select that cell before starting the recording process. This way, when you run the macro, it performs on the current selection.

You want to consider whether the macro uses *relative* or *absolute referencing*. The concept is the same as the absolute versus relative referencing discussed in copying formulas. If your active cell is A1 when you start recording the macro using absolute referencing and you click on cell D6, the first thing the macro does when played is move to cell D6. If you were using relative referencing—which is the default—the macro would move three columns to the right and five rows down, which is D6's relative position from A1. As a general rule, relative referencing allows your macros to operate correctly in a variety of situations.

Finally, you want to decide where the macro is to be stored. If you are creating a macro that is only applicable to the active workbook, you can have the macro stored there. You can also store macros in a new workbook, but then you have to open that workbook whenever you want to use that macro.

If you want to make your macros portable (usable in a variety of workbooks and situations) the best approach is usually to store them in the *Personal Macro Workbook*. The Personal Macro Workbook is a hidden workbook that is always available for use with any workbook you have open.

Let's start recording the cell formatting macro now.

1. Start Excel and open the BUDGET workbook if it isn't already on your screen. Click on the **Sheet3** tab so we can record this macro on a fresh worksheet.

    It isn't necessary to record the macro on an unused sheet, but doing so ensures that you won't mess up any existing worksheet data while recording your macro.

2. Click on cell **B2** to make it the active cell and then choose **Tools**, **Record Macro**, **Record New Macro** to display the Record New Macro dialog box, as shown in Figure 10.1.

    For this macro, any active cell works. Using a cell that is at least one row down and one column over allows us to see all sides of the border the macro adds.

    You could allow Excel to name the macro for you (in this case Macro1) but that's not very descriptive, so we give it a new name.

3. With the Macro Name text box highlighted, type: **CellFmt** and press the **Tab** key to highlight the contents of the Description box.

4. In the Description box, type: **Formats selection center aligned, places border and AutoFits column width**.

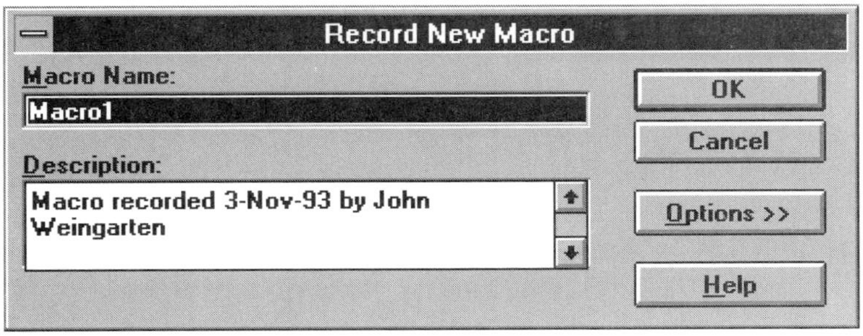

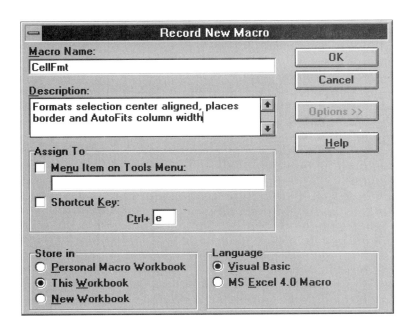

Figure 10.1 *The Record New Macro dialog box.*

This macro works on any group of selected cells, so we want to make sure it's available whenever we need it.

5. Click on the **Options** button to expand the dialog box so the Record New Macro options are visible, as shown in Figure 10.2.

Figure 10.2 *The expanded Record New Macro dialog box.*

We cover the Assign To portion of the dialog box later in the chapter. For now, let's make sure we are storing the macro in the Personal Workbook.

NOTE The Language section of the dialog box lets you choose whether you want to record the macro in Visual Basic or the MS Excel 4.0 Macro language. Unless you are sharing macros with users who haven't upgraded to version 5 yet, you should always use Visual Basic. Not only is Visual Basic a more powerful language, but it is also the language that will become the standard for all future Microsoft applications. You might as well get used to it.

6. Click on the **Personal Workbook** option button and then click on **OK** to begin the macro recording session.

    You can tell you are recording a macro because the status bar displays the message **Recording**. There is also a little toolbar floating on the screen with a Stop Recording Macro button, as displayed in Figure 10.3.

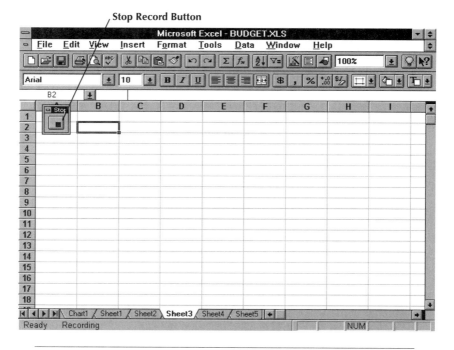

Figure 10.3   The Stop toolbar and the status bar displaying **Recording** *.*

Before performing the our macro tasks, we need to make sure we are using Relative References so the macro works on any group of selected cells and not just B2.

7. Choose **Tools**, **Record Macro**, **Use Relative References**, unless there is already a check mark in front of Use Relative References. If there is already a check mark, press **Esc** three times to back out of the menu.

   Now, we proceed to format the active cell for center alignment, place a single-line border around it, and AutoFit the selection.

8. Display the shortcut menu for the active cell by right-clicking on it. Choose **Format Cells**, click on the Alignment tab, and choose **Center** in the Horizontal area of the dialog box.

9. Click on the **Border** tab, then click on **Outline** in the Border section of the dialog box, and click on **OK**.

10. Choose **Format**, **Column**, **AutoFit Selection**.

11. Click on the **Stop Recording Macro** button in the floating Stop toolbar, and then click on another cell so you can see the border around the cell.

   You cannot tell if the type in the cell is centered or the width is adjusted to accommodate it, since the cell is empty. You see the complete results of the macro when you run it on a real selection.

RUNNING A MACRO

Now that we've recorded a macro, let's select some cells in the sheet containing our database and try it out.

1. Click on the **Sheet2** tab (the database sheet) to display it. If you already adjusted the width of column A and B to accommodate the largest entries, reduce their widths now so at least some of the text in each is obscured. Finally, if the Query and Pivot toolbar is still on your worksheet, remove it by clicking on the **Close Box** in its upper-left corner.

2. Select cells **A2** through **A11** and choose **Tools**, **Macro**. Click on **PERSONAL.XLS!CellFmt** so that it is highlighted, as shown in Figure 10.4.

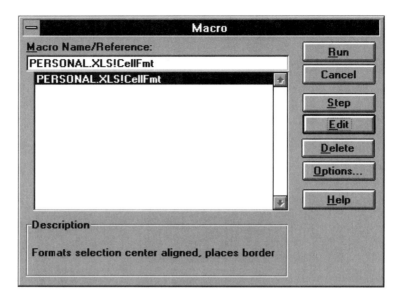

Figure 10.4   *The Macro dialog box.*

Your Macro dialog box may contain the names of other macros if there are any others that are stored in the PERSONAL.XLS dialog box or on any other open workbook.

N O T E

3. Click on the **Run** button to execute the macro.

The list of items in column A is now center-aligned, with a border around it and with the column width adjusted to fit the largest entry.

That's all there is to running a macro from the Macro dialog box. Next let's take a look at ways to make it even easier to run a macro.

ASSIGNING MACROS

The whole point of using macros is to save time. That being the case, choosing **Tools**, **Macro**, clicking on the macro name, and then the **Run** button is a far too tedious process for executing a simple macro.

In the expanded Record New Macro dialog box, there is an *Assign To* area. This area lets you assign the macro to a menu option, a shortcut key, or both.

Let's change the options for the CellFmt macro in the PERSONAL.XLS workbook. The PERSONAL.XLS workbook is hidden, so before we can make any changes to the CellFmt macro, we have to unhide the PERSONAL.XLS workbook.

4. Choose **Window**, **Unhide** to display the Unhide dialog box, as displayed in Figure 10.5.

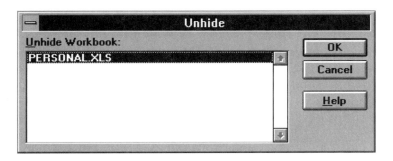

Figure 10.5 *The Unhide dialog box.*

If there are any other open but hidden workbooks, these are listed along with PERSONAL.XLS.

5. Click on **PERSONAL.XLS** if it isn't already highlighted, and then click on the **OK** button.

The PERSONAL.XLS workbook with one tab, Module1, is displayed, as shown in Figure 10.6.

If other macros have been recorded and stored on the PERSONAL.XLS workbook, they may be displayed on your screen and you may need to scroll down to view the CellFmt macro.

With the macro displayed, you could edit it to correct mistakes or add functionality. Even if you do not know the first thing about programming, you may find it interesting to look over the macro. You'll be surprised at how easily you'll understand what's going on.

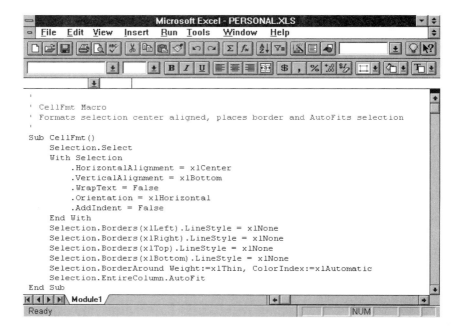

Figure 10.6 *The PERSONAL.XLS workbook.*

WARNING

Unless you know what you are doing and have a reasonable understanding of Visual Basic, you should not edit the macro in any way. Even making some seemingly innocuous changes could leave the macro completely useless.

Now that the workbook containing our macro is unhidden, we can switch back to the Budget workbook and change the macro's options.

6. Choose **Window**, and then click on **BUDGET.XLS** in the bottom portion of the menu.

7. Choose **Tools**, **Macro** and click on **PERSONAL.XLS!CellFmt**, then click on the **Options** button to display the Macro Option dialog box, as shown in Figure 10.7.

The Assign To portion of the Macro Options dialog box is the same as in the expanded Record New Macro dialog box. You can do everything before you start the recording process in exactly the same manner as you do after the macro is recorded.

Macro Options

Macro Name:
PERSONAL.XLS!CellFmt

Description:
Formats selection center aligned, places
border and AutoFits selection

OK

Cancel

Help

Assign To

☐ Me**n**u Item on Tools Menu:

☒ Shortcut **K**ey:

Ct**r**l+ a

Help Information

Status Bar Text:

Help Conte**x**t ID for this Macro:

Function **C**ategory:

Figure 10.7   The Macro Options dialog box.

By default, the Shortcut Key check box is unchecked, but Excel assigns
Ctrl plus the next available letter for the shortcut key combination. You
can use any of the 26 alphabet letters in either uppercase or lowercase,
giving you 52 possible shortcut key combinations. To change the shortcut
key, you highlight or delete the letter in the box and type the letter you
want. If you want to use the letter in uppercase, press **Shift** plus the letter. We accept the shortcut key Excel suggests, which is probably Ctrl+e.

WARNING

When Excel chooses the shortcut key, it's looking for the next
available letter. Available does not necessarily mean the next
consecutive letter. After Ctrl+e is used, Excel skips to Ctrl+g because
Ctrl+f is already assigned as the keyboard shortcut for Find. Press
Ctrl+f and the Find dialog box is displayed.

The bad news is that Excel lets you assign letters that have already
been assigned. If you choose Ctrl+f as the shortcut key combination
for a macro, then Ctrl+f is no longer the shortcut for Find. For this
reason, it is usually best to accept Excel's choice for a shortcut key.

We assign this macro to a menu item on the Tools menu and put a check in the Shortcut Key check box. In real life, you probably would not use both a shortcut key and assign the macro to a menu item. You'd most likely choose one or the other.

8. Click on the Shortcut key check box if it is not already checked.

N O T E   If Excel has assigned a different shortcut key to this macro, that's ok, but make a note of it so you'll be able to remember how to invoke the macro later. In fact, it's not a bad idea to keep a complete listing of all your macros and their shortcut keys handy. You could create the list in an Excel database or in your word processing program.

9. Click on the check box in front of Menu Item on the Tools menu and then click in the text box below and type: **Center/Border/AutoFit**. Click on **OK** and then the **Close** button of the Macro dialog box.

The text you typed—Center/Border/AutoFit—is the text that appears in the Tools menu. The menu width will adjusts to accommodate as much text as fits on one line across the screen. However, it's best to keep the menu text reasonably short so the menu does not obscure too much of the screen.

We now have two new ways to run the macro, from the Tools menu and the shortcut key. Let's use them both.

10. Select cells **B2** through **B11** (the category column) and choose **Tools** to display the Tools menu, as shown in Figure 10.8.

11. Click on **Center/Border/AutoFit** in the bottom portion of the menu.

There now, wasn't that easier? To use the shortcut key on a column that needs reformatting, we close the Budget workbook without saving it, and then open it again.

12. Close the Budget workbook by choosing **File**, **Close** and click on **NO** when asked if you want to save BUDGET.XLS. Then reopen the Budget workbook.

13. Once again, select cells **B2** through **B11** and press the shortcut key combination, **Ctrl+e** (or whatever your shortcut key is).

This is getting just a bit too easy, don't you think? Well, we're still not finished making life easier with macros. Next, assign the macro to a button, which will then add to the Formatting toolbar.

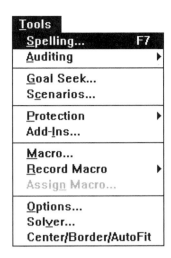

Figure 10.8   *The Tools menu with the new choice at the bottom of the menu.*

14. Close the Budget workbook again without saving and reopen it, as before.

15. Choose **View**, **Toolbars** to display the Toolbars dialog box, as shown in Figure 10.9.

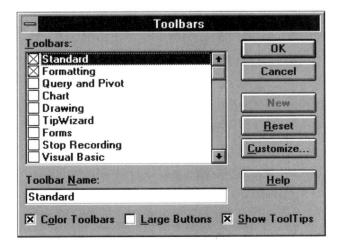

Figure 10.9   *The Toolbars dialog box.*

From this dialog box, you can add or remove any toolbars you want displayed on the screen by clicking in the check box next to the toolbar name. Remember, the more toolbars you display, the less screen *real estate* you are able to see.

N O T E

16. Click on the **Customize** button to display the Customize dialog box, as shown in Figure 10.10.

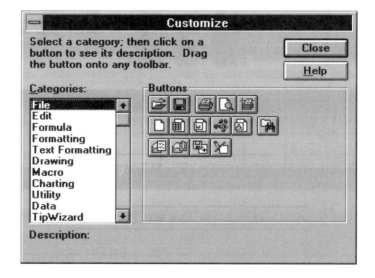

Figure 10.10   *The Customize dialog box.*

You can use the Customize dialog box to assign macros to any of the button icons used in any of the toolbars. Instead of using a button that is already used in another toolbar, it makes more sense to choose a button from the group of custom buttons that Excel supplies.

17. Scroll down to the bottom of the Categories list and click on **Custom** to display the group of buttons, as shown in Figure 10.11.

You can add any of the buttons to any visible toolbar by dragging it to the position you want on the toolbar. We drag a button onto the Formatting toolbar.

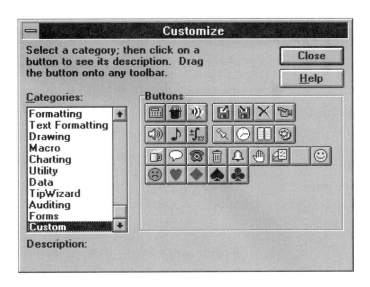

Figure 10.11 *The Custom buttons.*

N O T E

You can create some space on a toolbar for your new macro buttons, (or just remove some clutter) by simply dragging the button you want to remove down onto the worksheet and releasing the mouse button. We have enough room to add another button to the Formatting toolbar, so we won't remove any buttons from it.

18. Drag the button you want to add—let's use the *smiley face* that's on the right side of the third row of buttons—to the Formatting toolbar, between the Italic and the Align Left buttons. Release the mouse button to accept the new button position and display the Assign Macro dialog box, as shown in Figure 10.12.

You can assign any available macro in the Macro Name/Reference list to the button.

11. Click on **PERSONAL.XLS!CellFmt** and then click on **OK**.

12. Click on the **Close** button of the Customize dialog box to complete the toolbar button assignment.

13. Select **B2** through **B11** again and then click on your new smiley-face macro button.

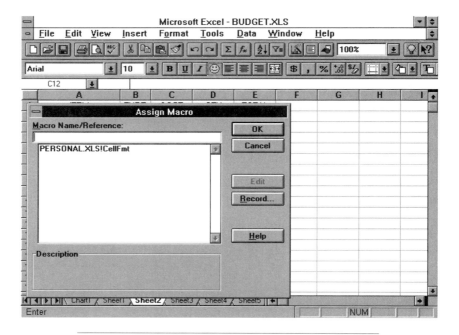

Figure 10.12 *The new button on the Formatting toolbar
and the Assign Macro dialog box.*

That's all there is to making macros easier to execute. You should have
no excuses for avoiding them anymore, even though they involve that
nasty programming stuff.

14. Choose **Window**, click on **PERSONAL.XLS**, and then choose **Window**,
    Hide.

15. **Save** your work and exit Excel if you are not proceeding to the next
    chapter now. Click on the **Yes** button to save the changes to the
    Personal Macro Workbook.

A FINAL THOUGHT

This chapter covered the basics of planning, recording and executing macros. I
strongly encourage you to invest more time and energy exploring the vast
power of macros and macro programming. It is time well spent.

The next chapter looks at the process of linking worksheets.

Chapter 11

Linking Worksheets

- ✳ UNDERSTANDING LINKING CONCEPTS
- ✳ CREATING LINKS
- ✳ UPDATING LINKS

UNDERSTANDING LINKING CONCEPTS

We have been working in only one workbook so far. The separate worksheets created within the Budget workbook have no special relationship to each other, except that they contain information about a single company.

There are many situations that call for tying data from two or more work-books together. This process of tying data together is called *linking*. You can also link data between worksheets in the same workbook.

There is nothing magical or mysterious about linking. When you link data from one worksheet to another, you are simply using the referencing concepts that have been discussed since we started creating formulas. However, when you create links to other worksheets—whether they are in the same or a different workbook—the reference includes the workbook name (if it's a different workbook), the sheet name, and then the cell address or range.

Linking is commonly used for a couple of different purposes. You can use linking to break a large, complex worksheet into smaller, more manageable chunks. You might want to keep some confidential data in a separate worksheet to keep prying eyes away, or you may want to segregate your worksheet by company, department, or activity.

A very good reason for linking to worksheets in different workbooks is to summarize data from several company divisions. Suppose your company has offices in three cities and each creates a worksheet detailing weekly sales activity. By linking, the manager at each location could send a disk containing the workbook to company headquarters, where the new numbers could be brought into the summary, or master worksheet.

N O T E   Of course, you don't have to place confidential information in a separate sheet. You can hide any portion of a worksheet that you do not want to be in plain sight. However, it can be less cumbersome to place the data in another worksheet so that it is available to you by switching to that sheet, rather than having to unhide and rehide it every time you want to see it.

When you create links, you are dealing with at least two worksheets, a *source worksheet* and a *dependent worksheet*. The source worksheet contains the data that you want to bring into the dependent worksheet. After a link is created, the linked data in the dependent worksheet is automatically updated when the linked data in the source worksheet is updated.

Linking worksheets is different than a simple copy-and-paste operation. If you copy a value from one worksheet and then paste it into another, you are simply copying the value and not establishing a link. If the value in the source worksheet (the one you copied from) changes, the value in the dependent worksheet does not change.

If you try to use copy and paste to copy a formula from one worksheet to another, it does not work at all. The requisite workbook and worksheet portions of the reference are not copied so you end up with an invalid formula.

CREATING LINKS

If the worksheets you want to link are already created, you can simply open them and create the link references from the source worksheets to the dependent worksheet.

We create three simple worksheets in separate workbooks to track sales data for Spokane Locks and Bagel's three locations. These are the source worksheets. We then create a dependent worksheet to let us summarize the data from the source worksheet.

1. Start Excel. If the BUDGET workbook or any other workbooks containing data are on your screen, close them and then click on the **New Workbook** toolbar button to open a fresh workbook.

2. In cell A1, type: **SALES**.

3. In cell A3, type: **Total Sales**, press **Enter** to confirm the entry, and then double click on the column heading border of column A to adjust the width to accommodate the entries.

    We copy the worksheet to two other sheets in two new workbooks. This worksheet is simple enough that we may as well enter the data manually into the other worksheets. But copying the worksheet can be a real time saver when you want to create multiple worksheets with an identical structure.

4. Choose **Edit**, **Move**, or **Copy Sheet** to display the Move or Copy dialog box, as shown in Figure 11.1.

5. Click on the **Arrow** next to the text box under To Book to display the list of books to which you can move or copy the worksheet, as shown in Figure 11.2.

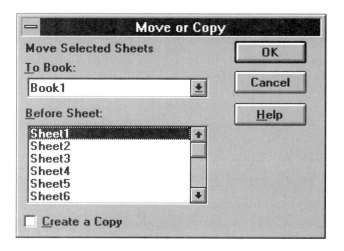

Figure 11.1   *The Move or Copy dialog box.*

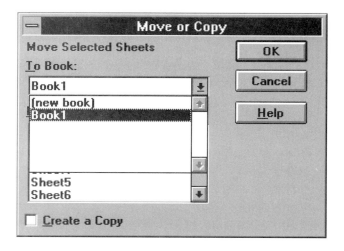

Figure 11.2   *The Move or Copy drop-down list of available workbooks.*

6. Click on (**new book**). Then click on the **Create a Copy** check box and click on **OK** to make the copy.

7. Repeat steps 4 through 6 to make another copy or the worksheet.

8. Click on the **New Workbook** toolbar button to display a new empty workbook so we can enter the structure for our summary sheet.

9. In cell A1, type: **MASTER SALES SHEET**.

10. In cell A3, type: **Downtown**; in A4, type: **Valley**; and in A5, type: **Northside**. Press **Enter** to confirm the entry.

    Now we enter the sales figures into our source worksheets and then create the links. We could switch to each of them one at a time, but it's often easier to be able to see a portion of all of the worksheets at once. To do this we use Windows' ability to organize the four workbook windows into four equal-sized tiles on the screen.

11. Choose **Window**, **Arrange** to display the Arrange Windows dialog box, as shown in Figure 11.3.

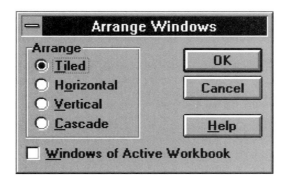

Figure 11.3   *The Arrange Windows dialog box.*

12. The Tiled option is the default, so just click on the **OK** button to tile the four windows, as shown in Figure 11.4.

    You can easily tell which window is active. It is the one with the highlighted title bar and the Scroll bars. You can change active windows by choosing **Window** and then the name of the window you want. The easiest way to change active windows is to simply click on it.

    Let's add location and sales information in cells B1 and B3 of each of the source windows.

13. Click anywhere in the window in the upper-right portion of the screen. In Figure 11.4 it is Book2.

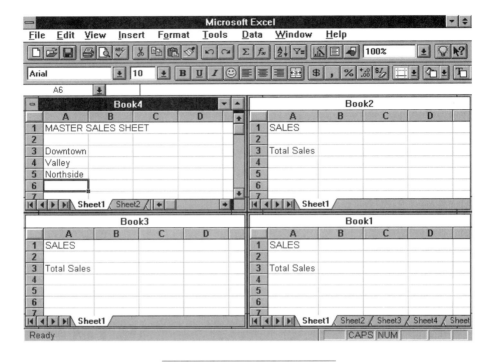

Figure 11.4 *The tiled windows.*

14. In cell B1, type: **DOWNTOWN**. In B3, type: **$31,000** and then click anywhere in the window below—Book1—to make it the active window.

15. In cell B1, type: **VALLEY**. In B3, type: **$27,500** and then click in the window on the lower left—Book3—to make it the active window.

16. In cell B1, type: **NORTHSIDE**. In B3, type: **$58,000** and then click in the Master Sales window in the upper-left.

    With the windows tiled, creating the links is a snap. All we need to do is start the formula as we would when creating any other formula—with an equal sign—and then point and click.

17. Click in cell **B3**, where the Downtown sales figure will be in the Master Sales sheet, and type: **=**. Make the Downtown sheet active by clicking in it, then click in cell B3 and click in the confirm box on the formula bar to accept the entry.

N O T E When creating a link reference, clicking on another worksheet does not *really* make it the active window. It just allows you to include references from the window and use scroll bars to find the portion of the sheet you want.

The formula in the formula bar is =[Book2]Sheet1!B3. Next we add the other links.

18. Press the **Down Arrow** key to make B4 (the Valley sales cell) active and type: **=**. Click in the Valley window and then on cell B3 of the Valley window, and press **Enter**.

19. With cell B5 in the Master Sales sheet selected, type: **=**. Click in the Northside window, then click on cell **B3**, and click on the confirm box to accept the entry.

The sales numbers for each location are now linked to the master sheet, as shown in Figure 11.5.

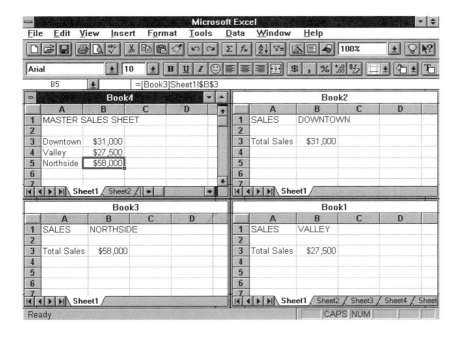

Figure 11.5 *The tiled windows with sales numbers.*

If any of the sales numbers in the source sheets changes, the numbers in the dependent Master Sales sheet also change. Let's try changing one of the numbers to see if it works.

20. Change the sales number in the Downtown sheet to $41,000 and notice the number in the Master Sales window change.

MAINTAINING LINKS

You'll often make changes in your linked worksheets that require them to be updated. If you save these workbooks and name them something other than Book1 through Book4, the link references are no longer correct. However, when you open the dependent document later, you are given an opportunity to have Excel automatically update the links.

Let's save and close the workbooks now.

21. Close the Downtown workbook, saving it with the name *Downtown*. Close the Northside workbook and save it with the name *Nside*. Use the name *Valley* to save the Valley workbook and, finally, save the Master Sales workbook with the name *Master*.

     Open the Master and Valley workbooks to see how Excel updates the links.

22. Open the MASTER.XLS workbook.

     Excel prompts you with a message dialog box asking if you want to update the automatic links, as shown in Figure 11.6.

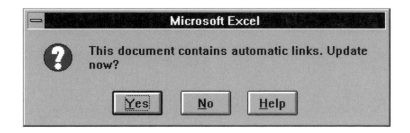

Figure 11.6   *The Excel message dialog box to update links.*

23. Click on the **Yes** button to update the links and open the workbook.

24. Click on cell B4 and notice that the reference now indicates the VAL-LEY.XLS workbook.

25. Open the VALLEY.XLS workbook and try changing the sales number to assure yourself that the link has been maintained.

26. Close all open workbooks and exit Excel if you are not moving on to the next chapter now.

A FINAL THOUGHT

In this chapter, you learned to take advantage of some of Excel's powerful features for working with multiple workbooks. In the next chapter, you learn about some of the ways you can customize Excel to make your working environment suit your requirements.

Chapter 12

Customizing Excel

* SETTING EXCEL'S OPTIONS
* USING AUTOSAVE
* CHANGING VIEWS

213

This chapter covers various ways of customizing your Excel environment. It is also something of a potpourri of Excel information that did not have a clearly logical location in any of the other chapters.

Some of the sections of this chapter, such as using AutoSave, can allow you to work in Excel with greater confidence knowing your data is automatically protected, even if you forget to save. Other sections show you how to specify such options as how Excel calculates formulas, whether you are prompted for summary information when saving workbooks and how many sheets there are in a workbook by default.

You also learn to alter your perspective of the worksheet by changing view options.

SETTING EXCEL'S OPTIONS

Excel's Options dialog box provides tremendous flexibility and allows you to change most of the ways you interact with the program. Take a look at some of these options now.

1. Start Excel, if it isn't already running, and make sure there is a work-sheet on your screen.

   Since we are not stepping through the procedures we are discussing in this chapter, it doesn't matter which worksheet is on the screen.

2. Choose **Tools**, **Options**, and then click on the **General** tab to display the General portion of the Options dialog box, as shown in Figure 12.1.

   We examine some of the more interesting options in the dialog box without changing them. However, I will offer some of my recommendations for these options.

   The Reference Style choices—A1 or R1C—determine how you refer to cells in the worksheet. You want to leave this as the default, A1, unless you are more comfortable with a fairly old spreadsheet program from Microsoft called Multiplan. Even if you *are* more familiar with Multiplan, you are still better off sticking with the default since that is the way all modern spreadsheet programs refer to cells.

   The Menus area of the dialog box provides two check boxes. The first lets you turn off the display of the last four recently used files at the bottom of the File menu. I cannot think of any reason to turn this option off. The other option lets you use the menus from the previous version of Excel, version 4.0. Again, I cannot think of a good reason to use this option. You may as well get used to the 5.0 menus since this book and all the documentation that comes with Excel 5.0 refers to them.

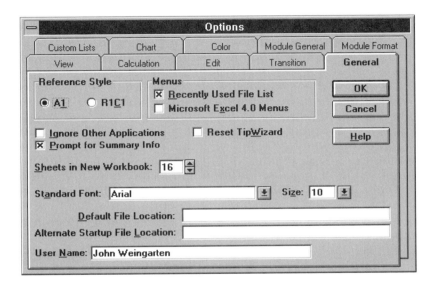

Figure 12.1 *The General portion of the Options dialog box.*

✳ **Prompt for Summary Info** may be turned off if you are not entering any information into the Summary dialog box and are not having trouble locating your files from their file names.

✳ **Sheets in New Workbook** default is 16. You can always add or delete worksheets from a workbook, so the value in this option does not matter too much. However, if you consistently use more or fewer worksheets in a workbook, you may want to increase or decrease the value to save you the trouble of doing it later.

✳ The **Standard Font** and **Size** lists let you specify which of your available fonts and sizes you want to use for future worksheets. Changing the defaults does not change the fonts or sizes on existing worksheets. You might consider changing the font or size if you find the default difficult to read on your screen. Keep in mind that, if you change to a larger size, you are not be able to see as much data on your worksheet at one time.

✳ The **Default File Location** and the **Alternate Startup File Location** let you specify which directories you want to use for your Excel files. The files in each of these directories appears when you choose **File**, **Open**. I recommend specifying a directory for Default File Location so your files are always where you expect them to be.

To enter a Default File Location, click in the text box and type the complete path where your files are stored. For example, if your files are stored on drive C in a directory called MYFILES, which is one level below the Excel directory, you would enter **C:\EXCEL\MYFILES** in the text box.

✳ **User Name** is the name that was entered when Excel was first installed on the computer. If you are not the person who installed the software, you can simply delete the name in the text box and enter yours. They can always change it back when they return from vacation.

Let's take a look at a couple of the options you might want to change in the Edit portion of the dialog box.

3. Click on the **Edit** tab to display the Edit portion of the Options dialog box, as shown in Figure 12.2.

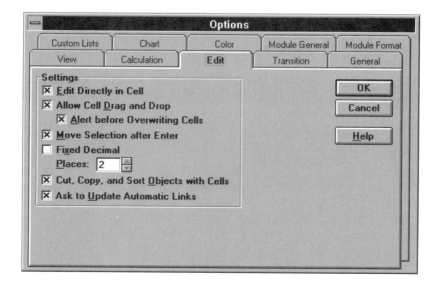

Figure 12.2 *The Edit portion of the Options dialog box.*

✳ The **Move Selection after Enter** (the default) causes the active cell to move one row down after you accept an entry by pressing **Enter**. If you want to be able to press **Enter** without changing the selected cell, click in the check box to remove the check.

If you almost always enter numbers with a certain number of decimal places, it can save you time if you do not have to enter the decimal point. If you specify a certain number of decimal places (2 is the default) and click in the **Fixed Decimal** check box, Excel enters your decimal point for you. You can always override this option by manually entering a decimal point.

Next, let's take a look at how Excel calculates.

4. Click on the **Calculation** tab to display the Calculation portion of the Options dialog box, as shown in Figure 12.3.

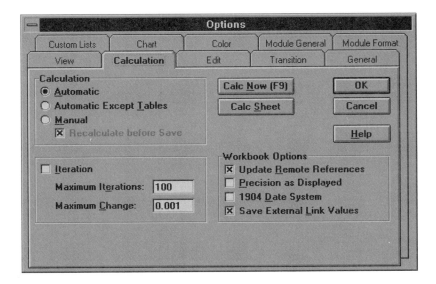

Figure 12.3 *The Calculation portion of the Options dialog box.*

The options in the Calculation area of this portion of the dialog box let you choose whether Excel calculates automatically (the default) or manually. You can also choose to have Excel calculate automatically except for tables (such as PivotTables).

As you have worked through the steps in this book, you probably noticed that when you changed numbers that formulas referred to, the recalculations occurred almost instantly. This is because the examples in the book are very simple and very small. However, if you are working with larger, more complex worksheets containing many formulas and functions requiring recalculation when numbers are changed, there can be quite a long delay while Excel performs the calculations.

The actual length of time required for calculations depends on the size and complexity of the worksheet, as well as the speed of your computer. If your computer is fast enough, even very large worksheets may recalculate fast enough to satisfy you. However, when you find that the delays become burdensome as you are entering or editing worksheet data, consider switching to manual recalculation by clicking in the **Manual** option button.

Be sure to keep the Recalculate Before Save check box checked so the numbers are brought up to date when you save the workbook. Whenever you want to perform a calculation to see the current state of your worksheet, you can use the keyboard shortcut key, **F9**.

Before leaving this dialog box, we take a look at one more part, the View portion.

5. Click on the **View** tab to display the View portion of the Options dialog box, as shown in Figure 12.4.

The View portion of the dialog box is a bit different than the other portions of the Options dialog box we have looked at. Any changes to the settings in the other portions of the dialog box become the new default settings for new workbooks. This is also true of the changes made in the Show area of the View portion of the dialog box. Changes made in the other areas of the View portion of the dialog box only affect the current worksheet.

For example, if you turn off the gridlines by clicking in the **Gridlines** check box, the gridlines are removed from the active worksheet, but not from other worksheets, even in the same workbook.

This dialog box lets you turn on or off various screen elements that can make it easier to navigate in Excel, but can also add clutter to your screen. A good rule of thumb is to remove any elements that you don't use. For example, in the Show area, you can uncheck the Formula Bar, the Status Bar, and Note indicators. These are all very useful elements and I recommend that you keep all of them on your screen.

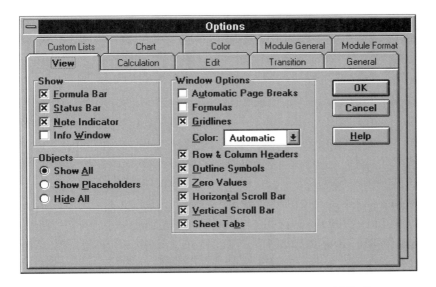

Figure 12.4 *The View portion of the Options dialog box.*

You can also add the Info Window, which is not checked by default. The Info Window displays the current active cell reference, any formula it contains, and any attached note. The Info Window does not take up any screen real estate since you have to switch to it to see it, which you can do from the Window menu.

SHORTCUT

All the options in the Show area of the View portion of the dialog box, except the Info Window option, can be turned on and off from the View menu. Since you may want to turn these elements off and on while working in a particular worksheet, the View menu is the fastest way to make these changes.

The Objects area of the dialog box lets you choose whether to show all objects, show placeholders (gray rectangles), or hide objects. The objects in question here are graphic elements such as charts and pictures. Showing all of them (the default) presents you with the most accurate representation of what your printed page will look like. Not surprisingly, though, it can slow down your navigation through the worksheet, especially on a slower computer. Showing the placeholder can speed things up and does not affect the printout. Hiding these objects causes them not to print at all.

A couple of the options in the Window Options area of the dialog box bear discussion. The Automatic Page Breaks check box allows you to choose whether Excel displays horizontal and vertical lines where your printed pages end. This can be a very useful option for determining where portions of your worksheets fall on the printed pages as you enter and edit data, without having to use Print Preview.

The Formulas option can be especially useful for finding and displaying all the formulas on a worksheet without selecting one cell at a time. It is easy to forget where you placed your formulas, particularly in larger worksheets, and this can shed some light on the situation. Figure 12.5 shows a portion of the budget worksheet with the formulas displayed.

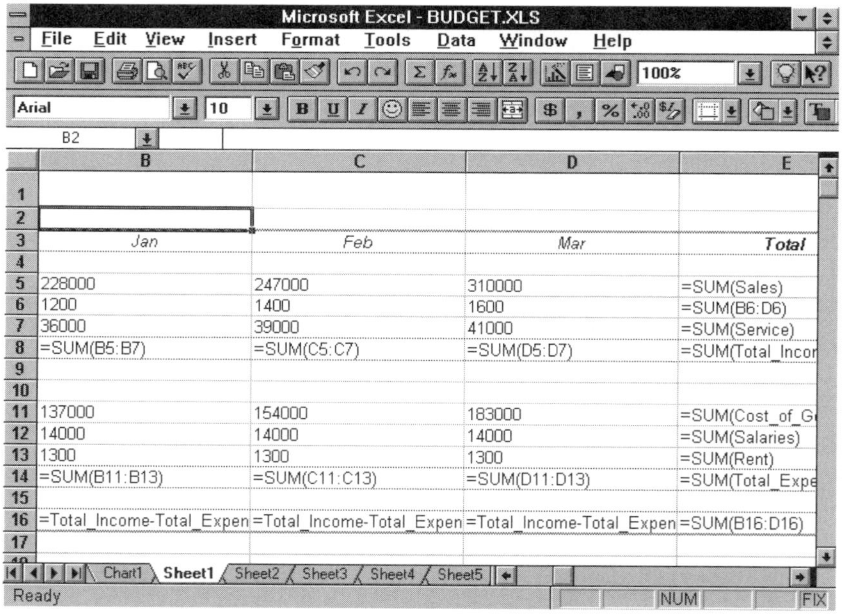

Figure 12.5 *Part of the budget worksheet with formulas displayed.*

There are many other choices in the Options dialog box for customizing your environment. In each portion of the dialog box, as in most other dialog boxes, you can click on the **Help** button to get explanations of the various options.

USING AUTOSAVE

Excel provides a host of *extra* little programs, designed to enhance Excel. We have already used one of these, the Scenario Manager, earlier in the book. Other add-ins include a program for creating slide shows from Excel screens, which you can use for presentations. There is a program for querying external databases that can be quite useful when data is kept in files created by other programs, such as dBase or Access.

The add-in we are going to discuss here is AutoSave. There is no more important procedure in Excel, or any other computer program for that matter, than saving your work. It does not matter which other skills you master or what sort of elaborate worksheets you create if you lose them to a power failure, or some other computer mishap.

Of course you can save your work manually, but anything that can be done to automate the process and relieve you of that burden is welcome. AutoSave does just that. With AutoSave you can instruct Excel to save your work automatically at specified intervals.

Let's take a look at AutoSave now. You can skip the first two steps if AutoSave is already one of the choices on your Tools menu.

1. Choose **Tools**, **Add-Ins** to display the Add-Ins dialog box, as shown in Figure 12.6.

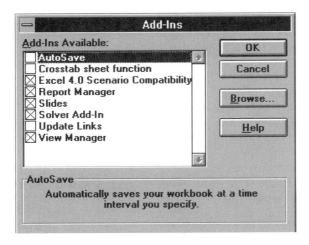

Figure 12.6   *The Add-Ins dialog box.*

This dialog box displays the add-in programs on your computer's hard disk. The ones with checks in their check boxes are currently available to Excel.

2. Click in the **AutoSave** check box (if it is unchecked) and then click on **OK** to make AutoSave available.

N O T E   Browse through the other add-ins to familiarize yourself with their functions. You can also use the Help button to learn more about each of them.

In addition to the add-ins included with Excel, several companies offer other add-in programs for performing many specialized tasks. You'll see ads for and reviews of these in some of the popular computer magazines. You may also receive offers for some of these through the mail after you send in your registration form.

3. Choose **Tools**, **AutoSave** to display the AutoSave dialog box, as shown in Figure 12.7.

Figure 12.7   *The AutoSave dialog box.*

By default, the check box in the upper-left portion of the AutoSave dialog box is checked and the default save interval is ten minutes. The rule of thumb for how often you should AutoSave is the same as for how often you should save manually. Save often enough that if you lose your work just before the next save, you won't be too upset. For most folks, that is between 10 and 20 minutes.

The Save Options area of the dialog box lets you choose whether AutoSave saves only your active workbook (the default), or all open workbooks. Since saving all open workbooks could cause each save to take a few extra precious seconds, it is usually best to have AutoSave just save the active workbook.

The final check box lets Excel prompt you before proceeding with a save. I strongly recommend that you use this option. In this way, if you have made some changes to the worksheet that you do not want saved, you can prevent the save.

If you choose to be prompted before the save, Excel displays the AutoSave confirmation dialog box, as shown in Figure 12.8, after the specified number of minutes.

Figure 12.8   *The AutoSave confirmation dialog box.*

If you want to proceed with the save, click on the **Save** button. If you do not want to save, click on **Cancel**. The Skip button also works, but its primary purpose is to allow you to skip saving certain workbooks and save others when you've chosen to have AutoSave save all open workbooks.

WARNING

Just because your work is saved to your computer's hard disk often, do not feel too secure about the safety of your data. If you have important data stored on your computer, you must also back it up to floppy disks or tape (if you have a tape back-up system). This is critical, because things can go wrong that are more serious than a power failure.

If your computer breaks altogether, is stolen, or burned in a fire you can at least restore your important data to another computer from your backups.

CHANGING VIEWS

There are a couple of options for changing the view of your worksheet that are not part of the Options dialog box. The first of these we discuss is another add-in called View Manager.

As you work with larger worksheets, you may find yourself jumping back and forth between the far reaches of the worksheet to view and edit different portions. You can use the Go To method we discussed earlier, but even that method can become confusing. An easier way to move around the worksheet is to assign names to the various views you want to move to in the View Manager.

To add a named view, move to the portion of the worksheet you want to be able to return to and then use View Manager to assign it a name. Let's take a look at View Manager.

1. Choose **View**, **View Manager** to display the View Manager dialog box, as shown in Figure 12.9.

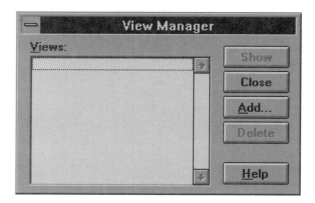

Figure 12.9 *The View Manager dialog box.*

2. Click on the **Add** button to display the Add View dialog box, as shown in Figure 12.10.

3. Enter a name for the view and click on **OK**.

    You usually want to keep the print settings and hidden rows and columns with your views, so keep these check boxes checked.

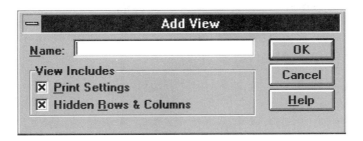

Figure 12.10   *The Add View dialog box.*

Figure 12.11 displays an example of the View Manager dialog box with several views from which to choose.

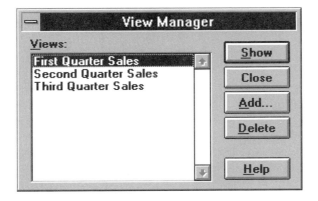

Figure 12.11   *The View Manager dialog box with several named views.*

The views you name in the View Manager only relate to the active worksheet. You can use View Manager to switch among workbooks, or even among worksheets in the active workbook.

N O T E

After you have added views, you can move to them by choosing **View**, **View Manager**, highlighting the desired view and clicking on the **Show** button.

Let's take a look at one other useful feature for changing the view of your worksheet, the Zoom feature. Until now, we have been looking at our worksheets at the default 100% zoom. If you want to step back from your worksheet to get a bigger picture, you can zoom out to a smaller percentage. You can also zoom in to see more detail in a smaller portion of the worksheet.

You can use the drop-down list on the Standard toolbar (the one that has 100% in it now) or the Zoom dialog box from the View menu to change your view. We'll take a look at the Zoom dialog box.

4. Choose **View**, **Zoom** to display the Zoom dialog box, as shown in Figure 12.12.

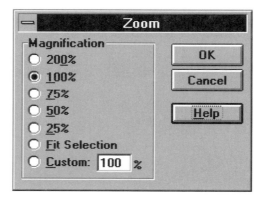

Figure 12.12 *The Zoom dialog box.*

5. Click in any of the option buttons next to the zoom sizes, or click in **Custom** and enter a number from 10 to 400, then click on **OK**.

The larger the number, the less worksheet area you are able to see. The Fit Selection option adjusts the selected cells to fit in the window. Figure 12.13 displays a portion of the budget worksheet zoomed to 200%.

N O T E

The zoom percentage you choose only affects the appearance of your screen. It has no effect on what is printed.

Also, zoom percentages are saved as a part of your named views in View Manager.

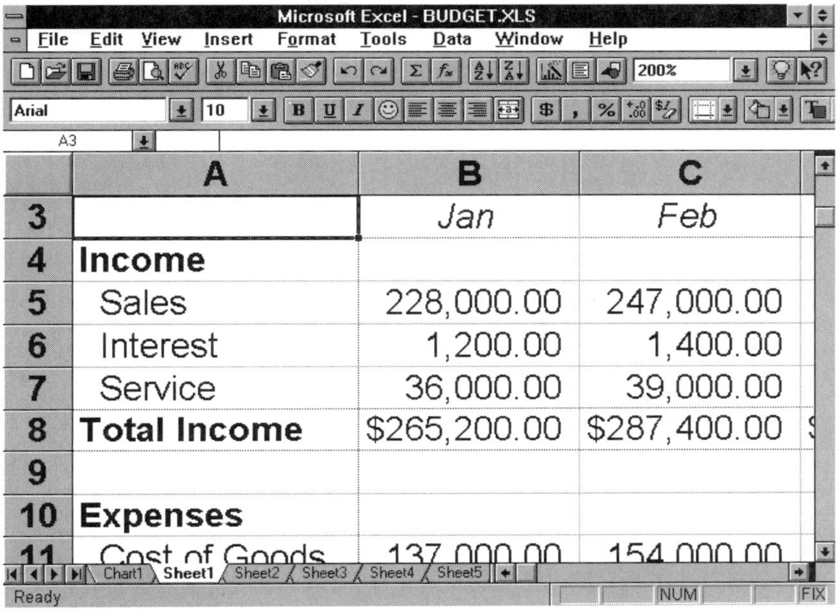

Figure 12.13   *An example of a 200% zoom.*

A FINAL THOUGHT

In this chapter, you learned to customize Excel in a variety of ways. Of course, there are no limits to the ways you can work with Excel and you should now have a good start on that journey of exploration. I hope this book has helped you to gain the skill and confidence to produce usable worksheets that make your life easier and more enjoyable.

Chapter 13

Switching and Customizing Toolbars

* DISPLAY AND POSITION TOOLBARS
* CREATE CUSTOM TOOLBARS
* DESIGN CUSTOM TOOLBAR BUTTONS

As you have seen throughout this book, toolbars are often the fastest and easiest way to initiate Excel tasks. With a click of the mouse, you are off and running with an operation that might otherwise take several mouse clicks or keystrokes.

You can make toolbars even more useful by customizing them to include just the buttons you use most often for a particular type of operation, or by creating custom buttons.

DISPLAY AND POSITION TOOLBARS

Excel automatically displays the Standard and Formatting toolbars and positions them at the top of the screen. You have also seen Excel display other toolbars such as the Chart toolbar when editing charts, and you have displayed the Drawing toolbar by clicking on the **Drawing** button on the Standard toolbar.

Let's see how you can choose other toolbars, and position them wherever you want them on the screen.

1. Start Excel, if it isn't already running, and make sure there is a worksheet on your screen.

    You don't need to have any particular workbook open since you are displaying and moving toolbars without actually using the buttons.

    The shortcut menu is the fastest way to choose which toolbars are displayed on your screen. There is also a Toolbars dialog box which makes additional toolbars available, as well as a few extra options. Start with the shortcut menu.

2. Right-click on any of the toolbar buttons on either toolbar to display the toolbar shortcut menu, as shown in Figure 13.1.

    The toolbars that are currently displayed have a check mark in front of their names on the shortcut menu. You can remove a toolbar from the screen by clicking on its name. Clicking on a toolbar name without a check mark will cause it to be displayed.

    If you frequently switch to other Microsoft applications, you find that the Microsoft toolbar is one of the most useful and time saving toolbars included with Excel. With this toolbar you can instantly switch to any of your other Microsoft programs at the click of a button. Most newer Microsoft applications also have Microsoft toolbars available so you can easily switch from them back to Excel or another program.

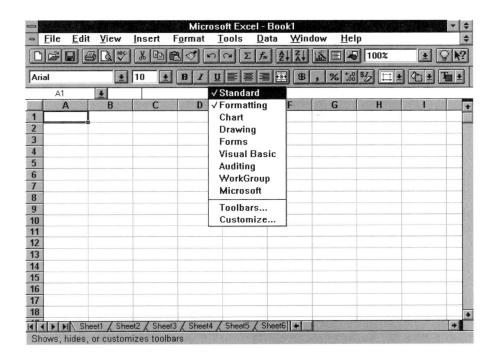

Figure 13.1   *The toolbar shortcut menu.*

Let's display the Microsoft toolbar now.

3. Click on **Microsoft** to display the Microsoft toolbar shown in Figure 13.2.

All the available toolbars and their respective functions are listed in Appendix D. You can mix and match buttons to create your own custom toolbars using any of the buttons or create your own custom buttons.

As with other toolbars, you can see what the function of each of these buttons is by simply moving the mouse over a button and reading the ToolTip. The lower-left portion of the status bar displays a longer description of the button.

Toolbars can be moved by moving the mouse pointer to one of the areas between a toolbar border and the buttons and then dragging. However, if the toolbar is floating, it is easier to move it the same way you move other windows—dragging it by the title bar. You can remove a toolbar by clicking on its name in the shortcut menu or by simply clicking on a floating toolbar's close box in its upper-left corner.

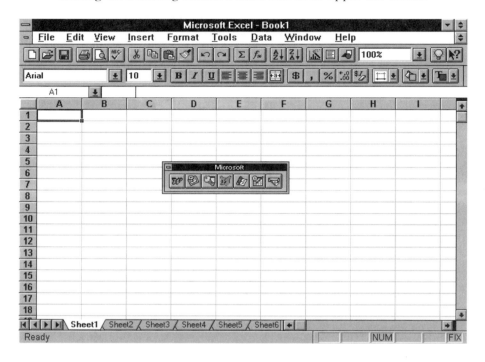

Figure 13.2 *The Microsoft toolbar.*

Often, having a toolbar floating on the screen obscures important information or is distracting, even if you move it out of the way. One solution to this problem is to dock it in one of the *docking positions.*

There are four docking locations: the top, bottom, and sides of the screen. In fact, the Standard and Formatting toolbars are docked at the top of the screen now. You can dock a toolbar by moving it to one of the docking areas. The exception is that you cannot dock a toolbar to the left or right side of the screen if it has buttons with drop-down lists (such as the Zoom Control button on the Standard toolbar) or buttons with tear-off palettes (such as the Borders button on the Formatting toolbar).

The Microsoft toolbar does not have any drop-down lists or tear-off palettes, so let's dock it to the left side of the screen.

4. Drag the Microsoft toolbar by the title bar to the left side of the screen until you see a vertically-oriented outline of the toolbar. Now release the mouse button.

The Microsoft toolbar is now docked on the left side of the screen, as shown in Figure 13.3.

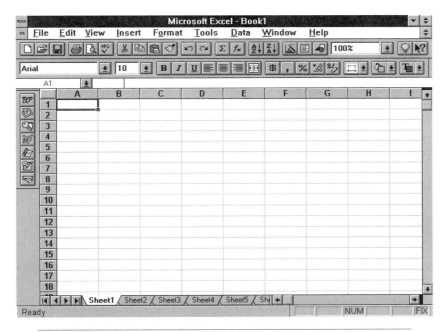

Figure 13.3 *The Microsoft toolbar docked on the left side of the screen.*

The vertical position depends on where the outline was when you released the mouse button. You can move the toolbar up or down by positioning the mouse over any space between the buttons and the edges of the toolbar.

For a toolbar with very few buttons, such as this one, it's a good idea to position it at the top or bottom of the docking area so there will be room for another toolbar, should you decide to add one.

N O T E

The Standard and Formatting toolbars, which are docked, can be undocked or docked in another position by dragging them to where you want them. Let's undock the Formatting toolbar and position it as a floating toolbar near the top of the worksheet.

5. Move the mouse pointer into the Formatting toolbar (but not on top of a button) and drag it down so the top edge of its outline is just below the column headings. Now release the mouse button.

The Formatting toolbar should be positioned approximately like the one in Figure 13.4.

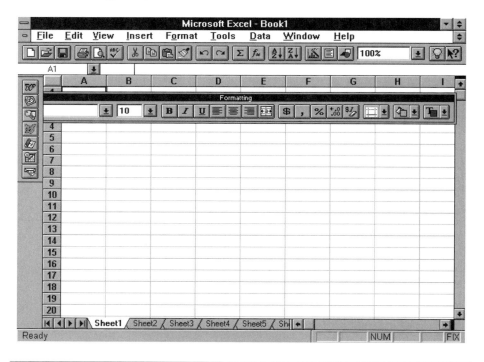

Figure 13.4 *The undocked Formatting toolbar positioned near the top of the worksheet.*

Now the problem is that part of the Formatting toolbar is obscured. Even if you move the toolbar to the left or right, you are not able to see all the buttons. Never fear. There is a solution. Excel allows us to change the shape of the toolbar. Instead of a single row of buttons, let's change it so there are three rows of buttons and the toolbar can fit comfortably in a corner of the worksheet.

6. Position the mouse pointer over the bottom border of the toolbar so it is a double-headed arrow. Drag it down about an inch and release the mouse button.

   The Formatting toolbar should look approximately like the one in Figure 13.5. If your toolbar is taller or wider, you can grab one of the borders and resize it until it is just the way you want it.

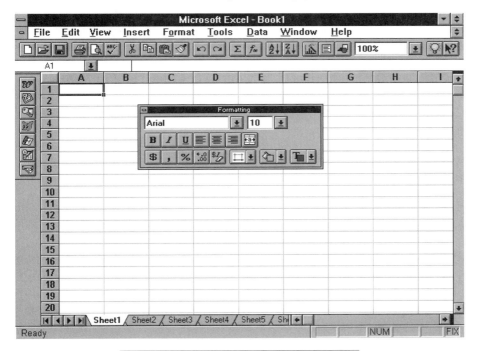

Figure 13.5 *The resized Formatting toolbar.*

Before moving on, let's redock the Formatting toolbar so it will be in its normal position the next time you use Excel.

7. Move the Formatting toolbar up to the top of its outline in the Formula bar, and release the mouse button to redock it below the Standard toolbar.

   Now let's check out the Toolbars dialog box, which is used to choose toolbars and change some of their options.

8. Choose **View**, **Toolbars** to display the Toolbars dialog box, as shown in Figure 13.6.

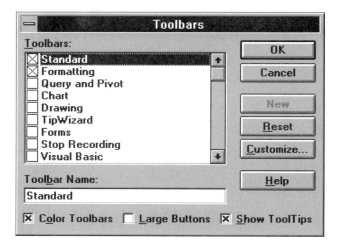

Figure 13.6 *The Toolbars dialog box.*

You can use the check boxes in the Toolbars dialog box to choose which toolbars to display. Notice that if you use the scroll bar to scroll down the list of toolbars there are more toolbars to choose from in the dialog box than are available from the shortcut menu.

The check boxes across the bottom of the Toolbars dialog box allow you to change several toolbar options.

The Color Toolbars check box lets you choose whether the toolbar button faces are displayed in color or black and white. You might want to use this option if you are using Excel on a laptop or notebook computer with a black and white screen.

The Large Buttons option lets you display extra-large toolbar buttons. This option can be useful if you use a high-resolution screen driver. Standard Windows resolution is called *VGA* (Video Graphics Array) and uses a resolution of 640 dots by 480 dots. In standard resolution, the buttons are usually large enough to see the detail without using too much screen real estate.

Many computer/monitor combinations are capable of higher resolutions such as 800 x 600 or 1024 x 768. If you are using one of these higher resolutions, you already know that the trade-off for the finer detail in the higher resolution is a smaller image, which can cause some difficulty in making out the detail of some screen elements. If you have a very large monitor (17" or more), you may find that the screen image, even at high resolutions, is large enough. If you have difficulty discerning the detail of the buttons, choose **Large Buttons**. Let's try it now to see its effect.

9. Click on the **Large Buttons** check box and then click on **OK** to enlarge all the toolbar buttons, as shown in Figure 13.7.

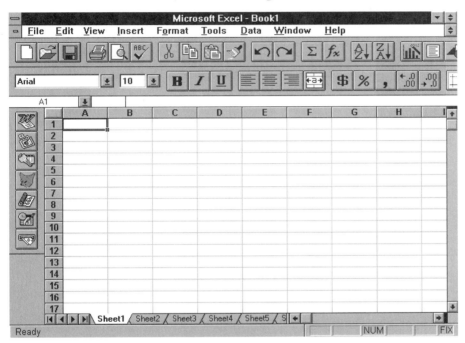

Figure 13.7 *Large toolbar buttons.*

N O T E

With large buttons in standard resolution, some of the buttons on the docked Standard and Formatting toolbars are not visible. At higher resolutions this is not a problem. If you want to display large buttons in standard resolution, just undock the toolbars. Of course that creates another problem. A great deal of your worksheet is obscured by toolbars.

One way to solve this problem would be to remove a few buttons so that all the remaining buttons are visible in their docked position. You learn how to do this in the next section—"Creating Custom Toolbars."

Before we move on, let's return to normal-sized toolbar buttons.

10. Choose **View**, **Toolbars**, or choose **Toolbars** from the toolbar shortcut menu to display the Toolbars dialog box.

11. Click on the **Large Buttons** check box to remove the check mark.

Before closing the dialog box, let's talk about the last check box in the dialog box. The Show ToolTips check box lets you turn off the tooltips feature, which shows what a button does when the mouse pointer is positioned over it. My advice is to leave this option checked. I can't think of any reason why you might want to turn this feature off.

12. Click on **OK** to remove the dialog box and return the toolbars to their normal size.

CREATING CUSTOM TOOLBARS

Now that you know how to display and position the toolbars supplied by Excel, let's look at how to customize toolbars. There are several ways to modify toolbars to suit the way you work. You can alter existing toolbars by adding, removing or changing the position of buttons. You can also start from scratch with a new toolbar equipped with your choice of buttons.

With the Toolbars or Customize dialog box on the screen, you can remove or reposition any button on a toolbar that is currently displayed by simply dragging it:

✳ Off the toolbar

✳ To a new position on its toolbar

✳ To any other visible toolbar

Let's try removing and repositioning some buttons. We use the Customize dialog box to perform some additional customization. You can open the Customize dialog box by clicking the **Customize** button on the Toolbars dialog box, or from the toolbar shortcut button.

1. Right-click on any of the toolbars to display the toolbar shortcut menu and then click on **Customize** to display the Customize the dialog box, as shown in Figure 13.8.

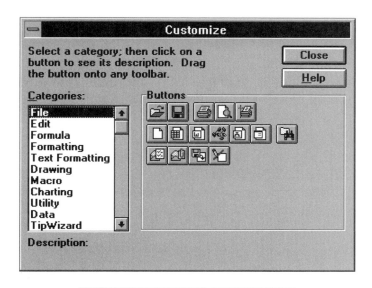

Figure 13.8 *The Customize dialog box.*

The Customize dialog box contains all the existing buttons you can use to add to a toolbar. The buttons are separated into logical categories to make it easy to find the button you want.

Before we add any buttons, let's make some room on the Formatting toolbar so we won't obscure any buttons when we add a new one to it.

Let's say you decide that you don't need the Bold, Italic, and Underline buttons because you have already memorized the keyboard shortcuts (Ctr+B for bold, Ctrl+I for italic, and Ctrl+U for underline). Let's remove these buttons from the Formatting toolbar now.

2. Drag the **Bold** button from the Formatting toolbar onto the worksheet and then release the mouse button. Repeat the process for the Italic and the Underline buttons so the toolbar looks like the one in Figure 13.9.

Let's add buttons for Double Underline, Strikethrough, and Rotate Text Down. All of these buttons fall within the Text Formatting category but you could, of course, add buttons from different categories.

3. Click **Text Formatting** in the Categories list to display the Text Formatting buttons, as shown in Figure 13.10.

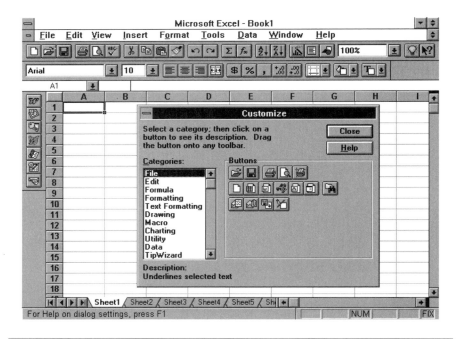

Figure 13.9 *The Formatting toolbar without the Bold, Italic, and Underline buttons.*

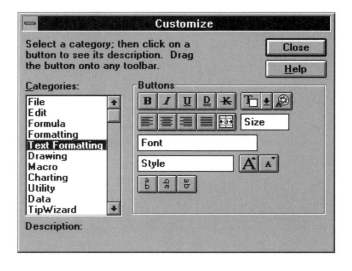

Figure 13.10 *The Text Formatting buttons.*

N O T E

You cannot see the ToolTips when you move the mouse pointer over a button in the Customize dialog box, but you can see a description of the button's function by clicking on it. The description appears in the Description area at the bottom of the dialog box.

4. Drag the **Double Underline** button (its description is "Double under-lines selected text") up to the Formatting toolbar, so its outline is between the Font Size and the Align Left buttons, as shown in Figure 13.11.

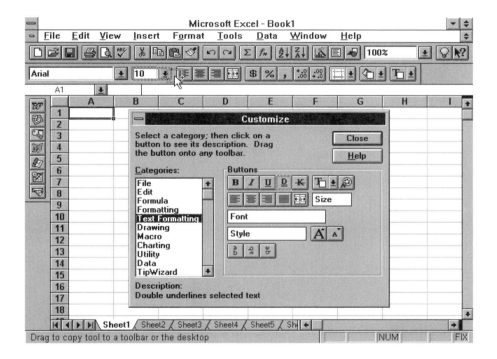

Figure 13.11   *The outline of the Double Underline button ready to be placed on the Formatting toolbar.*

5. Release the mouse button to accept the placement of the new button.

    If the button ended up to the left or right of its intended position, you can simply drag it left or right to reposition it where you want it.

6. Drag the **Strikethrough** button (its description is "Draws a line through selected text") to the position just to the right of the Double Underline button and release the mouse button.

7. Drag the **Rotate Text Down** button (its description is "Rotates text sideways, reading top to bottom") to the position just to the right of the Strikethrough button and release the mouse button.

The Formatting toolbar should now look something like the one in Figure 13.12.

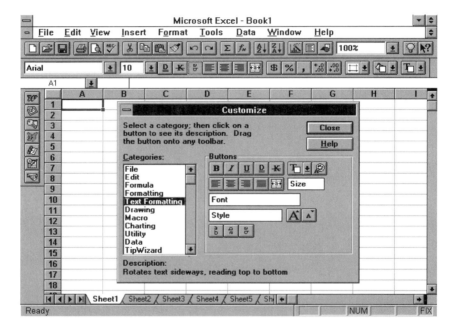

Figure 13.12 *The Formatting toolbar with its three new buttons.*

Now let's create a custom toolbar with just the buttons we want. We can simply drag a button from the Customize dialog box onto the worksheet to create a new toolbar named Toolbar 1, Toolbar 2, etc. However, it usually makes more sense to enter a name for the new toolbar before creating it, which is done from the Toolbars dialog box.

8. Click on the **Close** button to remove the Customize dialog box from the screen.

9. Choose **View**, **Toolbars** or click on **Toolbars** from the toolbar shortcut menu to display the Toolbars dialog box.

   When you create a new toolbar, choose a name that denotes the group or category of buttons you plan to add to it. If you are creating a toolbar with a conglomeration of buttons with no particular relation except for the fact that *you* want them on a toolbar, a name such as "My Toolbar" might be a good way to designate your toolbar. In fact, that's exactly what we'll do right now.

10. Select the text in the Toolbar Name text box by dragging the mouse over it and type: **My Toolbar**

   The Toolbars dialog box should look like the one in Figure 13.13.

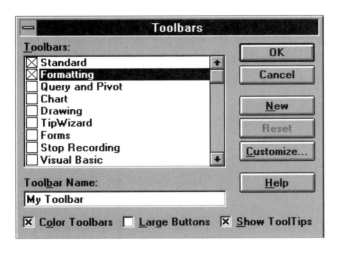

Figure 13.13   *The Toolbars dialog box with the name of our new toolbar entered in the Toolbar Name text box.*

Notice that as soon as you enter a name in the text box, the New button becomes available.

11. Click on the **New** button.

   The blank new toolbar appears and the Toolbars dialog box switches to the Customize dialog box, as shown in Figure 13.14.

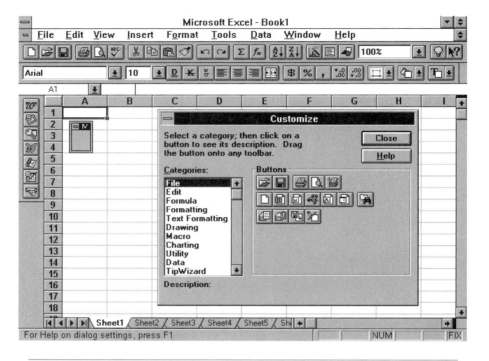

Figure 13.14   *The beginning of the new toolbar next to the Customize dialog box.*

N O T E   The toolbar will widen and lengthen as you add buttons to it. The way you see it now, it isn't wide enough to fit the entire title, "My Toolbar." If you only plan to add one or two buttons to a toolbar, use a very short name.

Let's add several buttons from several categories to the new toolbar. As you add them, don't worry too much about getting them positioned just right since you can always reposition them. Also, we are going to position the buttons in a single row. If some of them end up stacked vertically, you can resize the toolbar by dragging a border.

12. From the File category of buttons, drag the **Open** button onto the new toolbar and release the mouse button.

N O T E

Just because a button is already in use on one toolbar doesn't mean you wouldn't want it on another. You may want to equip My Toolbar with your most often used buttons so you won't need to display any other toolbars when it is displayed.

13. Click on **Drawing** in the Categories list and then drag the **Arrow** button (its description is "adds an arrow") to the right of the Open button on the new toolbar and release the mouse button.

14. From the Charting category, drag the **ChartWizard** button (its description is "Creates embedded chart or modifies active chart") to the right of the Arrow button and release the mouse button.

The new toolbar should now look like the one in Figure 13.15

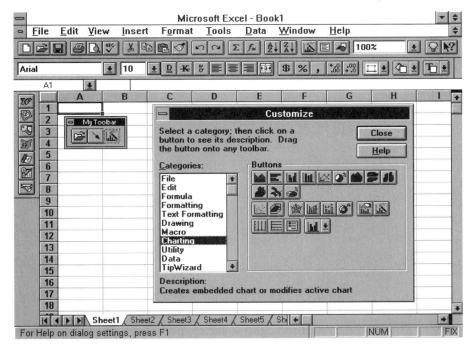

Figure 13.15 *My Toolbar with the three buttons added.*

The new toolbar will be listed on the toolbar shortcut menu and in the Toolbars dialog box, so you can display and remove this toolbar from your screen as you would any other toolbar.

Let's leave the Customize dialog box on screen as we will be using it in the next section.

DESIGNING CUSTOM TOOLBAR BUTTONS

If putting together your own collection of buttons does not provide you with enough customization, you can change the image of any of the buttons on any toolbar. The simplest approach, if you can find an existing image you like, is to copy the image to the button you want to change.

If you need an even more custom image than that, you can edit a button's image or design your own using the **Button Editor** or just about any other paint-type graphics program you like, including the Paintbrush program that comes with Windows.

WARNING

I'm not very creative when it comes to graphic design. On second thought, "not very creative" is an overstatement. Drawing stick figures is about as far as I got in art class. So don't expect any great-looking (or even good-looking) button images from these examples.

The first thing to do is to replace the image of one of the buttons on My Toolbar with one from the Customize dialog box. To do this, click on the button you want to use in the dialog box and copy its image to the Clipboard, then click on the button with the image you want to replace, and then paste the image from the Clipboard. It is easier than it sounds.

Let's replace the image on the Open button with an image from the Custom category. The Custom category buttons are normally used to attach macros, as you learned in Chapter 10, *Automating Your Work with Macros.* However, we can copy any image we want. Since these do not already have functions assigned to them, they are a natural choice.

1. Scroll down the Categories list until the Custom category is visible, then click on it to display the **Custom category** buttons, as shown in Figure 13.16.

   Let's use the heart image on the bottom row of buttons for our new image.

2. Click on the **heart** button just to the right of the frowning face button on the bottom row.

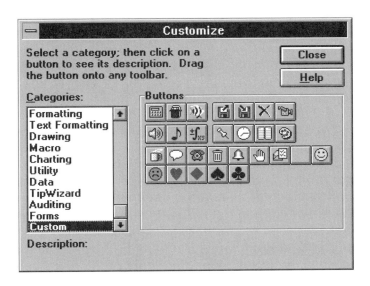

Figure 13.16 *The Customize dialog box with the Custom category buttons displayed.*

3. Choose **Edit**, **Copy Button Image**.

   The heart image is now stored on the Clipboard and ready to be pasted on top of another button.

4. Click on the **Open** button on My Toolbar and then choose **Edit**, **Paste Button Image**.

   The Open button in My Toolbar should now look like the one in Figure 13.17.

   With the Customize or Toolbars dialog box open, right-clicking on a button displays a special shortcut menu for customizing the button. Let's edit the heart button to customize it even further.

5. Point to the heart button on My Toolbar and right-click to display its shortcut menu, as shown in Figure 13.18.

6. Click on **Edit Button Image** to display the Button Editor dialog box, as shown in Figure 13.19.

   Each small box in the Picture portion of the dialog box represents one dot or pixel of the image. You can click on a color in the Colors portion of the dialog box and then apply that color to any dot in the picture by simply clicking on it. If you want to apply the color to a series of dots, you can drag the mouse over the dots to *paint* the color.

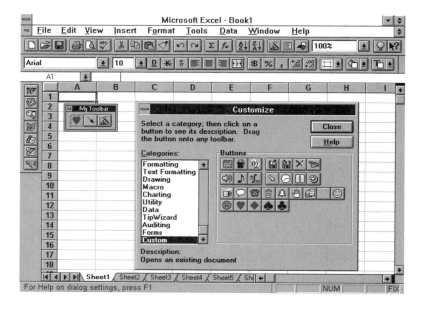

Figure 13.17   *Now My Toolbar has a heart.*

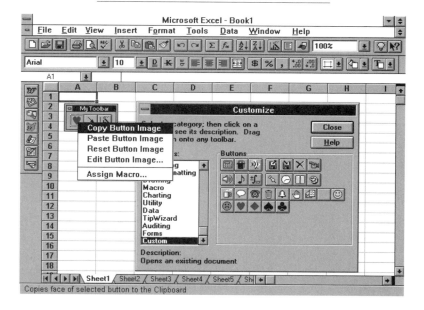

Figure 13.18   *The shortcut menu for customizing a button.*

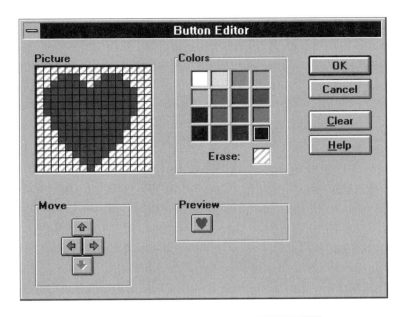

Figure 13.19 *The Button Editor dialog box.*

Clicking on the **Erase** box allows you to erase any of the dots that are filled with color by dragging or clicking on them.

You can use the arrow buttons in the Move portion of the dialog box to move the entire image up, down, left or right, if the image doesn't already extend to the edges of the Picture box.

The Clear button lets you remove the entire image so you can start fresh and create your own image.

Let's add a black horizontal line on the top and bottom rows and erase a few dots in the middle of the heart to create an *open* heart.

7. Click on the black box in the Colors portion of the dialog box and drag across the top and bottom rows of the Picture portion of the dialog box.

The Preview portion of the Image Editor dialog box shows, in actual size, what your button will look like as you edit it.

N O T E

8. Click on the **Erase** box and erase a few dots in the middle of the heart so the Picture portion looks like Figure 13.20.

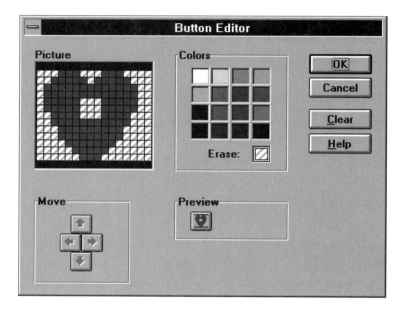

Figure 13.20 *The open heart with top and bottom borders.*

9. Click on **OK** to close the Image Editor dialog box and accept the modifications.

10. Click on the **Close** button to remove the Customize dialog box.

The Image Editor doesn't offer a wide variety of graphics tools to create complex images. If you want more design flexibility, consider using a more sophisticated paint-type program such as Paintbrush to create an image. You can then copy your design to the clipboard and paste the image onto the button of your choice using the technique just described.

Before we finish this chapter, let's get the screen back to normal. We'll remove the Microsoft toolbar, delete the "My Toolbar" toolbar, and reset the Formatting toolbar back to its original configuration.

11. Choose **View**, **Toolbars** to display the Toolbars dialog box.

12. Scroll down the Toolbars list until you can see the Microsoft and "My Toolbar" check boxes.

13. Click on **My Toolbar** in the Toolbars list to remove the check mark and, if you want to delete the toolbar, click on the **Delete** button to display the message dialog box shown in Figure 13.21.

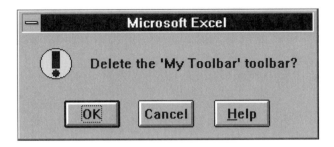

Figure 13.21 *The message dialog box confirms the toolbar deletion.*

14. Click on **OK** to confirm the deletion of My Toolbar.

15. Click on **Microsoft** in the Toolbars list to remove the check mark so the toolbar won't be displayed when the Toolbars dialog box is closed.

16. Finally, scroll back up the Toolbars list and click on **Formatting** twice so it is still checked and is highlighted. Then click on the **Reset** button to return it to its default setup.

17. Click on **OK** to remove the Toolbars dialog box.

Your screen should be back to the way it looked before you started this chapter.

A FINAL THOUGHT

In this chapter, you learned to display, position, and customize your toolbars to make them work as efficiently as possible for you. Don't forget to refer to Appendix D for a complete listing of Excel's toolbars and their button functions.

The next chapter covers some techniques for customizing your Windows environment.

Chapter 14

Customizing Windows

* TAMING THE MOUSE
* STRAIGHTENING THE DESKTOP
* COLOR YOUR WORLD

You learned in Chapter 2 (*Getting Started—Excel and Windows Basics*) to use Windows productively. In this chapter, you will explore several ways to make Windows behave just the way you want.

We will use the Control Panel, a program that comes with Windows, to alter mouse operations, the desktop environment, and Windows' colors.

TAMING THE MOUSE

The *Control Panel* is a Windows program that provides options for customizing such aspects of Windows' environment as fonts, sound, keyboards, and printers. You can find detailed information about these options in the Windows documentation and by using Help. There are also many good books that cover all these options and many more in depth.

We are just going to discuss a few of the more useful Windows customization options. One of the most useful options is customizing the mouse so you can work with it more easily. Let's start the Control Panel application and customize the mouse now.

1. Start Windows, if it isn't already running.

2. If Excel is running, switch to the Program Manager by pressing **Ctrl+Esc** and then double-clicking on **Program Manager** in the Task List dialog box.

    The Control Panel icon is normally found in the Main program group. Let's open that group now.

3. Double-click on the **Main program group** icon to display the Main group window, as shown in Figure 14.1.

4. Double-click on the **Control Panel** icon to start the Control Panel program, as shown in Figure 14.2.

    To enter one of the Control Panel's customization areas, double-click on its icon to open a dialog box. Let's go into the mouse dialog box now.

5. Double-click on the **Mouse** icon to display the Mouse dialog box, as shown in Figure 14.3.

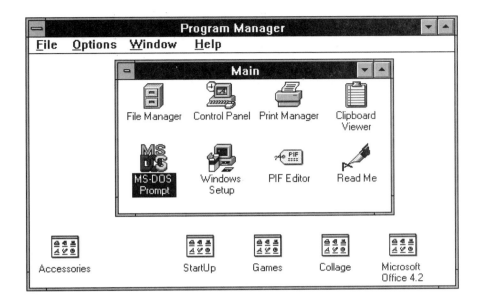

Figure 14.1   *The Main group window.*

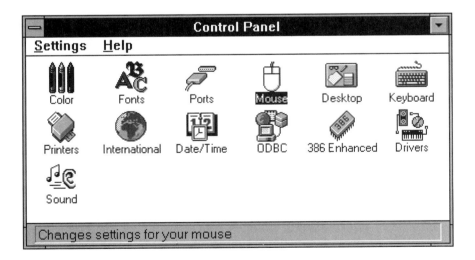

Figure 14.2   *The Control Panel program.*

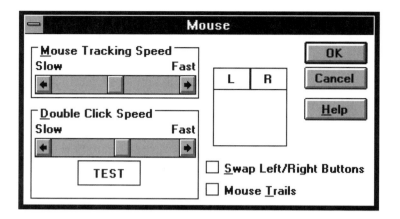

Figure 14.3 *The Mouse dialog box.*

N O T E Some mouse dialog boxes have more options than those shown in Figure 14.3. For example, some allow you to change the shape of the mouse pointer. If your dialog box has additional features and you don't know how to work with them, refer to the dialog box's Help facility for instructions.

The Mouse dialog box provides options for changing the mouse pointer *tracking speed* (how fast the pointer moves across the screen as you move the mouse), changing the *double-click speed* (how much time you can pause between two clicks and have Windows interpret it as a double-click instead of two single clicks), and *swapping left and right mouse buttons* (which may be useful for left-handed computer users).

There is also a feature called *Mouse Trails*, which leaves a temporary trail of mouse pointer images as you move the mouse pointer. This feature is often useful for laptop computers with *LCD* (Liquid Crystal Display) screens. The mouse pointer on some LCD screens has a *submarine* effect which can obscure the pointer as you move it from one place on the screen to another. Using the Mouse Trails feature can help you keep track of the mouse pointer in these situations. For standard desktop-type screens, this feature is usually more of an annoyance, though it can be amusing to try it out for a few minutes.

Let's try changing some of these options now to see what effect they have on mouse operations. We'll start with the tracking speed. If the tracking speed is too fast, you may have a difficult time accurately positioning the mouse pointer precisely. If the tracking speed is too slow, it will slow you down, causing you to make unnecessary mouse movements.

6. Move your mouse back and forth several inches on your desktop and notice how rapidly the on-screen pointer moves compared with how rapidly you move the mouse.

7. Move the scroll box in the Mouse Tracking Speed portion of the dialog box all the way over to the fast (right) side of the scroll bar and repeat step 5 to see the difference.

8. Move the scroll box in the Mouse Tracking Speed portion of the dialog box all the way over to the slow (left) side of the scroll bar and, once again, repeat step 5. Notice that the mouse pointer moves much more slowly.

9. Reposition the Mouse Tracking Speed scroll box so the tracking speed is comfortable for you.

Next let's take a look at the Double-Click Speed setting. The goal here is to set the double-click speed as fast as possible but not so fast that you cannot double-click. Most people have a tough time double-clicking when it is set at the fastest speed.

Setting the double-click speed too slow can be an equally bother-some problem. For example, you might click on one screen element then move to another element and click on it, and have Windows inter-pret that as double-clicking on the first element. You certainly don't want the double-click speed set so slow that you have to consciously wait before clicking again to avoid having the two clicks be a double-click.

10. Point to the TEST box below the Double-Click Speed scroll bar and double-click.

If you double-clicked fast enough, the box will be highlighted, as shown in Figure 14.4. The next double-click unhighlights the box.

11. If you had to try double-clicking several times before you could get the TEST box to highlight, move the Double-Click Speed scroll box a little to the slow (left) side. If you had no difficulty double-clicking at the cur-rent setting, move the scroll box to the fast (right) side until you do have some trouble and then back it off just enough that you can dou-ble-click comfortably.

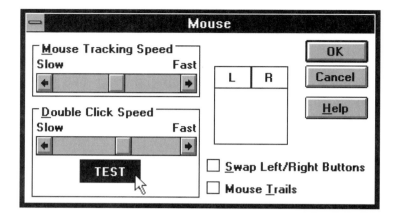

Figure 14.4 *The Mouse dialog box with the TEST box highlighted.*

If you want to use the Swap Left/Right Buttons or Mouse Trails options, simply click in the appropriate check boxes.

WARNING

If you swap the left and right mouse buttons, you can't undo the swap by clicking in the check box with the left mouse button. You need to use the right mouse button, which is now acting as the left mouse button.

12. Click on **OK** to accept any changes you made and close the dialog box.

STRAIGHTENING THE DESKTOP

The Control Panel's Desktop dialog box provides several options for enhancing the appearance of your desktop, such as adding background graphic images, adjusting the spacing of icons and windows and adjusting the blink rate of the cursor (insertion point).

You can also choose from several screen savers which will blank your screen and display moving images after a specified number of minutes of inactivity.

Let's take a look at these options and discuss their pros and cons.

1. Double-click on the **Control Panel's Desktop** icon to display the Desktop dialog box, as shown in Figure 14.5.

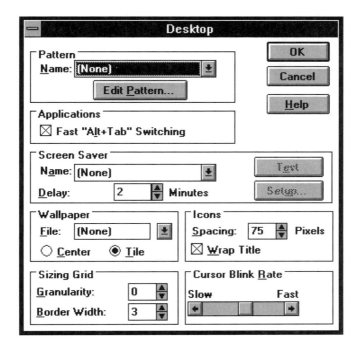

Figure 14.5 *The Desktop dialog box.*

Patterns and Wallpaper

Two Desktop options allow you to add a background to surround your windows: patterns and wallpaper. *Patterns*, as the name suggests, are designs made up of dots. These are generally not very intricate but can add a bit of visual appeal.

Wallpaper is actually a graphic file used as background. The graphic can be one of the supplied images or you can design your own in a program such as Paintbrush, which is included with Windows. Like the toolbar buttons we discussed in the previous chapter, wallpaper graphics can be extremely intricate. In fact, because wallpaper is displayed in a much larger size than toolbar buttons, you can use much more elaborate images for your wallpaper and still easily discern the details.

Let's start our desktop delving by choosing a pattern. To select a pattern, click on the arrow next to the Name drop-down list box and choose from one of the available patterns. You may then edit the pattern if you wish.

2. Click on the arrow next to the Name drop-down list in the Pattern portion of the dialog box to display the list of patterns, as shown in Figure 14.6.

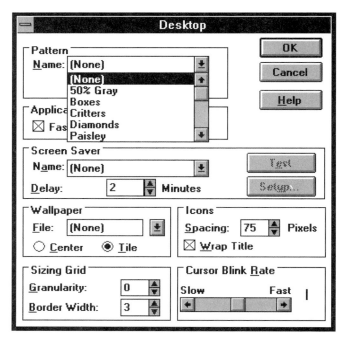

Figure 14.6   *The list of patterns.*

You can use the scroll bar to see additional pattern choices, but for now, choose one of the patterns near the top of the list.

3. Click on **Paisley** to choose the paisley pattern.

   Unlike actions in most other dialog boxes, you can't see the effect of your pattern choice until you close the dialog box.

4. With Paisley in the Name box, click on **OK** to close the Desktop dialog box and display the pattern, as shown in Figure 14.7.

N O T E   If you can't see the pattern, you may need to reduce the size of some of your open windows. For example, if you have Program Manager or Excel maximized, none of your desktop will be visible, so you won't see the pattern, just as you wouldn't be able to see the top of your desk if you had papers completely covering its surface.

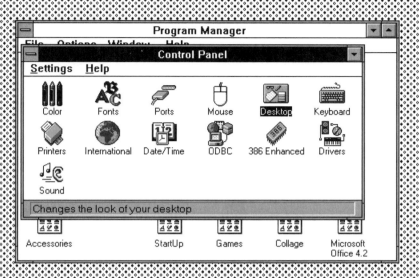

Figure 14.7   *The Paisley pattern covering our desktop.*

5. Double-click on the **Desktop** icon in the Control Panel program to display the Desktop dialog box once again.

   To edit a pattern, click on the **Edit Pattern** button and then use the mouse to add or remove dots in the pattern.

6. Click on the **Edit Pattern** button to display the Desktop-Edit Pattern dialog box, as shown in Figure 14.8.

   From this dialog box you can choose different patterns to edit by using the Name drop-down list. Choosing **None** from the list lets you create your own pattern from scratch.

   Each small square in the middle box of the dialog box represents one dot or pixel of the pattern. The Sample section on the left side of the dialog box lets you see what your modified pattern will look like as you make changes. Clicking the mouse in the large box adds a black dot if there isn't already one there, and removes a black dot if there is one there.

   The Add button lets you add a new pattern to the list after you enter a new name in the Name box. The Change button saves the changes you make to the pattern. The Remove option lets you delete a pattern from the list.

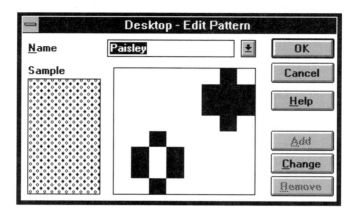

Figure 14.8   *The Desktop-Edit Pattern dialog box.*

We won't change the pattern, but let's see what a couple of the other supplied patterns look like in the next two figures.

7. Click on **OK** to close the Desktop-Edit Pattern dialog box.

8. Display the list of patterns and choose **None**.

Next, let's take a look at the wallpaper portion of the dialog box. The wallpaper images are color images and can add significantly greater visual appeal than the simple patterns we just looked at. If you want to edit one of the wallpaper images, you need to use another program, such as Paintbrush.

You can use the Center and Tile options to position the image on screen. The Center option centers the image on your screen. If the wallpaper image you use is large enough, this is a good choice. However, if you are using a small wallpaper image, it could be hidden behind some of your open windows. The Tile option places as many copies as required to fill the screen and reduces the chance that the wallpaper will be hidden.

Choosing a wallpaper image is just like choosing a pattern. Click the arrow to display the drop-down list of wallpaper images and choose the one you want.

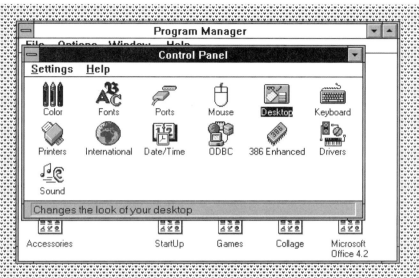

Figure 14.9   *The Critters pattern.*

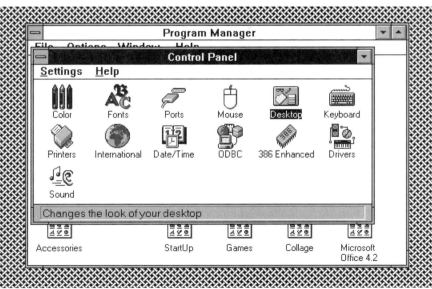

Figure 14.10   *The Thatches pattern.*

9. Be sure that the **Tile** option is chosen, then click on the arrow next to the File list box to display the drop-down list of wallpaper files, as shown in Figure 14.11.

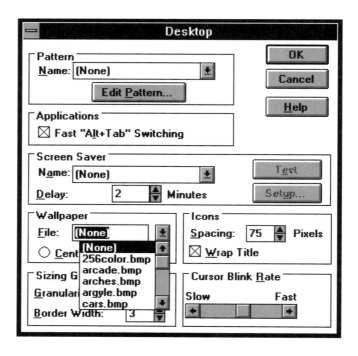

Figure 14.11   *The list of wallpaper files.*

All the wallpaper file names have a .bmp extension, which stands for bitmapped. This is a particular type of file format that can be created by most paint-type graphics programs. If you want to create your own wallpaper file, you need to save it as a .bmp file. You also need to save it in your main Windows directory, usually C:\WINDOWS, so that it will appear in the list of wallpaper files.

Windows performance can suffer if there isn't enough memory available, and using wallpaper uses memory. The more complex and larger wallpaper images use more memory than the smaller, simpler ones, but they all use memory. If you want to conserve as much memory as possible for your Windows programs and maximize performance, consider avoiding wallpaper.

10. Choose **cars.bmp** and then click on **OK** to close the dialog box and see what the cars wallpaper looks like, as shown in Figure 14.12.

Figure 14.12   *The cars wallpaper.*

11. Double-click on the **Desktop** icon, then choose **None** from the wallpaper drop-down list.

We'll discuss the next several features in the Desktop dialog box without performing any actions. Leave the Desktop dialog box open so you can refer to it as we look at the next few options.

The Screen Saver Option

At one time, screen savers were vital for protecting your screen from phosphor burn-in, which could occur if the same image remained on screen for long periods of time. Phosphor burn-in caused the image that was burned into the screen to appear as a *ghost image* even when another image should have been the only one on the screen.

Newer color monitors are much less susceptible to phosphor burn-in and make screen savers unnecessary. With standard VGA monitors, an image can remain on the screen for days or weeks without causing any problems. Also, like wallpaper, screen savers can decrease performance by using some of your computer's resources to monitor periods of inactivity. For example, if you set the screen saver to activate after ten minutes of inactivity, the computer must constantly time the length of inactivity.

My advice is to forget about screen savers unless you have a fast enough computer that the performance decrease is unnoticeable. To choose a screen saver, select from the list of screen saver names in the drop-down list in the screen saver portion of the Desktop dialog box and then specify the number of *delay minutes* (the number of minutes of inactivity Windows will wait before starting the screen saver). You can use the Test button to see what each of the screen savers looks like. The Setup button lets you specify some options for the screen saver that you have chosen.

There is one genuine advantage to using screen savers. They can help you protect confidential information by requiring a password to clear the screen saver. Normally, any keyboard or mouse activity clears the screen saver. However, with password protection enabled, you (or anyone else trying to use your computer) would need to enter the password that you had specified. This can be a nice little security feature.

Figure 14.13 shows the setup dialog box for the Marquee screen saver.

The Marquee screen saver lets you type your own text, which will be displayed as a moving marquee when the screen saver is activated. The setup dialog boxes for other screen savers provide different sets of options depending on the characteristics of the particular screen saver.

Figure 14.14 shows the Change Password dialog box.

For security purposes, asterisks appear as you type your password. This way, if someone is looking over your shoulder, they won't see your password. Also, you are told to type the same password twice, once in the New Password text box and once in the Repeat New Password text box. This ensures that you actually typed the password you intended to type. Also, if you already had a password set, type the old password in the Old Password text box.

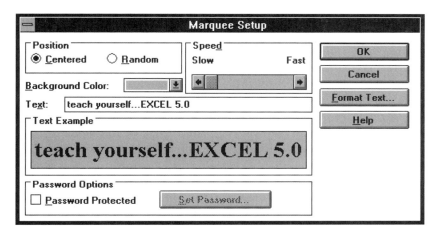

Figure 14.13   *The Marquee Setup dialog box.*

Figure 14.14   *The Change Password dialog box.*

WARNING

If you decide to set a password, make sure it's one you can remember. Otherwise, you will not be able to get back into Windows once the screen saver is activated.

Icons and Windows

The next couple of Desktop features we discuss control the spacing and labeling of icons, and the sizing and placement of windows.

The Icons portion of the Desktop dialog box lets you specify how many pixels (dots) separate your icons and whether the icon title can wrap onto multiple lines.

Unless you are using very tight icon spacing, you should keep the Wrap Title check box checked. The default 75-pixel spacing is generally appropriate, but you might find it more aesthetically pleasing to give the icons a little more space. On the other hand, you might want to give the icons less space if you want to be able to see more icons at one time.

Figure 14.15 shows the Main program group window with 150-pixel spacing.

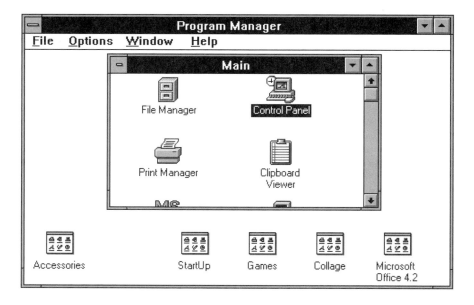

Figure 14.15   *150-pixel spacing.*

Figure 14.16 shows the Main program group window with 50-pixel spacing.

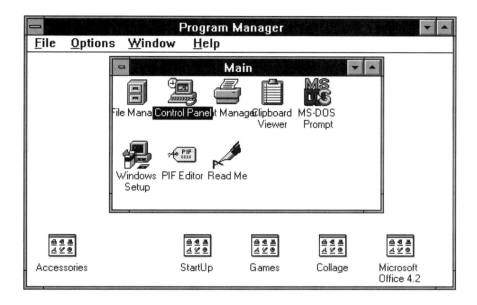

Figure 14.16 *50-pixel spacing.*

N O T E

The icon spacing you set does not take effect until you choose **Window, Arrange Icons**.

The Sizing Grid portion of the Desktop dialog box lets you specify where application windows and icons can be placed (*granularity*) and how wide the application and document window borders are.

Increasing the granularity makes it difficult to move windows small distances but makes it easier to position them precisely on the invisible grid. The default measurement of 0 lets you position windows wherever you want them on the screen.

The default Border Width setting of 3 is a good setting. Increasing this measurement generally results in a more cluttered screen appearance. Figure 14.17 shows several windows with a border width of 20.

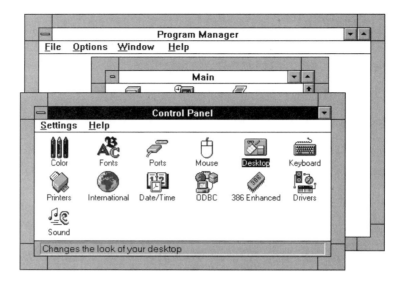

Figure 14.17   *Windows with 20-pixel border width.*

Cursor Blink Rate

The final Desktop option we look at is the *Cursor Blink Rate*. This setting affects how fast the cursor (insertion point) blinks. If it is blinking too fast it can be distracting and irritating. If it blinks too slowly, the cursor can sometimes be difficult to spot on the screen.

To change the blink rate, use the scroll bar to position the scroll box toward the fast (right) side or the slow (left) side. This is purely a matter of personal choice.

1. Click on the **OK** button to close the Desktop dialog box and accept any changes you have made.

COLOR YOUR WORLD

The Color option in the Control Panel lets you change the colors of various screen elements. Although the colors you choose are primarily an aesthetic decision, choosing unwise color combinations can make it hard to read portions of the screen. For example, if you choose black menu text and black menu bars, the menu text will be completely invisible.

Windows provides a variety of color combinations that makes it easy to spruce up your screen.

Let's take a look at the colorful options Control Panel provides.

1. Double-click on the **Color** icon in the Control Panel program to display the Color dialog box, as shown in Figure 14.18.

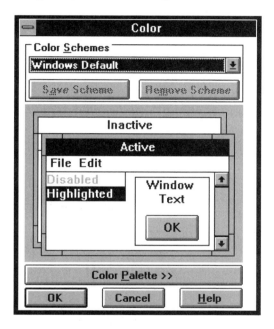

Figure 14.18   *The Color dialog box.*

The easiest way to make color changes is to choose one of the available color schemes from the Color Schemes drop-down list. To choose one of the color schemes, click on the arrow next to the Color Schemes box. Let's do that now.

2. Click on the arrow next to the Color Schemes list box to display the list of available color schemes, as shown in Figure 14.19.

I won't show you figures of different color schemes, since the figures in this book are in black and white. Try choosing several of the schemes to see their effect. When you click on a color scheme, you can see its effect by looking at the sample screen section of the dialog box just below the Save Schemes and Remove Schemes buttons. Of course, you won't really know how the color changes will affect your screen until you close the dialog box and start working in Windows with the new colors.

Figure 14.19 *The list of color schemes.*

3. Click on **Windows Default** (or whatever scheme was already in effect) to retain that as the color scheme.

You can also create custom color schemes and even custom colors by selecting colors for various screen elements from the Color Palette. Let's take a look at the Color Palette now.

4. Click on the **Color Palette** button to display the expanded Color dialog box with the Color Palette, as shown in Figure 14.20.

You can change a screen element's color by choosing the element from the drop-down list of screen elements above the color palette, as shown in Figure 14.21.

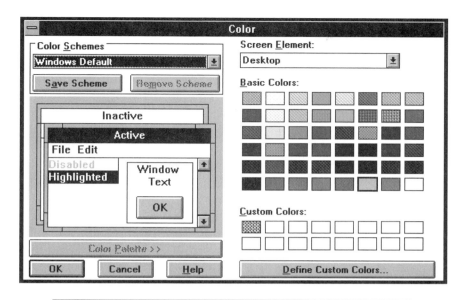

Figure 14.20   *The expanded Color dialog box with the color palette.*

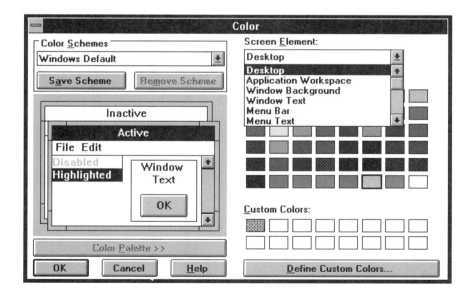

Figure 14.21   *The drop-down list of screen elements.*

SHORTCUT

Instead of choosing from the drop-down screen element list, you can simply click on the element you want to change in the sample portion of the dialog box. When you do, you'll know if you clicked on the correct element because the element's name will appear in the Screen Element box.

Having chosen the screen element you want to change, just click on the color in the color palette you want to use for that element. As you change colors for various screen elements, you can see the changes in the Sample Windows area on the left side of the dialog box.

After you change all the screen elements you want to change, you can close the dialog box and the changes will remain in effect. However, if you later choose a different color scheme, your changes will be lost unless you save them with a color scheme name.

To save a color scheme, click on the **Save Scheme** button to display the Save Scheme dialog box, as shown in Figure 14.22.

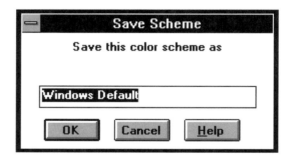

Figure 14.22   *The Save Scheme dialog box.*

You can then enter a name for your new color scheme. This name now appears on the color scheme drop-down list, so you can choose it in the future.

5.   Click on **OK** in the lower-left corner of the Color dialog box to close it and accept any color changes you made.

6.   Close the Control Panel program by choosing **Settings**, **Exit** or by double-clicking on the **Control-menu** box.

A FINAL THOUGHT

In this chapter, you learned to customize your Windows environment in several ways. The Control Panel offers other customization options that you might want to explore. Windows' Help facility includes information on the other Control Panel features, as does the Windows documentation.

Chapter 15

Using Excel with Other Programs

* WHY USE OTHER PROGRAMS WITH EXCEL?
* WHAT IS OLE AND WHY SHOULD I CARE?
* OLE SAMPLES

277

Few computer users rely solely on one program. If you are using Excel—and I think it's safe to assume that you are since you are reading this book—you have other programs at your disposal.

Even if all you have is Windows and Excel, you have the mini-applications that come with Windows, such as Write, Paintbrush, and Terminal. Chances are that you also have at least one other "major" application, such as Word for Windows.

WHY USE OTHER PROGRAMS WITH EXCEL?

In several places throughout this book I mention the value of using other, more specialized, programs for accomplishing certain tasks. For example, you can create and edit toolbar buttons with the Button Editor. However, using a more flexible program such as Paintbrush allows you greater freedom of expression and control.

Certainly Excel isn't the best tool for every job. It is an incredible spreadsheet program and clearly excels at creating and formatting number-oriented documents. But when it comes to creating text-oriented documents, you may want to use a word processing program with all the tools for formatting words such as Word for Windows.

"Use the best tool for the job" may just sound like common sense. And it is. Of course you would use a word processing program if you were writing a report for your company proposing to hire some new employees for your department. You would want to format the report so it would be as attractive—and persuasive—as possible.

But words alone probably won't make this proposal fly. The words will likely need to be backed up by some numbers demonstrating the various costs and benefits these proposed new employees will bring. I hope you realize by now that the best tool for that job is a spreadsheet program such as Excel.

You can create and print the report with your word processing program. Then you can create and print a worksheet, and perhaps a chart for emphasis, from Excel, and insert the worksheet and chart pages into the report. But imagine how much more professional-looking and convincing the report would be if the worksheet and chart were integrated into the body of the report.

Right in the middle of a beautifully formatted word-processed page, you place your worksheet and your chart, as if you had used scissors and paste, but without the muss and fuss. And the worksheet and chart can be linked to the report document so that, when the data is changed in the worksheet, the changes will be instantly reflected.

What is OLE and Why Should I Care?

In Chapter 11, *Linking Worksheets*, you learned how to use a simple form of linking to tie several source worksheets to a dependent worksheet. This is a valuable form of linking, but is only the beginning.

Most major Windows applications support a technology for sharing data with other Windows applications that are similarly equipped. Some early Windows programs used a linking technology called *DDE* (Dynamic Data Exchange). DDE worked, but was rather clunky in its implementation. In order to edit DDE linked data, you had to switch to the source application, make your edits, switch back to the dependent application and tell the application to update the link. This was quite cumbersome.

In the last couple of years a new technology has become available in numerous programs. The new technology is called *OLE* (Object Linking and Embedding). Linking allows the data to be updated when the source data changes. Embedding places a copy of the source data in a new location without a link. OLE is really an extension and refinement of DDE, but it offers more than a slight improvement in functionality. The first version, OLE 1.0, was a significant step forward. The second version, OLE 2.0, took another leap toward the goal of seamless integration of Windows applications.

N O T E
I shouldn't be talking about DDE only in the past tense. There are still many current Windows programs that have not yet moved beyond basic DDE. And certainly there are many programs still in use by people who have not yet upgraded to newer versions.

If you are using an older program and you can upgrade to a newer version that supports OLE, I strongly suggest that you do so.

So, what does OLE do that regular DDE doesn't? Without getting into the overly technical details, it makes linking and embedding data easier and editing the data much easier. To edit OLE source data in a document, simply double-click on the data and you are ready to edit.

What actually happens after you double-click is one of the main differences between OLE 1.0 and 2.0. In OLE 1.0, double-clicking switches you to the source application with the source document open. In OLE 2.0, double-clicking on embedded data replaces the menus in the current application with the menus from the application in which the data was created.

For example, suppose you have on your screen the report we discussed earlier. The report is in Word for Windows and a portion of an Excel worksheet is inserted in the middle of it. When you double-click on the worksheet, it looks as if you are still in Word for Windows. But, if you take a closer look, you see that the Word menus and toolbars have been replaced with the Excel menus and toolbars and the Excel formula bar.

Word for Windows comes with a few utility programs that might be useful for Excel. WordArt is a Word program that lets you add text with special effects. Using OLE, you can add some fancy text to an Excel worksheet and when you double-click on the WordArt text to edit it, the Excel menus are replaced with the WordArt menus.

N O T E The only applications that currently support OLE 2.0 are from Microsoft Excel 5.0, Word for Windows 6.0, and PowerPoint 4.0. Many other applications are sure to adopt this standard shortly. However, these are pretty terrific choices. If you don't have programs in these other categories and need to choose word processing and presentation programs, you can't go wrong with these Microsoft programs, which are part of the Microsoft Office suite of applications.

Another reason you might want to use these other Microsoft programs is that they are all designed to work in a similar fashion and have virtually identical menus. Toolbars and shortcut menus work the same way and the overall logic of the programs have much in common. Unless you have a good reason for using a word processing or presentation program from another manufacturer, stick with Microsoft.

OLE Samples

Describing how OLE works is not nearly as effective as actually seeing a couple of examples of OLE in action. First, let's look at an example of an Excel worksheet in a Word for Windows document. Then I will show you some WordArt text linked to an Excel worksheet.

Figure 15.1 displays a sample Word for Windows document with a portion of our Spokane Locks and Bagel budget worksheet.

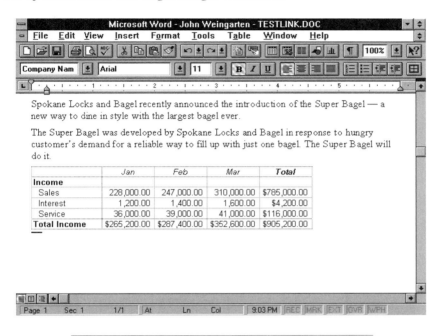

Spokane Locks and Bagel recently announced the introduction of the Super Bagel — a new way to dine in style with the largest bagel ever.

The Super Bagel was developed by Spokane Locks and Bagel in response to hungry customer's demand for a reliable way to fill up with just one bagel. The Super Bagel will do it.

	Jan	Feb	Mar	Total
Income				
Sales	228,000.00	247,000.00	310,000.00	$785,000.00
Interest	1,200.00	1,400.00	1,600.00	$4,200.00
Service	36,000.00	39,000.00	41,000.00	$116,000.00
Total Income	$265,200.00	$287,400.00	$352,600.00	$905,200.00

Figure 15.1   *A Word document with an Excel worksheet.*

The worksheet looks like it's just part of the Word document. But double-click anywhere on it. As you can see in Figure 15.2, the Excel menus, toolbars and formula bar are available and you can edit the worksheet as though you were in Excel.

Figure 15.3 shows the Excel program with our budget worksheet on screen but with the title replaced with some fancy WordArt text.

Figure 15.4 displays the same worksheet after double-clicking on the WordArt text. The WordArt program menus and dialog box replace the Excel menus and toolbars.

I haven't given you the specific steps to complete these operations since you need other programs in addition to Excel to perform these feats. The instructions for OLE are provided in the Excel documentation and the documentation for other programs that support OLE.

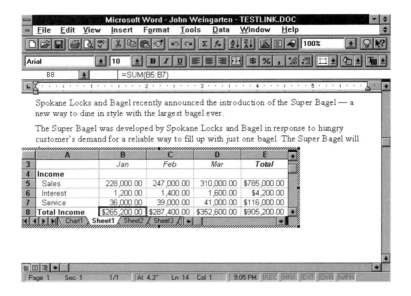

Figure 15.2 *The embedded worksheet is ready to be edited.*

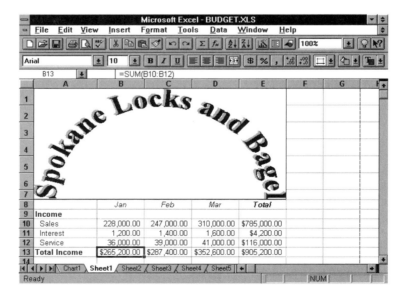

Figure 15.3 *Excel with embedded WordArt text.*

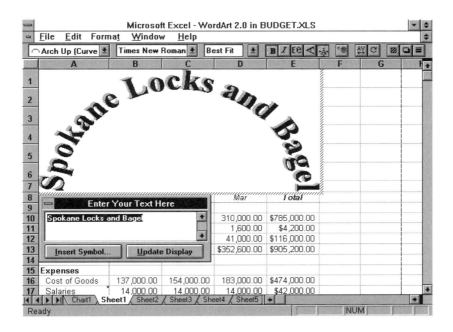

Figure 15.4   *WordArt text in Excel, ready to be edited.*

A FINAL THOUGHT

In this chapter, you learned some of the basic concepts of using Excel with other programs and using OLE to share data between applications. This just scratches the surface of Excel's ability to work with other Windows programs. You may find that combining Excel with other programs adds up to more than the sum of the programs and greatly enhances your ability to create complex documents.

Appendix A

Installing and Optimizing Excel

INSTALLING EXCEL

Those nice folks at Microsoft have made installing Excel just about automatic. In this appendix, you learn to install Excel on your computer.

NOTE

These instructions assume you are installing Excel on a stand-alone (not connected to a network) computer. If you are on a network, contact your network administrator for instructions on using Excel from the network.

To start the installation process:

✳ Insert Microsoft Excel Disk 1 into floppy drive A or B. If you are using 5.25" disks, do not forget to close the drive door latch.

✳ From Windows' Program Manager, choose **File**, **Run**, and type: **a:setup** (or **b:setup** if you are using drive b).

Figure A.1 displays the Run dialog box with the command to begin the installation process.

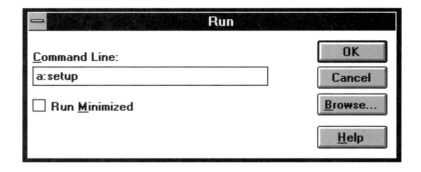

Figure A.1 *The Run dialog box with the setup command entered.*

✳ Click on **OK** to begin the installation.

After a short time, Excel will display the Microsoft Excel 5.0 Setup dialog box, as shown in Figure A.2.

If the installation disks have been previously installed, you receive a dialog box displaying the name of the previous installer and asking you to confirm that you want to continue. Click on **OK** to proceed.

✳ The next dialog box asks you to enter your serial number. Enter it and then click on **OK**.

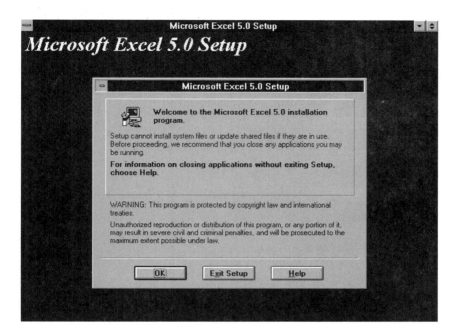

Figure A.2 *The Microsoft Excel 5.0 Setup dialog box.*

✳ The next dialog box asks you to confirm the directory where you want to install Excel. The default is C:\EXCEL. Unless you have a good reason for choosing another directory, click on **OK**. If you want to change the installation directory, click on the **Change Directory** button and then specify the directory you want to use in the Change Directory dialog box.

✳ A dialog box with three large buttons for specifying the type of installation you want is displayed in Figure A.3.

The *Typical installation option*, as the name implies, installs all the essential Excel elements and the most commonly used add-in programs, such as AutoSave, Scenario Manager and View Manager. If you are not sure what portions of Excel you want to install, this is the choice that makes the most sense.

The *Complete/Custom installation option* lets you choose which portions of Excel to install. If you have lots of available hard disk space, you can choose this option. Excel displays the Microsoft Excel 5.0 Complete/Custom dialog box, as shown in Figure A.4.

Figure A.3 *The Setup dialog box with the three installation choices.*

Notice that the bottom portion of the dialog box tells you how much disk space is required for the portions of Excel you have chosen to install and how much space is available. If you click on the check box of an option you do not want to install, the number for the amount of space required changes.

You can click on the **Continue** button to install everything, or you can click in any of the check boxes next to items you do not want to install and then click on the **Continue** button. The one item on the list that you must install for Excel to run is Microsoft Excel.

You can also choose which parts of the various programs you want to install. For example, you can highlight Add-ins and click on the **Change Option** button to see a dialog box that lets you choose which add-ins you want installed.

The *Laptop (Minimum) option* only installs the essential files required for Excel to run. If you are really pressed for disk space, this is the option to choose. However, even if you are installing on a laptop computer, you may have enough free disk space to choose one of the other installation options.

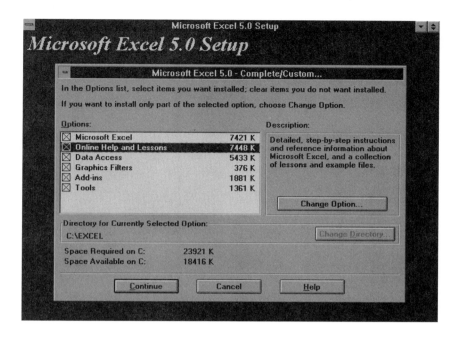

Figure A.4 *The Complete/Custom dialog box.*

N O T E

Do not be too concerned about making a mistake when you choose which installation method to use. You can always return to the setup program later and add or remove portions of the program as your requirements change.

Finally, you see a dialog box asking the program group in which you want to install Excel, as displayed in Figure A.5.

The list of existing groups in your list may differ from those in the figure. You can type in the name of a program group you want to use or highlight one of the existing groups and then click on the **Continue** button.

Now, just feed the disks into your drive as you are prompted for them and click on **OK** after each is inserted. Once Excel is installed, you are asked to restart your computer so the changes to some of the startup files can take effect.

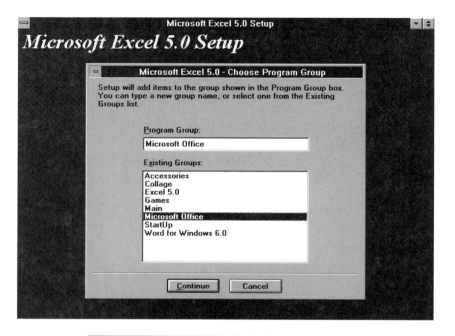

Figure A.5   *The Choose Program Group dialog box.*

OPTIMIZING EXCEL

The steps you can take to maximize Excel's performance are, for the most part, the same steps that maximize the performance of most Windows programs. If you have an incredibly fast computer and you are working with relatively small worksheets, you may have no need for optimization. Everything already happens in a flash for you. If, on the other hand, you want any little performance boost you can get, read on.

The first thing is to consider how much *RAM* (Random Access Memory) your computer has and how it is configured. Windows programs (and Excel is no exception) perform best with lots of memory. While you can get away with 4Mb (megabytes) of RAM, Excel is much happier with 8. If you do not have enough memory, Excel is forced to store portions of the worksheet data on the hard disk, which, no matter how fast it is, is many times slower than memory.

Also, the kind of memory Windows programs use is called *extended memory*. Refer to your computer's instructions for information on how to set up your memory as extended. If you are running DOS 6 or higher, the included program called MemMaker helps you configure your memory properly. Your DOS instructions tell you how to use MemMaker.

If your Excel operations are unacceptably slow—and you have the funds—consider upgrading your computer. If you are still working with a 286 or slower 386 machine (these numbers refer to the type of main processing chip in the computer), it may be time to upgrade to a fast 486 or Pentium machine.

If you can not afford more memory or a faster machine, here are a few tips for making the most of what you have. First, don't use large fonts or graphics unless absolutely necessary. These graphic elements slow you down as you work in Excel. You can always use the Show Placeholder option in the View portion of the Options dialog box to speed up worksheets that require graphics. Also, if calculations are causing you to spend too much time waiting, choose **Manual** from the Calculation portion of the Options dialog box.

If you still find the program too slow, just remember how long it took you to perform calculations like these before you had a computer! Don't you feel better now?

For Lotus 1-2-3 Users

There are many Lotus 1-2-3 users switching over to Excel, so Microsoft has included some tools to help former 1-2-3 users over the hump. If you are one of these, you'll be delighted at how easy it is to learn Excel. In fact, you won't even have to learn too much of Excel. You can just let Excel's help for 1-2-3 users guide you through your Excel tasks.

The first place to go to see what sort of help is available to you is the Excel Help system. Choosing **Lotus 1-2-3** from the Help menu displays the Help for Lotus 1-2-3 Users dialog box, as shown in Figure B.1.

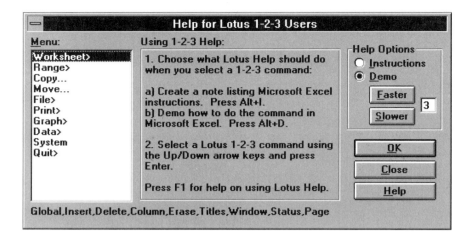

Figure B.1   *The Help for Lotus 1-2-3 Users dialog box.*

In the Help Option area of the dialog box in the upper right, you can specify whether Excel gives you instructions or demonstrates how to perform a 1-2-3 task in Excel, leading you by the hand as the task is carried out. You can also enter a number in the box just below the two option buttons to specify how quickly or slowly Excel carries out the demonstration.

If you choose Instructions, the steps for carrying out the task appears in the middle portion of the dialog box.

In either case, you choose the command you want to learn about from the Menu list. For example, if you want to learn how to perform the /Worksheet, Insert, Column command in Excel, you would click on **Worksheet** and then **OK** (or double-click on **Worksheet**) to display the list of Worksheet commands. Next, double-click on **Insert**, and then on **Column**.

If you have chosen the Demo option, you are be asked to confirm or change where the columns are to be inserted, as shown in Figure B.2.

After entering the required information, clicking on the **OK** button causes Excel to carry out the task, using the Excel procedures.

If you have chosen the Instructions option, a note appears on your screen telling you how to perform the task, but letting you do it on your own.

Figure B.3 displays an example of an instruction note.

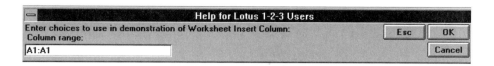

Figure B.2 *A Lotus 1-2-3 demo help dialog box.*

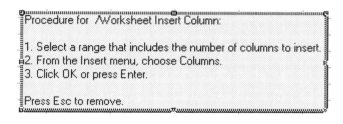

Figure B.3 *An instruction note for inserting columns.*

You can drag the note to any portion of the screen you want so it is not in the way. When you are finished with the note, you can clear it from the screen by pressing **Esc**.

If even this much help is not enough, you can have Excel use your actual 1-2-3 commands to carry out tasks in Excel. You can even set up Excel to allow you to enter formulas in the 1-2-3 format and have Excel translate them for you. All these options are specified in the Transition portion of the Options dialog box, as shown in Figure B.4.

In the Settings area of the dialog box, you can choose the **Lotus 1-2-3 Help** option to have Excel display the 1-2-3 help dialog box when you press the **Slash** (/) key. The Transition Navigation Keys check box lets you use 1-2-3 keyboard navigation keys in Excel.

The Sheet Options area of the dialog box lets you specify how you want formulas handled. Choosing **Transition Formula Evaluation** causes Excel to evaluate formulas entered in Excel using 1-2-3's rules. Transition Formula Entry lets you enter formulas as you would in 1-2-3.

WARNING

While all these help facilities for former 1-2-3 users are very nice, they can slow down your learning process by insulating you from the real Excel commands. If you need to use them because you have been forced to use Excel against your will and you have to get a project completed before you have time to really learn Excel, fine. Otherwise, bite the bullet and stick with the normal Excel commands. You'll thank me later.

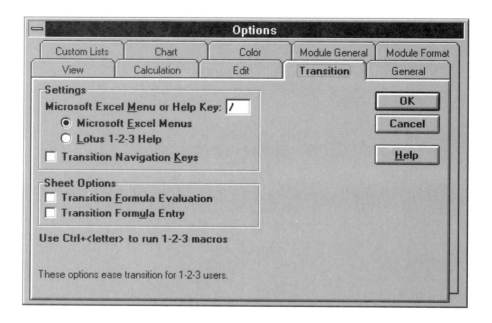

Figure B.4 *The Transition portion of the Options dialog box.*

In addition to all the help facilities, you'll be pleased to know that all the 1-2-3 files you have created can be opened directly into Excel. You are prompted with a dialog box asking if you want to open the 1-2-3 version *xx* file. That's all there is to it. All the formatting and formulas you used in 1-2-3 are retained. You can even use most of the macros you created in 1-2-3 version 2.01 and some from 2.2.

Keyboard Shortcuts

Excel provides keyboard shortcuts for almost everything you can do with the mouse. I concentrated on the mouse actions to accomplish most tasks in the book. However, you save time if you use some of the keyboard shortcuts, particularly if you are a touch typist. Good typists find that removing their hands from the keyboard to use the mouse slows them down. Using keyboard shortcuts allows you to keep your hands on the keyboard.

This list of keyboard commands is not comprehensive. These are just some of my favorites. You'll find a complete guide to the keyboard commands in Excel's help facility. To view the keyboard commands in help, choose **Help**, **Contents**, click on **Reference Information**, and then on **Keyboard Guide**. You are then able to choose among a variety of keyboard guides in different categories.

FUNCTION KEYS

To	Press
Get help	**F1**
Get context sensitive help	**Shift+F1**
Edit cell	**F2**
Display Info Window	**Ctrl+F2**
Display the Function Wizard	**Shift+F3**
Switch between relative and absolute reference while editing	**F4**
Repeat last action when not editing	**F4**
Close active window	**Ctrl+F4**
Close application	**Alt+F4**
Display Go To dialog box	**F5**
Check Spelling	**F7**
Calculate all sheets in open workbooks (when manual calc is turned on)	**F9**
Calculate active sheet	**Shift+F9**
Save As	**F12**
Save	**Shift+F12**
Open	**Ctrl+F12**

INSERTING, DELETING, COPYING AND MOVING

To	Press
Cut selection	**Ctrl+X**
Copy selection	**Ctrl+C**
Paste selection	**Ctrl+V**
Clear selection contents	**Del**
Undo last action	**Ctrl+Z**

MOVING AND SELECTING

To	Press
Extend selection one cell	**Shift+Arrow**
Move up or down to edge of current data region	**Ctrl+Up Arrow key or Ctrl+Down Arrow**
Move left or right to edge of current data region	**Ctrl+Left Arrow key or Ctrl+Right Arrow**
Move to beginning of row	**Home**
Select to beginning of row	**Shift+Home**
Move to last cell in worksheet	**Ctrl+End**
Select entire column	**Ctrl+Spacebar**
Select entire row	**Shift+Spacebar**
Select entire worksheet	**Ctrl+A**
Move down one screen	**Page Down**
Move up one screen	**Page Up**
Move right one screen	**Alt+Page Down**
Move left one screen	**Alt+Page Up**
Move to cell A1	**Ctrl+Home**

MOVING WITHIN A SELECTION

To	Press
Move down	**Enter**
Move up	**Shift+Enter**
Move left to right	**Tab**
Move right to left	**Shift+Tab**

FORMATTING DATA

To	Press
Apply Currency format	**Ctrl+Shift+$**
Apply Percent format	**Ctrl+Shift+%**
Apply Date format (Day+Month+Year)	**Ctrl+Shift+#**
Apply two decimal place format with commas	**Ctrl+Shift+!**
Apply or remove bold	**Ctrl+B**
Apply or remove italic	**Ctrl+I**
Apply or remove underline	**Ctrl+U**

Toolbar Reference

Here are all the toolbars included with Excel. Each button is labeled with its tooltip. Don't forget that you can create your own custom toolbars using these and many other buttons available in the Customize dialog box.

THE STANDARD TOOLBAR

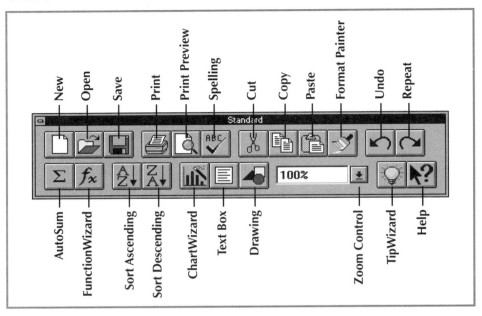

THE FORMATTING TOOLBAR

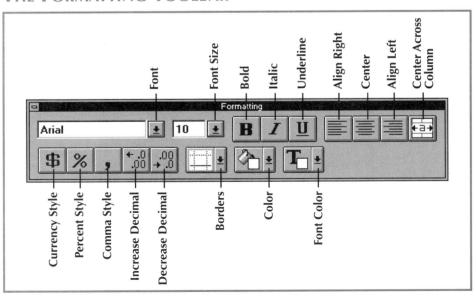

THE CHART TOOLBAR

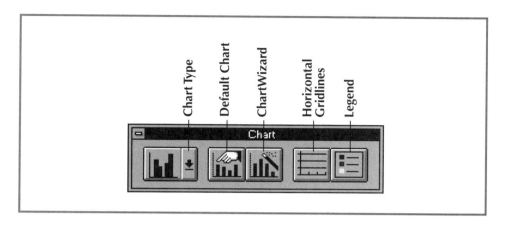

THE DRAWING TOOLBAR

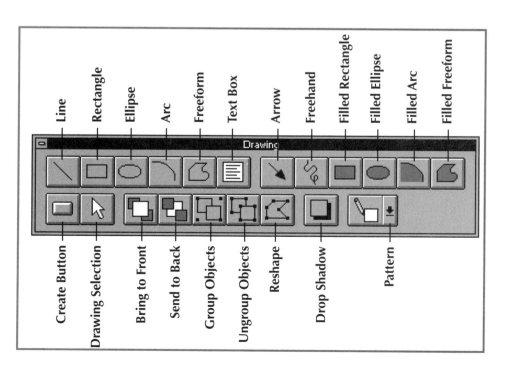

THE FORMS TOOLBAR

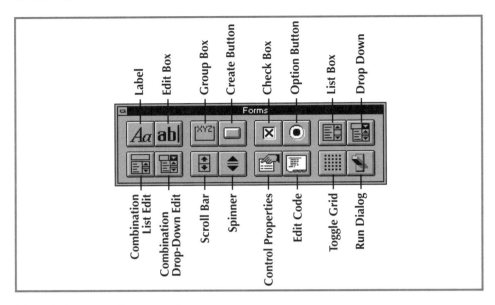

THE VISUAL BASIC TOOLBAR

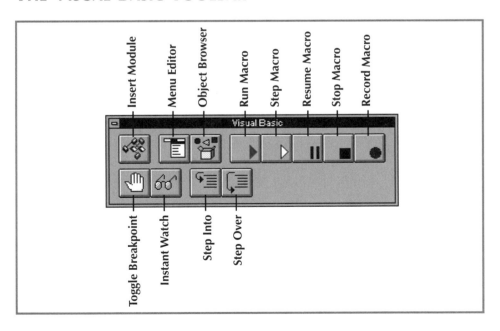

THE AUDITING TOOLBAR

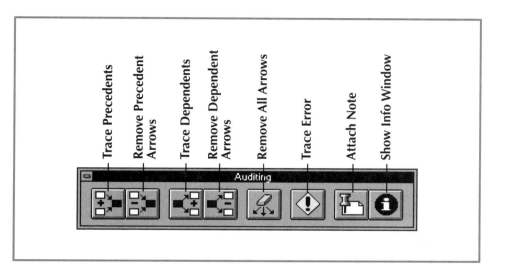

THE WORKGROUP TOOLBAR

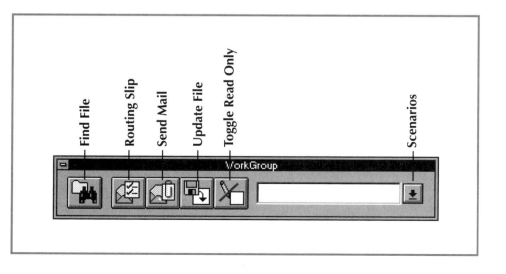

THE MICROSOFT TOOLBAR

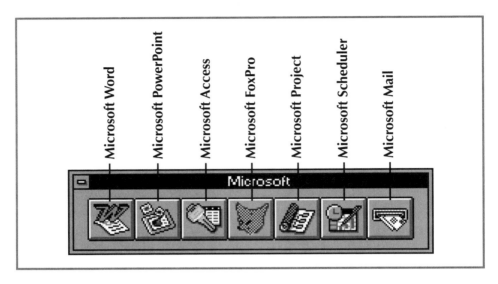

THE FULL SCREEN TOOLBAR

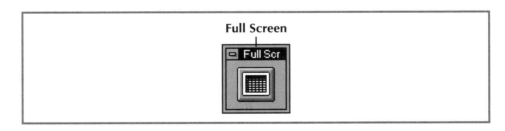

THE STOP RECORDING TOOLBAR

Glossary

active window

The window that is currently in use or selected.

active cell

The worksheet cell that is currently selected.

application window

The window containing the menu bar for an application.

cell formatting

Appearance changes applied to cells, such as alignment, fonts and borders.

cell

The rectangular area on a worksheet that is the intersection of a column and a row.

307

comparison operators

> Symbols used to compare values, such as > (greater than), = (equal to) etc.

comparison criteria

> A set of search conditions used to find the data you're looking for in a list or database.

Control menu

> The menu that contains commands for manipulating the active window. The Control menu is opened by using the Control-menu box.

Control-menu box

> The icon in the upper-left corner of a window used for opening the Control menu. Double clicking on the Control-menu box closes the window.

data series

> A group of related data points that are plotted in a chart.

data point

> A piece of data that is represented in a chart.

default

> Settings that are preset. Excel comes with default settings for many options, such as column width. Most defaults can be changed.

dependent worksheet

> A worksheet that uses linked data from one or more source worksheets.

document window

> A window within an application window. An Excel workbook is a document window. There can be multiple document windows within an application window.

drop-down menus

> A list of commands that is opened by choosing its name from the menu bar.

field names

> The label in the first row of an Excel database list used to name the fields.

field

> A category of information in a database list. A column in an Excel database is a field.

fill handle

> The handle in the lower-right corner of the active cell or selection used for moving, copying, and filling data from the cell or selection into other cells.

group icons

> Icons containing program icons, usually in Windows' Program Manager.

header row

> The first row in an Excel database containing labels for the field names.

hotkey

> The keys used to initiate a command. The sequence of underlined menu letters are hotkeys.

icon

> A pictorial representation of an object or element. Excel is started from an icon. The toolbar buttons are icons.

insertion point

> The flashing vertical line indicating where text is inserted. The insertion point is sometimes called a cursor.

link

> A reference between two worksheets. Useful for summarizing or consolidating data from multiple worksheets or workbooks.

macro

> A series of actions that has been recorded, or programmed, and

named, which can be executed by running (playing) the macro. An Excel macro is really a small program within Excel.

mouse

A hand-held pointing device that you move across your desktop to control the on-screen pointer. A mouse usually has two or three control buttons.

name list

The list of names assigned to cells or ranges of cells on the worksheet. The name list is opened from the name box on the left side of the formula bar.

Personal Macro Workbook

A workbook for storing macros that you want to be available all the time. The Personal Macro Workbook is usually hidden, but is always opened when you start Excel.

point

A size measurement, usually referring to font size. One point is approximately .72 inches.

program

A sequence of instructions that can be run by a computer. Excel is a program.

proportional fonts

Fonts with variable-width characters. Proportional fonts usually look more professional than monospaced fonts, in which each character occupies the same width.

record

A collection of fields pertaining to one database entry.

relative reference

A cell reference that determines its position relative to the original location. Relative referencing allows formulas to work properly, even when they are copied to other areas of the worksheet.

restore button

A double-headed arrow button in the upper-right corner of a window, used to restore the window to its previous size.

scroll bars

Devices used for navigating vertically and horizontally in a window. Vertical scroll bars are usually on the right side of the window. Horizontal scroll bars are usually on the bottom.

shortcut menu

A list of commands that is relevant to a particular area of the screen. Shortcut menus are opened by right-clicking on that area.

sort key

The field used as the basis for a database sort. Up to three sort keys can be used at one time in an Excel sort.

source worksheet

A worksheet with linked cells or ranges that provide variable information to the dependent worksheet.

tool tip

A short description of a toolbar button that appears just below the mouse pointer when it is on a toolbar button.

TrueType fonts

A particular type of font that is scalable to practically any size on the page and the screen.

user interface

The kind of menus, dialog boxes, and other elements used to interact with the program. Windows is a graphical user interface because it incorporates many graphical elements for your interaction.

VBA

Visual Basic for Applications. This is the primary programming language used for Excel macros.

workbook

A collection of sheets (worksheets, chart sheets) that is saved with one file name. A workbook can contain up to 255 sheets.

x-axis

The horizontal plane of a chart. Sometimes called the category axis.

y-axis

The vertical plane of a chart. Sometimes called the value axis.

Index

A

313

F